Three Hundred Years
at the Keyboard

Three Hundred Years At the Keyboard

A Piano Sourcebook From Bach to the Moderns

Historical Background,
Composers, Styles, Compositions,
National Schools

Compiled and Annotated by

Patricia Fallows-Hammond

Ross Books   Berkeley, California

Patricia Fallows-Hammond was born in New York City. As a resident of California, she attended Mills College where she holds the degrees of Bachelor of Arts and Bachelor of Music. She studied with the late Albert Elkus of the music department of the University of California, Berkeley. Upon graduation from Mills College, she was awarded the Certificate of Proficiency in Piano and first prize in composition.

She later studied in France with Ennemond Trillat of the Lyons Conservatory and with Alfred Cortot in his Master Class at Ecole Normale in Paris. Further study in Paris included private lessons with Marguerite Long and Yvonne Lefébure. While residing in Honolulu, she was a founder of the well known Chamber of Music Series and performed extensively as the pianist of the Honolulu Chamber Trio.

Ms. Fallows-Hammond currently lives and performs in the Bay Area and continues to coach with Adolph Baller, Professor of Piano at Stanford and pianist of the Alma Trio.

My profoundest gratitude goes to Betty Bacon and Elizabeth Davidson for their material and technical help in putting an idea to work. I am indebted to Ann Nutting and the staff of the Art and Music Department of the Berkeley Public Library for their untiring assistance. Rex Uhl of the Berkeley Music House generously provided important source information. Jane Galante, in detailed reading of the manuscript, made invaluable musical suggestions which helped shape the book. Others who offered encouragement are Rosalyn Pollycove, Carol Snell, Marianne Thompson, Elizabeth and Park Chamberlain, Dolly Du Prau, and Olga Scheuermann. I give special thanks to my daughter, Patty, who has read the proofs. My husband and daughter, Katharine, provided the gift of time without demands.

Fallows-Hammond, Patricia
    Three hundred years at the keyboard.

    Bibliography: p.

    Includes index.

    1. Piano music--Analysis, appreciation. 2. Piano music--Bibliography. I. Title. II. Title: 300 years at the keyboard.
MT140.F2 1984   786.4'041'01   83-23056
Paper ISBN 0-89496-043-1
Hard ISBN 0-89496-045-6

In Honor of Adolph Baller,
     Albert Elkus, and Yvonne Lefébure

Preface

There are many facets of music which the piano student needs to know to become a rounded musician as well as a skillful performer of pieces. To this end, I have asked my students to look up background information on the composers' lives and the musical traits that distinguish one from another. As the students progress, they learn the extent and variety of each composer's compositions. They find that piano repertoire does not exist in a vacuum but reflects the historical and cultural changes of each generation, most important of all, their own. In other words, they find that piano study involves not only the basics of keyboard harmony, ear training, and technique but also ideas and emotions generated by a changing world.

This book is my answer to the "whole" approach to piano study. It reminds me of what my own teacher said before the first big recital when I couldn't decide what dress to wear. "If you can't find it, make it." I have looked for a book like this one for a number of years. I didn't find it; I had to make it.

In simple and convenient form, the book brings into focus the last 300 years of piano activity. As a short cut from reference shelf to music rack, it provides essential information on the major composers for the piano, including their styles, works, and editions. Final sections discuss the message of contemporary trends; salient musical developments within each major country from harpsichordists and early guitarists to the present; interaction of composers, teachers, and virtuosos; modern international exchange; and suggested 20th Century repertoire for piano and for harpsichord.

I have added single musical examples for each composer discussed in individual chapters. Obviously, a few pages of music cannot represent scope, but they can give flavor and a sense of style. I have referred to all the examples in the body of the text. My hope is that as you play the music, you will say eventually, "Why, of course, that *has* to be Haydn!" (or Schumann, or Debussy). Have fun with your learning; that's what this book is for. To students, teachers, listeners, and indeed anyone interested in the development and potential of the piano, please be seated for *your* enjoyment.

Berkeley, 1984

CONTENTS

1 | FROM THE BEGINNING

Evolution of the Piano

The word "piano" is the English term for the familiar keyboard instrument whose full name is "pianoforte" (from the Italian, soft-loud). It has basically evolved from the *dulcimer, clavichord,* and *harpsichord,* instruments in use in the 14th and 15th Centuries. In its present form, it is built on an iron frame and is either a *grand* (horizontal) or an *upright.* Its standard compass is 7-1/3 octaves (88 keys), but some models by Bösendorfer have 8 octaves. [1]

The *dulcimer,* a closed shallow box over which were stretched wires to be struck with two wooden hammers, was a forerunner of the *clavichord* of the 14th Century. The *spinet, virginal, clavecin,* and *gravicembalo* were predecessors of the *harpsichord* of the 15th Century. As keyboard music assumed importance in the 16th and 17th Centuries, its chief instruments became refined versions of the *clavichord* and *harpsichord.*

The idea for the piano was inspired by the action of the clavichord and the substantial sound projection of the harpsichord. The conception of the clavichord's hammer action and the level of volume possible with the harpsichord were carried over into an instrument created by the Italian, Cristofori (1655-1731). First exhibited in Florence in 1709, Cristofori's instrument was called *gravicembalo col piano e forte,* a harpsichord with soft and loud tone. (His first surviving piano dates from 1720 and can be seen in New York's Metropolitan Museum.) Cristofori's ideas were then used by a German organ builder, Gottfried Silberman (1683-1753) who incorporated further improvements in the new instrument.

---

[1]   See *Concise Oxford Dictionary of Music,* 3rd Ed., 1980, Piano.

During the last quarter of the 18th Century and the first part of the 19th, piano construction developed rapidly in Austria, England (John Broadwood and Sons), France (Pleyel, Érard), and later in America (Chickering, Steinway).[2] The most acceptable piano which evolved after Silberman's was made by his disciple, Stein. When factories moved from Augsberg to Vienna, the Stein pianos incorporated a further improvement in mechanism called the Viennese action. It was the Stein Viennese action piano which Mozart adopted in 1777. He also knew, played, and owned a fortepiano (c. 1780) by Anton Walter which some contemporary musicologists feel should be used in replica to reproduce the piano music of Haydn, Mozart and early Beethoven. Mozart's endorsement of the Stein piano and fortepiano gave other keyboard instruments a less important role except for special effects and historical interest. The evolving instrument was eventually called simply a piano, or a grand piano because of its increased length and breadth.

The years between 1709 when Cristofori exhibited the first piano, and 1777 when Mozart adopted it, determined the future of piano playing and composing. Bach was acquainted with the instrument but preferred the harpsichord and clavichord. Haydn was not primarily a keyboard artist – nevertheless, he was aware of the extensive developments of the piano during his lifetime when he composed his later works. Mozart, a superb performer and daring innovator, adopted the piano when he was twenty-one and used it exclusively in his concerts. He composed the majority of his keyboard works with the advancements and advantages of the piano in mind.

Beethoven in turn discarded the light action piano employed by Mozart for the weightier English Broadwood, but he did not live to see the keyboard range enlarged to its current maximum of 7-1/3 octaves. From Beethoven's time until the present, demands of composers and resourcefulness of manufacturers have combined to produce increasingly satisfying pianos, remarkable for sonority and tonal contrast.

Changing Styles in Piano Technique

If you sat at the middle of the keyboard or a little to the left or right; if your bench was high or low; if you played with flat or curved fingers; if you covered the notes first or dropped from a height; if you used the sustaining pedal generously or lightly; if you strove for mellowness or brilliance of tone – you had successful and convincing examples from each generation of keyboard performers from the 17th Century onward. Each outstanding individual had his own characteristics or *method*. Keyboard technique changed as musical ideas and instruments developed.

The piano owes its development to the limitations of the clavichord and harpsichord. The clavichord was extremely soft and essentially unusable in public performance; the harpsichord, although brighter, could not vary tone. Bach and Handel used the clavichord and harpsichord, but filled their keyboard music with *ornaments* (trills,

[2]   The piano which Steinway and Sons first exhibited in 1855 was essentially the present form of the grand piano.

turns, grace notes, mordants) which were a substitute for sustained sound and gradation of dynamics.

With the development of the piano, the quantity of tone could be altered by the pressure of fingers. This eliminated the need for busy ornaments and pointed toward pure melody. One of Bach's sons, C.P.E. Bach (1714-1788), spoke of a *cantabile* singing style and of *singing* on a keyboard instrument. He was one of the first composers to use definite melody and accompaniment[1] and thus influenced directly the development of sonata form. He also published a treatise in two parts (1753 and 1762) on the *Art of Clavier Playing* which was the original methodical guide to keyboard performance. Because of the technique he developed and the music he wrote to support his theories, he may be considered the father of piano playing.

With the advances of the Viennese light action piano, Haydn and Mozart were able to determine one of the building blocks of *sonata form* – individualized melody standing out clearly from its surroundings. Although Mozart adopted the piano exclusively over all earlier keyboard instruments, he continued to use the harpsichord style of keyboard control, quiet and close, with only occasional bravura effects.

Clementi (1752-1832), whose *Gradus ad Parnassum* was a kind of Bible of technique, followed Haydn and Mozart in his theories of tonal equality, speed, and of melody as distinct from accompaniment.[2] He also presented a system for strengthening the weak fingers. Unlike Haydn and Mozart, Clementi preferred the hammer fall of English pianos which produced a larger, more penetrating tone.

Beethoven also preferred the heavier English piano. An exceptional performer, he demanded sonority from music rather than elegance, and an urgent quality of sound growing out of profound emotion. His contemporaries, von Weber (1786-1826) and Czerny (1791-1857), also supported Beethoven's revolutionary strength and expressiveness. Von Weber, a concert pianist and composer, added technical ideas quickly incorporated by contemporary composers – bold use of the left hand apart from accompaniment figures and scattered, wide spread chords. Czerny added exercises for the development of speed and smoothness.

Consistently delicate use of the sustaining pedal allowed Schumann and Chopin to establish the artistic value of gossamer, poetic tone.[3] Chopin recognized the essential weakness of the hand and built his technique around it. His technical studies, *Etudes Opp. 10* and *25,* show inspired use of the natural conformation of the hand. Another pianist, Thalberg (1812-1871), developed a remarkable ability to make piano sound sing and inspired Mendelssohn's melodic strength in many of the *Songs Without Words.*

Liszt proceeded along the lines of Chopin but demanded larger tone. He sat higher at the keyboard to take advantage of the added fall of gravity from shoulder and arm. He freed his hands for renewed attack by use of the sustaining pedal. And he incorporated these revolutionizing ideas for increased volume in *Twelve Transcendental Studies R. 2b.* To support the bravura style of Liszt and his followers, piano makers in-

---

[1] This was impossible on the harpsichord without using two manuals.
[2] His pupil Cramer (1771-1858) furthered these ideals in his 84 *Studies* of 1804 which are still in use.
[3] Ironically, this quality of tone was originally considered the chief defect of the evolving piano.

creased key resistance with weights measured in ounces. In the case of Liszt's immediate followers, technique became important for its own sake, and loudness was often achieved at the expense of rich quality.

Brahms by-passed exterior brilliance for interior motivation; technical flourishes alone rarely existed in his music. His technical contributions grew from a consistent musical idiom, polyphonic interweaving of voices within harmonic, or chordal, structure. His *Fifty-One Exercises* demonstrated for pianists the technique necessary for developing finger strength and independence to meet his unique approach.

After Liszt's era, there was a reaction against "thumpers," and a controlled style set in. (The nature of Brahms's writing in general put him beyond charges of excessive sound.) Tchaikovsky returned to a modified approach as did the great teachers of the 19th Century, Leschetizsky and I. Phillip. Franck, in turn, employed forceful, fluent technique to support serious musical ideas and gave a new dignity to technical means used in this way.

Debussy provided the piano with a new technique by floating notes above the sustaining and forte pedals to capture sounds descriptive of nature (water, wind, rain), of exotic Eastern instruments (bells, gongs, gamelans), and of instruments of the orchestra (flutes, horns, drums, brass, celesta). His precise technique, Romantic in its dexterity, called for a touch to match the moment's expressiveness, a feat for the imagination ahead of the fingers and pedals.[4] His *Twelve Etudes* furnish the basic technical and musical equipment for his special approach.

Heralded by Bartók, much contemporary music treats the piano as a purely percussive instrument. Bartók diagrammed in *Mikrokosmos* a ground plan of piano writing and performance which continues into the present generation. Angular and dissonant, contemporary music is also strongly individualized and frequently oriented to expressiveness. Without key or time signature and without conforming to usual hand patterns, today's piano music is in transition. Experiments beyond traditional piano resources and capabilities of the hand involve electronic devices and computers, setting the stage for an entirely new family of wired instruments with or without keyboard.

Based on the best results of the past, current piano teaching has the benefits of approximately 300 years of development from the birth of Bach to the present. For the traditional repertoire there is a premium on perfection of execution, with a minimum of sentimentality. The arm is used freely for agility; fingering is skillful; resonant as well as percussive tone quality is produced by finely calculated muscular control. Present pianists have developed extraordinary technique which has been matched by the development of powerful, responsive instruments.

---

[4]   This technique is explained by the French pianist, E. Robert Schmitz, in his book, *The Piano Works of Claude Debussy,* Duel, Sloan and Pearce, New York, 1950, p. 39.

2 | THE BAROQUE ERA

The term "Baroque" originated in the 17th Century and was first applied to architecture. Its initial reference to music was made by the author Noel Antoine Pluche in his *Spectacle de la Nature* in 1746. By then, for practical purposes and before being identified as such, the Baroque period in music was well underway. It extended roughly from 1600 to 1750. Included in these years were the important contributions of the first Baroque composers which culminated in the supreme achievements of Bach and Handel. (For a more detailed division, Willaert's *Musica nova* written in 1540 may be considered the bridge between the preceding *Renaissance* period and the *Baroque* period which followed. Works written between 1540-1600 by Claudio Monteverdi and Orlando di Lasso, for example, suggest characteristics of both periods. For the sake of convenience, the following divisions can be made: *pre-Baroque* from 1540-1600; *middle* or *full Baroque* including Lully, Purcell, and Alessandro Scarlatti from 1600-1700; and *late Baroque* including Vivaldi, Telemann, Bach and Handel from 1700-1750.)

For the pianist, the entire Baroque period lies somewhat in shadow since keyboard music did not yet have its most important instrument: the piano. Nevertheless, for the development of music, the Baroque era was enormously important. By its close, it had defined *melody with thorough-bass accompaniment,*[1] true polyphony,[2] concertante style,[3]

---

[1]   A bass line which played as an accompaniment the lowest notes without break from beginning to end.

[2]   Music of a composition that combines simultaneously 2 or 3 voice parts of individual design. It is distinct from *monophony* or *monody* which consists of a single melody with accompaniment and from *homophony* which combines several voice parts of similar, and rhythmically identical, design.

[3]   An 18th Century style of writing for orchestra which included parts for several solo instruments, or for several solo instruments without orchestra.

and *tonic-dominant as central chords of harmony. Melody with accompaniment* (called monody) became the basis of later opera, oratorio, cantata, and recitative; *polyphony* reached perfection with Bach as a fundamental principle of composition; *concertante style* with its foundation of contrasting instruments and tempo appeared in the concerto grosso style of Bach's Brandenburg Concertos and in the later "true" concerto style of solo instrument and orchestra; *tonic-dominant* key relationship furnished the framework for Handel's *operas* and *oratorios* and became an important element in the development of *sonata form*.

The Baroque years were fruitful and yeasty, filled with contrasts of exuberance and self denial, longing and ecstasy, heavenly clouds and the gates of Hell.

Born in Eisenach, Germany,
March 21, 1685

Died in Leipzig, Germany,
July 28, 1750,
Age 65 years

Johann Sebastian Bach

Historical Sketch

The achievements of Johann Sebastian Bach hold a place without parallel in music history. With the universality and vision of his genius, Bach fused the contributions of 16th, 17th, and early 18th Century composers in Italy, England, and France in terms of his own technique and style. With this synthesis, he created a musical mother tongue which has formed the basic language of western music to the present day.

Bach's musical heritage was unique. His ancestors were outstanding performers and composers for 200 years before his birth, and in his youth the distinguished family numbered over 100 active musicians. Left virtually an orphan at 10, young Bach went to live with an older brother, Johann Christoph, in Ohrdruf. Johann Christoph, also a musician, arranged for Bach's early education with a general curriculum. At 15, Bach moved to Lüneburg to begin formal musical training at St. Michael's School. Here he studied singing, organ, violin, clavier, and composition. And here his first works, preludes and sets of variations, appeared. The organ became his favorite instrument, and organists famous for their style and technique soon exerted an influence on his maturing genius. The best known of these were Reincken in Hamburg and Buxtehude at Lubeck.

Bach left St. Michael's School in 1703 for brief appointments in Arnstadt and Mühlhausen. It was in Arnstadt that he wrote in 1704 the delightful *Capriccio on the Departure of a Beloved Brother*. A few years later, in 1708, he secured his first important position as Court Organist and Musical Director at Weimar. Twenty-three at the time, he was already renowned as an organ virtuoso and master of improvisation.

In 1717, Bach moved to Cöthen to become Director of Music for Prince Leopold in whose service he wrote largely for clavier, for orchestra, and for the combinations of instruments comprising chamber music. At Cöthen, he finished in 1722 the first book of the *Forty-eight Preludes and Fugues for the Well-Tempered Clavier*. This work was written as his acceptance of the system of tuning, or tempering, which made it possible to play in all twelve major and minor keys on any one clavier.[1]

Bach's last position, in 1723, was as Director of the St. Thomas School of choir singers in Leipzig. He became organist at the St. Thomas Church and lived in Leipzig until his death. At this time, he also held the office of Musical Director for three other churches[2] planning and often writing the music for all four churches every Sunday. Here he composed his greatest choral works, among them the *St. John Passion* (1723), *St. Matthew Passion* (1729), and the *Mass in B minor* (1733-38).

Bach became blind the year before his death. Nevertheless, he had the satisfaction of knowing that his musical line extended through three sons who were outstanding composers: Wilhelm Friedemann, Carl Philipp Emmanuel, and Johann Christian Bach.[3]

For over seventy-five years, Bach's music was little known since his fame as a virtuoso eclipsed his greatness as a composer. Mendelssohn "discovered" his musical legacy and arranged the first posthumous performance of the *St. Matthew Passion* in 1829.[4] The public awakened at last to Bach's universality and accorded his genius a place unchallenged in the musical world.

Style

If all the music in the world but Bach's were destroyed, so the saying goes, the whole system of romantic and modern harmony could be re-established from it. Beethoven felt that Bach's writing uncovered the roots of all music when he said, "Play a great deal of Bach and everything will become clear to you."

Bach's many-sided nature included discipline, drama, and poetry: as disciplinarian, he required clarity; as dramatist, he understood bravura and the emotional impact of climax building; as poet, he wrote with lyricism which went beyond personal expressiveness and suggested a universal source.

[1]   Before the adoption of this system, it was impractical to play in more than a few keys on a single instrument.
[2]   St. Nicholas, St. Matthew, and St. Peter.
[3]   The last was called the "English Bach" because of his twenty year residence in London.
[4]   At Berlin's Singakademie, March 11, 1829.

Universality may explain the ease with which Bach's music is transcribed; Bach concerned himself with the idea rather than the instrumentation of it. Organ works can be exchanged with clavier or piano, and stringed works given to the keyboard. Ideas for the limited range and resources of the harpsichord and clavichord expand naturally to the versatility of the modern piano.[5]

With Bach, melody was an outgrowth of counterpoint[6] as well as a statement of its own individuality. His melodies, especially in the free forms, were expressive and singable, and even in contrapuntal context were warm and flexible. Except in the slow movements, rhythm in general was devoid of complications and advanced steadily to the climax with the same pattern often repeated throughout the work. Foreshadowing contemporary harmonies, modulations involved remote and unexpected keys.

Although Bach was at heart an innovator, he did not create new forms; he expanded and raised existing forms to perfection. His innovations were poured into molds already made, and out of them he created enduring works through contrapuntal skill. His favorite structural method was probably the fugue. (Fugal medium has never been more beautifully or intricately developed.)

In keyboard technique, Bach's contributions were original and far reaching. Early keyboard execution embodied flat fingers and excluded use of the thumb which hung away from the hand. Bach added the thumb and curved the fingers, revolutionizing, expanding, and strengthening keyboard technique. The resulting new system of fingering is basically the one used today.

Compositions

Bach's works are divided into three periods: *Weimar* (1708-17) when he wrote largely for organ; *Cöthen* (1717-23) when he composed many works for clavier; and *Leipzig* (1723-50) when he produced the choral masterpieces. The divisions are a matter of convenience for general reference. The keyboard works listed below appeared before, during, and after the fertile Cöthen period.

Capriccio on the Departure of a Beloved Brother (1704) BWV 992

At the beginning of Bach's residence in Arnstadt he wrote a rare example of program music inspired by his brother Jacob's departure for Poland. It is a charming picture of leave-taking, depicting "the dangers of foreign lands" and the pleading of friends "to remain with us." The second movement, titled *Sorrow and Regret*, is a forerunner in idea of Beethoven's *Sonata in E flat Op. 81, Farewell, Absence and Return.* The last movement, a fugue, is built on the notes of the postillion's horn.

[5]   Bach severely criticized the earliest pianos, finding the keyboard touch "heavy" and the upper notes "feeble."
[6]   Music made up of single lines where the interest is in horizontal relationship as opposed to harmony which is considered vertical, i.e., a fugue vs. a Protestant hymn.

Inventions: Two Part (15) (1723) BWV 779-86; *Three Part* (15) also called *Sinfonias* (1723) BWV 787-801

The *Two* and *Three* Part Inventions are studies in contrapuntal technique. Bach took an interest in musical education and recommended learning the *Inventions* "to attain a good cantabile manner of playing." The Bach scholar, Spitta[7] describes the learning process as running the gamut from grace and dignity through sad expressiveness to honest German fun.

Collections of dance forms, combined, extended, and balanced, became the basis for three sets of *Suites*, six in each set, the *English Suites, French Suites,* and *Partitas* (sometimes called the *German Suites*). These contain rhythmic variety, contrapuntal dexterity, and harmonic freedom surpassing any previous works in this form, including Handel's *Suites* with which they were contemporary. The *English* and *French* Suites follow the so-called ACSOG pattern of Couperin and Rameau which incorporates an Allemande, Courante, Sarabande, Optional menuet, Gavotte, and Gigue.

English Suites (1715) BWV 806-11

The *English Suites,* composed in Weimar, are larger in outline than the *French,* using the ACSOG pattern and adding an opening *Prelude* in each case. The *Preludes* are striking for breadth of melody, good examples of Bach's organ style applied to clavier.

French Suites (1722-25) BWV 812-17

Bach composed the *French Suites* in Cöthen for his youthful second wife.[8] The *Fifth* comes close to the bright, melodious style of Handel.

Partitas or *German Suites* (1731) BWV 825-30

Freer in form than the *French* or *English Suites,* the *Partitas,* written in Leipzig, approach the contrasts of the later classical sonata through variety of character and tempo.

Bach's love of the organ is shown by his adaptation of certain organ forms to the harpsichord, *Toccatas, Fantasias,* and *Fugues.* Making the changes demanded by harpsichord technique, Bach composed in these forms for the smaller instrument with the dramatic sweeping style of the organ. The influence of the organ is particularly noticeable in the recitative passages. These are followed by bravura sections which usually lead into the closing fugue. There are seven *Toccatas,* including the familiar and

---

[7]   Spitta, Philip, *Johann Sebastian Bach,* Vol. 2, Dover Publications, Inc., New York, 1951, pp. 61, 62
[8]   Anna Magdelena, for whom he wrote the simple and charming *Notebook (Clavierbuchlein)* in 1722. Bach also wrote a *Clavierbuchlein* in 1720 for his son, Wilhelm Friedemann, and another for Anna Magdelena in 1725.

spirited one in *C minor* of 1717, BWV 911. Among the *Fantasias* and *Fugues*, the remarkable *Chromatic Fantasia and Fugue* is unique.

Chromatic Fantasia and Fugue (1720) BWV 903

This work is one of Bach's most moving and unusual compositions. Chromaticism for its own sake was not widely used before Chopin, Franck and Wagner. But here is a composition written many years earlier which explores fully the emotional as well as the technical aspects of the chromatic scale.

Of all the keyboard works, *The Well-Tempered Clavier* is first in importance. Bach composed two *Preludes* and two *Fugues* for each major and minor key, bringing the total to forty-eight. These are published in two volumes of twenty-four each.

The Well-Tempered Clavier: First Book (1722) BWV 846-69; Second Book (1738-42) BWV 870-93

Schumann referred to this musical monument as the "musician's daily bread." It is a work of infinite musical knowledge and imagination which has no peer. The nature and quality of each key are established through continuous variety of mood, construction (i.e., free form or strict style), tempo, and technical demands. Some of the *Preludes* are fugal, others graceful and fluid, and still others dramatic and emotionally searching. The *Fugues*, anywhere from 2 to 5 part, are equally diverse – serious, merry, and triumphant by turn. The continuous freshness of each work is a testament to the mind and heart of unsurpassed genius.

Following the *First Book* of *The Well-Tempered Clavier*, Bach produced an entirely different work, the *Italian Concerto*. For keyboard alone, it was the counterpart of Bach's *Brandenberg Concertos* for orchestra and his concertos for solo instruments with orchestra.

Italian Concerto (1735) BWV 971

Although writing for piano without orchestra in this work, Bach achieved the quality of solo and accompaniment by marking contrasting sectons *forte* and *piano*. The *Concerto* is in the Italian style of two quick movements with an intervening slow one. The *Andante* has singular freedom of form and expression.

Seven years after he finished the *Italian Concerto*, Bach wrote a set of variations which constitute the most remarkable harpsichord collection in the history of music, the *Goldberg Variations*.

Goldberg Variations (1742) BWV 988 (Aria with 30 variations)

One of the few works which Bach wrote to order, the *Variations* involved several people. J.T. Goldberg, a concert artist, was Bach's pupil. Goldberg's employer, Count Kaiserling, commissioned Bach to write the *Variations* as he wished to have a lengthy piece which Goldberg could play to him on sleepless nights. Many variations have been written through the years, but the Goldberg set, every third variation a canon, represents one of the classics in this form.

Two impressive works which do not fit into any previous grouping are *The Musical Offering on a Theme of Frederick the Great* (1747) BWV 1079 and *The Art of Fugue* (1748-50) BWV 1080. *The Musical Offering* appears in two versions, Bach's original six part fugue played extempore to Frederick the Great, and his *Trio* arrangement for flute (Frederick the Great was a flutist), violin, and clavier. *The Art of Fugue* contains every possible fugal device. As scored for keyboard, it suggests a theoretical work, but theory comes to life even here for the attuned listener and certainly in later versions for stringed instruments where each voice has its own setting and timbre.

Bach's numerous keyboard *Concertos* are written in the style of chamber music where all instruments, including the solo instrument, are interdependent. They are similar to his 6 *Brandenburg Concertos* for orchestra which also provide occasional solo passages of professional virtuosity. Among them are arrangements of works by other composers, including Vivaldi and Telemann, as well as transcriptions of original concertos for other instruments, mainly violin. Among the eight *Concertos* for solo clavier and orchestra written between 1735-1740 which hold a place in the current repertoire are those in D minor, E, D, A, F minor, and G minor. Bach also wrote or transcribed three concertos for two harpsichords, two for three harpsichords, and one for four harpsichords. A masterpiece of contrapuntal writing, the *Concerto in D minor for Three Harpsichords* (1733) BWV 1063 was first performed by Bach's sons at the University of Leipzig concerts. When Mendelssohn revived Bach's music, he included a performance of this *Concerto* in London with himself, Moscheles, and Thalberg as soloists.

Editions:

J.S. Bach: Werke, ed. Bach-Gesellschaft, i-xvii (Leipzig 1851-99)   BG

Neue Bach-Augsabe, ed. Johann Sebastian Bach Institut, Gottingen and Bach-Archiv, Leipzig, ser. 1-VII (Kassel and Basle 1954-   )   NBA

Listings are abbreviated as BWV following the Thematisch-systemlisches Verzeichnis der musikalisches Werke: Johann Sebastian Bach (Leipzig 1950, 3/1966, revised and enlarged 4th ed. in preparation).   BWV

Schmieder, Wolfgang: (1901-   ) Systematic Thematic Index of the Musical Work of Johann Sebastian Bach, Breitkopf and Härtel.   S

Selected Works for Keyboard[9]

Capriccio on the Departure of his Most Beloved Brother, BWV 992 (1703,4 or 6)
6 English Suites, BWV 806-11 (1715)
Chromatic Fantasy and Fugue, BWV 903 (1720)
Well-Tempered Clavier with Appendix
    Volume I, BWV 846-69 (1722)
    Volume II, BWV 870-93 (1738-42)
Anna Magdelena's Music-Books (1722-5; 1725)
6 *French Suites*, BWV 812-17 (1722-25)
15 *Inventions*, BWV 772-86 (1723)
15 *Symphonies* (3-part *Inventions*), BWV 787-801 (1723)
6 *Partitas*, BWV 825-30 (1731)
Partita in B minor BWV 831
Toccata in F sharp minor BWV 910
Toccata in C minor BWV 911
Italian Concerto, BWV 971 (1735)
Clavierbuchlein for W.F. Bach (1720)
Suites, Toccatas, Preludes, Fugues, Fantasies
Air, with 30 Variations (Goldberg), BWV 988 (1742)
Musical Offering, BWV 1079 (1747)
The Art of Fugue, BWV 1080 (1748-50)

For Keyboard and Orchestra

Concertos for clavier and orchestra, BWV 1052; *E minor*, BWV 1053; *D minor*, BWV 1054; *A minor*, BWV 1055; *F minor*, BWV 1056; *F minor*, BWV 1057; *G minor*, BWV 1058; *D minor*, BWV 1059[10]

3 *Concertos for 2 claviers and orchestra:* *C minor*, BWV 1060; *C minor*, 1061; *C minor*, BWV 1062

2 *Concertos for 3 claviers:* *D minor*, BWV 1063; *C minor*, BWV 1064

Concerto for 4 claviers (after Vivaldi) *in A minor*, BWV 1065

[9] For complete listing, see *New Grove 1980*.
[10] These *Concertos*, including the numbers BWV 1052 - BWV 1065, were written in Leipzig, 1735-40.

Prelude and Fugue in B flat minor
from *Well-Tempered Clavier Book I*

1) In Hoffmeister, an *f* is added. 2) *d flat* is missing in 'D.' 3) In Kirnberger and in No. 49 of the "Amalienbibliothek" the *g flat* and *f* are written as eighth notes. The latter note appears similarly in 'D,' where it is joined to the *b flat*. 4) The *e flat* is missing in Hoffmeister, both *e flat* and *c* in Altnikol. Instead of *g flat* there is an *f* in 'D.' 5) [music example] Nägeli. 6) *e flat* is a quarter note, *d flat* is missing in Schwenke. 7) According to many sources, (including Kroll), there is a tie between the two *f's* which is not indicated in 'A,' 'B,' 'C,' and 'D.' 8) In 'D,' Kirnberger, Schwenke and No. 49 of the "Amalienbibliothek": *g flat* without a natural sign. 9) Middle voice in 'C' [music example] In Hoffmeister [music example]. 10) The two *f's* and the two *e's* are tied in Kirnberger and Hoffmeister; also in Schwenke there appear some ties, which are missing in 'A,' 'B,' 'C' and 'D.' 11) The two *d flats* and the two *c's* are tied in Hoffmeister. 12) *f* instead of *e*, Nägeli. 13) The tie between the two *a flats* is missing in Kirnberger and in No. 49 of the "Amalienbibliothek". 14) In 'A,' there is a subsequently added natural sign before the *a*, which is missing in 'B,' 'C' and 'D.' However, it is to be found in other good sources. 15) [music example] Schwenke, (not in Simrock.) There is a similar correction in '205.' The continuation of Gerber's copy has the same reading.

16) Variants of the middle voice: ♪ . 17) In 'D', natural before *d flat*, an error in script.

18) Some notes are missing in 'D'. 19) The two *f*'s are tied in Hoffmeister. 20) In the second quarter there is no *a* in Altnikol.

21) Spitta's assertion (Bk 1 pg. 844) that the fermata is missing in 'D', is erroneous. This fermata appears somewhat unclearly just above the treble staff. 22) In 'D', Kirnberger and in No. 49 of the "Amalienbibliothek" only the two *g flats* are tied.

1) The tie between the two *f♯*'s is missing in Simrock, '205'. 2) [music example] Variant in 'D'. 3) One should observe that because of the resolution of the seventh, *e flat* to *d*, the crossing of the second and third voices (counting from above) extends throughout eight measures. Kroll's annotation--(Bach-Gesellschaft XIV, 237)--is therefore untenable. 4) *d flat* instead of *e flat*, with a tie to the preceding *d flat* in 'B'; originally (before correction,) in 'A'.

5) Hoffmeister has instead of the ensuing 4 measures: [music example] 6) *f* instead of *ff lat*, 'D', '208'.

7) In connection with note 3, it is to be noted that the following phrase continues in the 2nd, 4th and 5th voices. 8) One must assume that the third voice succeeds the fourth voice at this point, as Kroll correctly states; the latter must be free to assume the entrance of the theme seven measures later. This also promotes a more natural resolution for the stretto at 9. 9) Kroll's explanations of this stretto, the second of which is at least interesting, raise the question of the possibility that the f should appear in the third voice-- on the basis of the omitted crossing of voices at 3. These explanations contradict the notation of the autographs. The worthy editor has suggested the correct solution without adopting it. Even the notation given under 10--derived from 'D'--is in harmony with our interpretation.

10) in Schwenke--also in Simrock, though here the f is written as a whole note(!). The third quarter appears in Hoffmeister:

In 'D', the f is a whole note, the b flat has only one stem; the stretto is, therefore, missing.

11) The two b flats are tied in Hoffmeister and Nägeli; similarly in 'C' though perhaps in a strange handwriting. 12) The flat missing before the c in 'B', 'C', 'D', and others, has later been added in 'A'; it is present in Kirnberger and Altnikol. 13) According to Kroll, d flat instead of d. In 'B', 'C' and 'D' there is undoubtedly a natural sign, as there is also in most of the good manuscripts. In 'A' one can read two accidentals, a natural as well as a flat. We adhere to the manuscripts, though we admit in consideration of the tonality of the alto a flat would be justified. The cross-relation would surely offer no obstacle to this interpretation. 14) The ties between the two c's are missing in 'B', '205'. 15) c instead of c flat, Nägeli, '417'.

16) Variants: Simrock, Schwenke. Hoffmeister. Nägeli, '417'.

17) The tie is missing in 'D'.

Born in Halle, Germany,
February 23, 1685

Died in London,
April 14, 1759,
Age 74 years

George Frideric Handel

Historical Sketch

Of all the great composers, Handel is one of the very few to come from a family devoid of musical background. Handel's father, a barber and minor surgeon, hoped his son would become a lawyer. His parents consented to Handel's lessons with the organist Zachau only upon the insistence of a royal patron, the Duke of Saxe-Weissenfels. Some years later, as a consequence of Handel's visit to the Court of Berlin, the Elector invited Handel to remain as court musician. But Handel preferred to stay near his ailing father in Halle and took the position of church organist there.

Seven years after his father's death in 1696, having completed the study of law, Handel set out for the commercial and cultural city of Hamburg. He then attached himself to the Hamburg opera as violinist and harpsichordist and two years later in 1705 produced his first opera, *Almira*.[1] With good fortune rare in the music world, this opera brought him immediate fame. Feted by the musicians Corelli, the Scarlattis, and others, Handel spent several years in Italy from 1706-1710, notably in Florence and Rome. He rapidly mastered the Italian style in opera, chamber music, and vocal music. At the end of this period, he travelled to England where he was warmly received.

---

[1] Later operas include *Agrippina* (1709), *Giulio Cesare* (1724), *Alcina* (1735), and *Serse* (1738).

Except for an occasional return to Germany, Handel spent the rest of his life in England. He was granted a substantial annual pension, first by Queen Anne in 1713, and after her death by George I.[2] A few years later, Handel began his most important keyboard works, the *Suites* for harpsichord. They were written in part as lessons for the royal Princesses but were also extremely successful with the public.

A year before publication of the *Suites* in 1720, Handel became musical director of a new opera venture, the Royal Academy of Music. It was popular and successful for a number of years until 1729 when the vogue for Italian opera, Handel's model, was exhausted. The Academy failed, but Handel was able to salvage funds to begin a new opera venture at the King's Theatre in the same year. When the King's Theatre was taken over in 1734 by a rival group called the "Opera of the Nobility", Handel was forced to move his location, this time to Covent Garden. After some success, the Covent Garden season closed in 1737.

With the need to turn his genius in a new direction, Handel began to write the *Oratorios* which combined his innate feeling for drama with the strength and universal appeal of Biblical narrative. *Saul* and *Israel in Egypt* were both produced in 1739, followed by *L'Allegro, il Penseroso et il Moderato* in 1740.[3] In 1742, Handel wrote in 23 days the most popular of all his *Oratorios*, the *Messiah*. The first performance took place in Dublin during the same year. Annual performances became a tradition which Handel maintained (and the Western world has upheld). He conducted them in spite of age, poor health, and blindness. In tribute, England honored its adoptive citizen by burial in Westminster Abbey.[4]

The outward similarities of the Baroque style which Bach and Handel shared are obvious, and their names are frequently linked. Both men were born in the same year, became organ virtuosos and celebrated composers, and were blind by the end of their lives. Yet no artists were less alike in temperament. Bach chose the provincial atmosphere of small towns and cared nothing for cosmopolitan life. He preferred to work quietly, secluded from the world. Handel, on the contrary, drew strength from personal contacts and enjoyed the acclaim of artistic success. The two men never met, and it is questionable that the works of one directly influenced the other. However unknowingly, they combined their gifts to close the Baroque Era with far-reaching contributions which opened the way for Classicism.

---

[2]   On August 1, 1714, Queen Anne died and was succeeded by the Elector of Hanover who became King George I. Handel had abandoned a post in Hanover for England where he preferred to live. Now he found himself under the patronage of a man he had slighted. Legend has it that he wrote his famous *Water Music* to win George's forgiveness. At any rate, it is certain that on July 17, 1717, the King and his court sailed from Whitehall to Chelsea where they had supper before sailing back. A second barge contained 50 musicians who played music especially composed by Handel for the occasion. Much later, Handel composed the *Royal Fireworks Music* in celebration of the Treaty of Aix-la-Chapelle in 1749.

[3]   Other celebrated *Oratorios* include *Samson* and *Semele* (1743), *Judas Maccabaeus* (1746), and *Solomon* (1748).

[4]   Handel became a naturalized Englishman in 1726.

Style

The vocal polyphonic era of the 16th Century, the Golden Age of polyphony, produced works dependent on single melodic lines in combination with other lines. These combinations in turn suggested the richer sonorities which were the beginnings of harmony. Handel, well-versed in polyphony, embraced the new sounds. With innate harmonic feeling, he created masterpieces of choral writing in the *Operas* and *Oratorios.* In choral writing, even more than instrumental, he reached a full expression of his genius. By temperament he was a composer of the theatre who understood the expressive possibilities of vocal sound.

Where Handel's vocal and instrumental means were tonally varied, unexpected, and dramatic, his keyboard resources were simpler by contrast. He introduced no complexity for its own sake and often wrote interchangeably for organ or harpsichord, as in the *Concertos.* However, in the *Suites* for harpsichord, Handel caught the lively spirit of the dance forms of the day and wrote idiomatically for the harpsichord with its quick repetitions and rapid scale passages. With strong melodic feeling and polyphonic skill, he created short, well-defined works including the dances and contrapuntal forms which played up the brightness, directness, and beauty of the style itself and of the harpsichord as an instrument.

Handel's melody is forthright with emphasis on beauty of line and interval. It hints frequently at the broad, singable Italian style of the operas. The keyboard harmony contains frequent dominant-tonic progressions which suggest the chordal accompaniment of operatic vocal lines. Dotted notes and repeated rhythmic patterns create vitality and as a favorite device often appear throughout complete sections.

Compositions

Handel's most important keyboard compositions are the two volumes of *Suites* (also called *Lessons*) published in 1720 and 1733 respectively, and the *Chaconne with 62 Variations in G* published in 1732. Each volume has 8 *Suites.* A third collection is made up of *Six Fugues,* 1735. The *Suites* do not generally have the cohesion or musical depth of Bach's *French* and *English Suites* and *Partitas.* Almost all contain good individual movements, however, some of them outstanding. Paul Henry Lang[5] suggests that their somewhat sparse and austere writing came from Handel's habit of improvising in public performance, using the written music only as a sketch. Of the three volumes, the first is the best; the second and third have certain distinguished movements but are less consistently interesting than the first. In addition to the three volumes and the *Chaconne* mentioned above, there are two other *Chaconnes with Variations, Suites,* and *Suite* movements.

The suites are collections of short forms treated contrapuntally. They include *Preludes, Fugues, Dances, Airs with Variations, Passacaglias,* and *Chaconnes.* The number of

---

[5]   Lang, Paul Henry, *George Frideric Handel,* W. W. Norton and Co., Inc., New York, 1966.

movements varies from four to six for each *Suite.* The order is flexible; in general, the rule of contrast of feeling and tempo is followed.

The *Preludes* are free in form; the *Fugues* generally simple. The *Dances,* including *Allemandes, Courantes, Sarabandes,* and *Gigues* follow two part form, each coming to a complete cadence, repeated. The *Allemandes,* dances of German origin in 4/4 time, involve complex contrapuntal writing. The *Courantes,* in 3/4 or 3/8 time, are of the Italian type, simple and flowing.[6] Derived from the French verb *courir* (to run), they are cheerful and energetic. The *Sarabandes,* in 3/4 or 3/2 time, originated in an ancient, measured dance introduced into France in the 17th Century by a dancer named Sarabanda. The form gave Handel an excellent opportunity to write broad melodies in his favorite Italian style. The *gigues,* in 6/8 or 12/8 time, are merry and bright. *Airs with Variations* were popular for their ability to combine interesting themes with a variety of technical display in composition and performance. *Passacaglias* were early Italian or Spanish dances similar in character to *Chaconnes.* In the *Passacaglia,* the theme was used in any part of the contrapuntal web making up the variations, often so disguised as to be hardly recognizable, while the *Chaconne* became a series of variations on a theme kept invariably in the bass (ground bass).

Volume I HG ii, 1-60; HHA iv/1 (1720)

Suite No. 5 in E

The Air with Variations from Suite No. 5 is Handel's most popular harpsichord work. Two choir singers of the Chapel Royal trumped up and supported with spurious evidence the story of the origin of the title, *Harmonious Blacksmith.* The story involved Handel in a sudden storm. To avoid the storm, he stepped into a blacksmith's shop and listened to the blacksmith sing as the sparks flew from the anvil. This chimerical song is the theme, or *air,* of the five variations which make up the last movement and bring it to a close in a climax of rushing scales.

Suite No. 7 in G minor

The *Passacaglia* from *Suite No. 7* is one of the most celebrated *Passacaglias* in keyboard literature with a theme of strength and nobility. The *Suite* itself most nearly approaches the monumental style of Handel's choral writing with unity of feeling which raises it above the works in either volume.

Suite No. 8 in F minor

Suite No. 8, like *No. 5,* is a fine work from beginning to end, with polyphony well suited to the keyboard, graceful melodies, attractive *Dances,* and a brilliant *Fugue.*

---

[6] Bach, on the contrary, chose the French type in 3/2 or 6/4 time, with heightened rhythmic and melodic intricacies.

Volume II HG ii, 63-122; HHA iv/5 (1733)

Suite No. 1 in B flat

The *Aria* from *Suite No. 1* became the theme of Brahms' celebrated work, *Variations and Fugue on a Theme by Handel, Op. 24.*

Chaconne with 62 Variations in G HG ii, 110; HHA iv/5, 77 (1732)

The *Chaconne with Variations in G* (which also appears as *Prelude* and *Chaconne with 62 Variations Op. 1*) shows to perfection the virtuoso display of the harpsichord age and remains among the finest examples of chaconne writing.

Volume III HG ii, 161-74; HHA iv/6, 1-23 (1735)

The *6 Fugues* or *Voluntarys for the Organ or Harpsichord* are grateful to play, witty and vigorous. Handel used them as a kind of reservoir for later choral ideas.

In Handel's time, *Concerto Grosso* meant a small group of instruments playing in contrast to a larger body of strings.[7] However, Handel's numerous keyboard *Concertos*, organ, or harpsichord, incorporate clearly the idea of soloist and orchestra, a concept which Mozart was to develop later. There are three sets of *Concertos: 6 Concertos Op. 4* (1738); *6 Concertos Op. 6* (1740); and *6 Concertos Op. 7* (1761). Handel played the *Concertos* between the acts of his *Oratorios* to furnish relief from the dramatic tension of the larger works. There are still occasional performances of at least two of these *Concertos*, those in *F major, Op. 4 No. 4* and *B flat major, Op. 4 No. 6.*

Editions:

Handel's works are identified by two main catalogue systems: G.F. Händels Werke; Ausgabe der Deutschen Händelgesellschaft, ed. F.W. Chrysander Leipzig 1858-1894, abbr. HG; and Hallische Händel-Ausgabe im Auftrage der George Friedrich Händel-Gesellschaft, Kassel, 1955, abbr.   HHA

Selected Works for Keyboard

New Grove 1980 lists the following, with the *Suites* and *Fugues* detailed below:
Suite de Piéces pour le Clavecin Vol. I (8), HHA iv/1   (1720): *A; F; D minor; E minor; E minor; F sharp minor; G minor; F.*

[7] Concertante style developed during the Baroque Era. It combined solo instruments with or without orchestra.

Prelude and Chaconne with 62 Variations, HHA iv/5 (1732)

Sonata for the Clavecin Op. 2 (1732)

Capriccio for the Clavecin Op. 3 (1732)

Preludio and Allegro for the Clavecin Op. 4 (1732)

Fantasie for the Clavecin Op. 5 (1732)

Suite de Piéces Vol. II (8), HHA iv/5 (1733): *B flat; G; D minor; D minor; E minor; G minor; B flat; G.*

Fugues Vol. III (6) HHA iv/6,1-23, (1735): *G minor; G; B flat; B minor; A minor; C minor.*

For Keyboard and Orchestra

Concertos for Organ or Harpsichord: Set I (1738): 6 *Concertos,* Op. 4: *G minor; B flat; G minor; F; F; B flat.* Set II (1740): 6 *Concertos,* Op. 6: *F; A; D minor; G; D; G minor.* Set III (1761): 6 *Concertos,* Op. 7: *B flat; A; B flat; D minor; D minor; B flat.*

Sarabande, Gigue and Passacaglia
from *Suite VII Vol. I*

Sarabande.

Gigue.

*) Die Halben sind zu zählen, sodass das | *Count the half notes; which means* | Compter par blanches, le morceau
Stück ein ziemlich rasches Tempo er- | *that the piece is played in rather* | demandant un tempo assez rapide.
fordert. | *fast time.* |

a)   b)   c)   d)   e) siehe d)

Allegro commodo.

Passacaglia.

a)

Allegro con brio.

a) Als Pralltriller auszuführen. | *To be executed as transient shake.* | Exécuter comme mordant.

3 | THE CLASSICAL AGE OF SONATA FORM

Haydn and Mozart were almost singlehanded in establishing the major forms of instrumental music which define the Classical Age. Their contribution was so vast that it is without parallel in music history. Through the creation and development of *sonata form*, they unified and perfected the structure of the *symphony, concerto, quintet, quartet, trio*, and the *sonata* itself.[1] The word *sonata* or *sound-piece* was used originally to distinguish it from *cantata* or *song-piece*. *Sonata* and *sonata-form* were purely instrumental conceptions built largely on the principle of contrasting themes against harmonic background. The early sonatas, *sonatas da camera*, were interchangeable with the *suite*, an instrumental form patterned after dances of the day. However, the *sonata* was soon separated from the lighter dance forms, as it became musically more and more serious.

Domenico Scarlatti, born the same year as Bach and Handel, was a pioneer in writing some of the earliest *sonatas*. Unlike his great contemporaries, he was not content to stay within the contrapuntal forms. He had an extraordinary gift for simple, joyous melody which he used in short pieces he called *sonatas*. He developed only one theme at a time, and that not in depth, in a single movement.

Other early composers added details to the emerging *sonata form*. Among them were two of Bach's sons, C.P.E. Bach and Johann Christian Bach. C.P.E. Bach's *sonatas* were written in three movements, fast, slow, fast. The first movement was built on one theme and developed in the free fashion of a *fantasia*. The themes were in-

---

[1]   The distinction between *sonata form* and *sonata* is that of theory and application. *Sonata form* is the genre, the pattern, the collection of rules which may be applied regardless of the medium whether symphonic or chamber music. The *sonata* as it eventually evolved is an individual work built on the rules of sonata form.

strumental in character, chosen with an eye to increasing possibilities for development.

In the Baroque age, before *sonata form,* the binding force of contrapuntal writing was the *fugue.* [2] Its strong lines were the predecessors of the distinctive melodies of *sonata form.* Haydn and Mozart added the elements of key relationship, tonal contrast, and balance of phrase. Sonata form has been expanded by succeeding composers, but its principles as defined by Haydn and Mozart remain essentially unchanged. Like all great composers, Haydn and Mozart looked back as well as forward. They incorporated frequent contrapuntal writing and startling personal expressiveness – but always within the framework we now define as Classical.

Mozart kept C.P.E. Bach's basic conception of tempo contrast, but he developed each movement with greater length, complexity, ingenuity, and expressiveness. The *first movement* was the most elaborate. A second theme, based on the important Classical element of tonal contrast, was added to the single one originally employed by Scarlatti and C.P.E. Bach. Forming a contrast to the opening theme, it provided additional material for the development section. The first movement conformed to this plan:

Exposition: The basic pattern of the *opening movement* contained the statement of the themes, the first theme in the tonic, the second in the dominant or relative major if the first theme was in minor. Between the two themes was a transitional passage.

Development: Here, the themes of the exposition or motifs from them were developed and contrasted in free form.

Recapitulation: This final section brought back the two themes introduced in the exposition, both stated in the tonic key.

The *second movement,* usually slow, stressed melody and expressiveness. Frequently it was written in simple two-part form[3] as used in the *Suites* of Handel and Bach; sometimes it was composed in three-part form, sometimes as *Theme and Variations.* The *last movement,* or *Finale,* was occasionally in the form of the first movement, but more often was a bright, quick *Rondo.*[4]

A broken chord type of accompaniment suitable as background for melody became an important feature of Classical music in the first half of the 18th Century. While this device has been attributed to the Italian, Domenico Alberti (1710-40), he probably did no more than give it a certain notoriety through overuse in his own compositions. At first, the *Alberti bass* was considered revolutionary; later, Haydn, Mozart, and Beethoven found it indispensable.

[2]   The *fugue* is not considered a form but a method; as such, it reached its highest development with Bach.

[3]   Two-part form (binary) may be explained as two sections of related music played consecutively (a b). Three-part form (ternary) contains a repetition of the original section after the contrasting section (a b a). Various repeats of the sections may be made.

[4]   In the *rondo,* the original theme *a* alternates with different episodes (a b a c a d a etc.).

Beethoven moved ahead of traditional classicism, introduced exceptions to rules established by Haydn and Mozart, expanded early keyboard resources, and enlarged personal expressiveness. He brought *sonata form* to its zenith and heralded the stirrings of Romanticism. Great changes were in store in the two centuries to come, but to this day the essential qualities of the *Classical Age of Sonata Form* continually reappear, a heritage of clarity, order, and balance.

Born in Rohrau, Austria,
March 31, 1732

Died in Vienna, Austria,
May 31, 1809,
Age 77 years

Franz Joseph Haydn

Historical Sketch

Franz Joseph Haydn was born in the Croatian village of Rohrau near the boundary between Austria and Hungary. His father was a journeyman. His mother, burdened by a large family and a small income, was a religious woman who gave Haydn a sense of divine power which stayed with him through life. Her influence appeared frequently in his compositions, from the opening *In nomine Domini* to the closing *Laus Deo.*

When Haydn was six, a relative named Johann Mathias Frankh took him to the neighboring town of Hainburg for music instruction. Under Frankh's discipline, he learned to play the harpsichord and violin and developed a good singing voice. Two years later, in 1740, he was accepted at St. Stephen's Cathedral Choir School in Vienna.[1] He remained in Vienna for twenty years developing from a talented choirboy into a serious musician and composer.

One of his first teachers in Vienna was the Italian composer Porpora, a contem-

[1] In the 18th Century, it was the custom for every cathedral to maintain a choir school where boys were trained to sing the masses, oratorios, cantatas, and requiems which accompanied the cathedral's regular services. The choir boys began their training when young, customarily staying until they were fifteen or sixteen years old. With practical and thorough teaching, they learned various branches of music: violin, organ, and harpsichord playing, singing and composition.

porary of Handel who introduced Haydn to the melodic style developing in Italian opera. As his reputation grew, Haydn was asked occasionally to direct a small orchestra at Edler von Fürnburg's musical gatherings. Through von Fürnburg, Haydn met his next patron, Count Morzin, and became musical director of Morzin's estate outside Vienna. Two years later, he was sponsored by Count Esterházy whose noble Hungarian family was outstanding among music patrons. Under Haydn, first in Eisenstadt and later at Süttör, the Esterházy orchestra became one of the finest in Europe.[2]

Haydn remained with the Esterházy family for almost thirty years. While patronage strained his innate good fellowship, it also gave him the opportunity for constant musical experimentation. Haydn's remarkable defining of the basic forms of the symphony, string quartet, piano trio, and piano sonata was accomplished during this period.

When Prince Nicolaus Esterházy died in 1790, Haydn visited London under contract to the music manager Solomon. During this and a second trip a few years later, he wrote twelve new symphonies, bringing his total to one hundred and four. The optimism and musical energy of his youth were undimmed by age or long years of work. To climax his public recognition, he was given the degree of Doctor of Music at Oxford.

Returning to Vienna after his second London visit, he wrote in 1798 a work new to his style, the oratorio, *The Creation*. Adding to the enthusiastic reception of *The Creation* and the popularity of numerous symphonies and quartets, he wrote three years later another oratorio, *The Seasons*. This was his last great work. At sixty-nine his strength began to fail. He lived quietly eight years longer, making a few public appearances at concerts.

Style

A classicist, Haydn created absolute music[3] through the definition and development of sonata form where interest lay in tonal development (key relationship), balance of phrase, design, and architecture. Applying sonata form to piano composition, Haydn wrote numerous keyboard *Sonatas* which had a profound influence on the direction Mozart and Beethoven took in bringing the form to its fullest expression. Between the years of 1766 and the early 1770s, Haydn went through a period of "romantic crisis" which was part of the larger "Sturm und Drang" (Storm and Stress) which

[2]   In Europe at this time there were many private orchestras owned by the music loving nobility. An outstanding composer was engaged as director whose duty it was to write and conduct the music performed by the orchestra. Members of the orchestra lived on the family estate as virtual servants. They were required to live among the household staff and wear uniforms which distinguished them as a class. This system of patronage had existed to a certain extent during the youth of Bach and Handel, was widely accepted in the time of Haydn and Mozart, but disappeared by Beethoven's time as a result of extensive social changes, among them the American and French Revolutions.

[3]   "Pure" music as opposed to "programme" music which tells a story, illustrates action, or evokes a scene.

affected German literature and music from roughly 1760-1780. It was most marked in his symphonies and string quartets of these years, although the *Sonatas*, particularly *Hob.XVI:20 in C minor* and *Hob.XVI:46 in A flat,* also show strongly the trend toward emotionalism and new formal and harmonic approaches. Other features which Haydn developed at this time were a wider use of minor keys, specific dynamic marks, sharp contrasts of volume, syncopated patterns, and wide leaps within the themes.

Haydn's steady musical growth during his whole life embraced new styles and ideas. Expanding pure Classicism with harmonic and structural originality, he created toward the end of his life a youthful freedom in instrumental and choral writing. The late piano *Sonatas* share the remarkable daring of his last years.

Haydn's rhythmic vitality is probably a counterpart of his own energy. Alive and compelling, it permeates his compositions with strength and directness. Broad and singable melodies stem from the Italian school and early association with Porpora. Melodic cheerfulness and humor reflect a vigorous Croatian heritage. Keyboard harmony is essentially simple, but its strength of key relationships establishes the formal structure developed and furthered by Mozart and Beethoven.

The most numerous of the piano works are the *Sonatas*. As with symphonies and quartets, Haydn wrote piano sonatas his entire musical life; they provide an almost visible diagram of his development. Lacking a performer's virtuosity, he adapted to his own use the keyboard style of C.P.E. Bach, incorporating repeated notes, ornaments, chordal effects, recurring triplet figures, and a free ranging use of the keyboard. Only the earliest *Sonatas* show in short answering phrases and changes of register the influence of the harpsichord. By the 1780's, the piano began to replace the harpsichord. Haydn took advantage of the developing piano's greater versatility in his later *Sonatas,* utilizing the fortepiano and the larger, more resonant English instruments made by the London firm of John Broadwood and Son.

Compositions

Haydn's keyboard works are overshadowed by the pianistic appropriateness and freshness of Mozart. Nevertheless, certain individual compositions in free form and some of the *Sonatas* are undisputed masterpieces which cast their shadows into the Romantic era.

The Sonatas preceding *Sonata in D Hob.XVI:19* (1767) follow the character of the suite. This *Sonata* itself is more mature, closer in style to the sonata pattern of C.P.E. Bach. *Sonata in C minor Hob. XVI:20* (1771), one of the few in minor key, casts off charm and grace in favor of intensity.

Sonata in D Hob.XVI:19 (1767)

The year 1767 marked a growth in power and concept of Haydn's succeeding *Sonatas*. The *D major* is larger and more heroic than any of the previous *Sonatas*.

Sonata in C minor Hob.XVI:20 (1771)

The *C minor Sonata* is a strong, tragic work where Haydn's piano technique matches the depth of his emotion. The outer movements display unbroken tension, while the *Andante con moto* forms a slow movement of perfect proportion.

Four sets of *Sonatas,* along with individual *Sonatas Hob.XVI:33-34* of 1777 and 1778, form a middle period between the trailblazers, *Hob.XVI:19* and *20,* and the last five *Sonatas, Hob. XVI:48-52.* The first set of 6, *Hob.XVI:21-26* (1773) contains in *Hob. XVI:24 in D* a *Sonata* which is well balanced with an unusual, dark *Adagio* in D minor. A second set, *Hob.XVI:27-32* (1776) includes the *Sonata Hob.XVI:32 in B minor,* a stormy work only slightly less intense than *Hob.XVI:20 in C minor.* A third set, *Hob.XVI:35-39* (published in 1780) incorporates bravura writing and contrasting ornate slow movements; both *Hob.XVI:37 in D* and *Hob XVI:38 in E flat* share these qualities. A fourth set includes *Hob.XVI:40-47* (all preceding 1789), notably the great *Sonata in A flat Hob.XVI:46.*

The last five *Sonatas Hob.XVI:48-52* (1789-1794) are a remarkable final group where Haydn's poetry and imagination are at full strength.

Sonata in C Hob.XVI:48 (publ. in 1789)

Bold originality lies in the design of this two movement *Sonata* which opens with an extended *Andante con espressione* and closes with a bright *Presto Rondo* in the spirit of the late *Symphony* finales.

Sonata in E flat Hob.XVI:49 (1789/90)

Dedicated to Marianne von Genzinger

Von Genzinger, physician to Prince Esterhazy, and his wife Marianne were connoisseurs of music. Their home in Vienna was a gathering place for people of discrimination and an artistic refuge for Haydn. Frau von Genzinger was an excellent pianist who pleased Haydn by playing with and for him. Haydn wrote this *Sonata* for her as a musical supplement to his other expressions of affection and respect.

Conflict and its resolution have long been the subject of art; Haydn used it in this *Sonata.* From the outset the themes show individuality, their role well marked in the struggle. The first movement presents the conflict, heightened in the *Adagio,* which Haydn considered the climax. The resolution comes in the cheerful flow of the *Finale.*

Sonata in C Hob.XVI:50 (1794-1795?)

Dedicated to Therese Jansen Bartolozzi[4]

The dry, witty opening *Allegro* and scherzo-like *Finale* are balanced by the middle movement *Adagio* which has the character of a fantasy. This *Sonata* and the two which follow show the influence of the new English pianos on Haydn's late pianistic style of sharp dynamic contrasts.

Sonata in D Hob.XVI:51 (1794)

Dedicated to Therese Jansen Bartolozzi

Rosemary Hughes[5] points to this *Sonata* as showing "the Haydnishness of Beethoven" where both men create fiery, restless movements against a background of quick harmonic progressions. Like Haydn's *Sonata No. 48, Sonata No. 51* is also in two movements. H.C. Robbins Landon[6] suggests that it stands between the big *Sonatas No. 50* and *No. 52* in the trilogy as a slow movement between powerful outer sections.

Sonata in E flat Hob.XVI:52 (1794)

Dedicated to Therese Jansen Bartolozzi

The virtuoso *Sonata in E flat* shows the monumental quality of Haydn's last keyboard style which runs the course of technical demands for massive brilliance. The first movement is compact to the point of tautness, but the modulations are startling in their freedom. The rhapsodic second movement *Adagio* has extraordinary rhythmic flexibility while the *Finale,* again like the first movement, is compact and technically demanding. H.C. Robbins Landon speaks of this *Sonata* as probably the greatest of Haydn's solo keyboard *Sonatas,* one of three[7] which were the most influential on the last part of the 18th Century. All three had a profound effect on early Romantic composers and established different but equally important approaches to the piano and its capabilities.

Among individual fine works in free form are *Capriccio in G Hob.XVII:1* (1765), highly thought of by Haydn himself, *Fantasia in C Hob.XVII:4* (1789), and the incomparable *Andante varié in F minor Hob.XVII:6* (1793)

---

[4]   A celebrated pianist, Therese Jansen, later married Bartolozzi whom Haydn met in London.
[5]   Hughes, Rosemary, *Haydn,* The Master Musician's Series, J.M. Dent and Sons Ltd., London, 1962, p. 146.
[6]   Landon, H.C. Robbins, *Haydn: Chronicle and Works,* Vol. III, Indiana University Press, Bloomington and London, 1976, p. 448.
[7]   The others are Mozart's *Sonata in C minor K.457* (1784) and Beethoven's *Pathétique Sonata Op. 13* (1799).

Fantasia in C Hob.XVII:4 (1789)

The *Fantasia* is one of Haydn's most humorous works with its sudden contrasts in texture and dynamics.

Andante varié in F minor Hob.XVII:6 (1793)

Dedicated to Barbara Ployer[8]

Of Haydn's several individual sets of variations, the F minor is outstanding. It is not only a masterpiece among Haydn's works, but one of the finest examples of theme and double variations in piano literature. The elements of contrast are set forth with refinement and balance. The *Variations* mark the beginning of the final period of Haydn's interest in the piano, the same period which produced the late *Sonatas*.

It was for Mozart rather than Haydn to establish the nature and importance of the piano concerto. Nevertheless Haydn, however superficially, first turned his genius in this direction. Many of the *Concertos*, also called *Concertinos* and *Divertimentos* and scored for organ or harpsichord, show a decided trend toward chamber music and are not distinguished as individual works. Those from the 1770's onward, however, reflect Haydn's growing perception of true concerto function. In 1784, he wrote a work of unmistakable maturity, the *Concerto in D Hob. XVIII:11*.

Concerto in D Hob. XVIII:11 (1784)

The most successful of the *Concertos*, the *D major* is a work which stands on its own, the climax of Haydn's writing in this form. The solo part is effective and the orchestral accompaniment is expanded beyond the usual strings to include oboes and horns. The final movement is the celebrated *Rondo all'Ungarese*.

In *duet* form, the *Master and Scholar Variations Hob. XVIIa:1* have charm and imagination.

Editions:

Haydn's works are identified by several catalogue systems including the Collected Edition; Haydn's own Catalogue (J. Haydns Werke, Leipzig); the Haydn Society; and Wiener Urtext Edition, Vienna, ed. by Christa Landon. Landon uses the further identification of Anthony van Hoboken (Hob.), an eminent Dutch musical bibliographer born in 1887. His collection contains a large number of works by Haydn as well as first editions of Handel. There is still some discrepancy in the total number of *Sonatas*. The

[8]   Daughter of the Salzburg "Hofagent" in Vienna, her pianism was admired also by Mozart and Beethoven. Hoboken gives the dedication to Mme. Joseph de Braun.

Collected Edition lists 52, while Wiener Urtext counts 49 as indubitably genuine.[9] The *Sonatas* presented here and in the complete listing follow the Wiener Urtext Edition with the Hoboken identification, ed. Christa Landon, 1973.   HOB

Selected Works for Keyboard [10]

Sonata No. 1 in G, Hob.XVI:8 (before 1766)

Sonata No. 2 in C, Hob.XVI:7 (before 1766)

Sonata No. 3 in F, Hob.XVI:9 (before 1766)

Sonata No. 4 in G, Hob.XVI:G1 (before 1766)

Sonata No. 5 in G, Hob.XVI:11 (?)

Sonata No. 6 in C, Hob.XVI:10 (before 1766)

Sonata No. 7 in D, Hob.XVII:D1 (before 1766)

Sonata No. 8 in A, Hob.XVI:5 (before 1763)

Sonata No. 9 in D, Hob.XVI:4 (before 1766)

Sonata No. 10 in C, Hob.XVI:1 (before 1766)

Sonata No. 11 in B flat, Hob.XVI:2 (before 1766)

Sonata No. 12 in A, Hob.XVI:12 (before 1766)

Sonata No. 13 in G, Hob.XVI:6 (before 1766)

Sonata No. 14 in C, Hob.XVI:3 (before 1766)

Sonata No. 15 in E, Hob.XVI:13 (before 1766)

Sonata No. 16 in D, Hob.XVI:14 (before 1766)

Sonata No. 17 in E flat, Hob. deest (?)

Sonata No. 18 in E flat, Hob. deest (?)

Sonata No. 19 in E minor, Vol./Cf., Hob.XVI:47 (before 1776)

Sonata No. 20 in B flat, Hob.XVI:18 (ca. 1766/67?)

Sonata Nos. 21-27 (the lost works): in D minor, Hob.XVI:2a; *in A*, Hob.XVI:2b; *in B*, Hob.XVI:2c; *in B flat*, Hob.XVI:2d; *in E minor* Hob.XVI:2e; *in C*, Hob.XVI:2g; Hob.XVI:2h

Sonata No. 28 in D, Hob.XIV:5 (ca. 1765/66?)

Sonata No. 29 in E flat, Hob.XVI:45 (1766)

Sonata No. 30 in D, Hob.XVI:19 (1767)

Sonata No. 31 in A flat, Hob.XVI:46 (ca. 1767/68?)

Sonata No. 32 in G minor, Hob.XVI:44 (ca. 1768/70?)

---

[9]   Wiener Urtext brings the total in Christa Landon's edition to 62, including fragments of 8 ''lost'' *Sonatas*.

[10]   The Arabic numerals which identify the *Sonatas* appear here as they are used in the thematic index of the Weiner Urtext Edition, Christa Landon, Ed. They do not always correspond to the Hoboken numbers.

Sonata No. 33 in C minor, Hob.XVI:20 (1771)

Sonata No. 34 in D, Hob.XVI:33 (ca. 1771/73?)

Sonata No. 35 in A flat, Hob.XVI:43 (ca. 1771/73?)

Sonata No. 36 in C, Hob.XVI:21 (1773)

Sonata No. 37 in E, Hob.XVI:22 (1773)

Sonata No. 38 in F, Hob.XVI:23 (1773)

Sonata No. 39 in D, Hob.XVI:24 (1773)

Sonata No. 40 in E flat, Hob.XVI:25 (1773)

Sonata No. 41 in A, Hob.XVI:26 (1773)

Sonata No. 42 in G, Hob.XVI:27 (1776)

Sonata No. 43 in E flat, Hob.XVI:28 (1776)

Sonata No. 44 in F, Hob.XVI:29 (begun in 1774)

Sonata No. 45 in A, Hob.XVI:30 (1776)

Sonata No. 46 in E, Hob.XVI:31 (1776)

Sonata No. 47 in B minor, Hob.XVI:32 (1776)

Sonata No. 48 in C, Hob.XVI:35 (ca. 1777/79?)

Sonata No. 49 in C sharp minor, Hob.XVI:36 (ca. 1777/79?)

Sonata No. 50 in D, Hob.XVI:37 (ca. 1777/79?)

Sonata No. 51 in E flat, Hob.XVI:38 (ca. 1777/79?)

Sonata No. 52 in G, Hob.XVI:39 (1780)

Sonata No. 53 in E minor, Hob.XVI:34 (ca. 1781/82?)

Sonata No. 54 in G, Hob.XVI:40 (ca. 1782/84)

Sonata No. 55 in B flat, Hob.XVI:41 (ca. 1782/84)

Sonata No. 56 in D, Hob.XVI:42 (ca. 1782/84)

Sonata No. 57 in F, Hob.XVI:47 (1788)

Sonata No. 58 in C, Hob.XVI:48 (1789)

Sonata No. 59 in E flat, Hob.XVI:49 (1789/90)

Sonata No. 60 in C, Hob.XVI:50 (1794/95?)

Sonata No. 61 in D, Hob.XVI:51 (1794/95?)

Sonata No. 62 in E flat, Hob.XVI:52 (1794)

Capriccio in G, Hob.XVII:1 (1765) (for harpsichord)

Arietta con variazioni in G major, Hob.XVII:2[11] (before 1765?)

12 *Variations in E flat major*, Hob.XVII:3 (before 1774) (for harpsichord)

Fantasia in C major, Hob.XVII:4 (1789) (for piano)

Andante con variazioni in F minor, Hob.XVII:6 (1793) (for piano)

Adagio in F major, Hob.XVII:9 (1786) (for harpsichord or piano) (attributed to Haydn)

32 *pieces for Mechanical Clocks*

[11]   Hob.XVII:2 also lists Arietta with 12 variations in A.

For Keyboard and Orchestra

Concertos, Concertinos, and Divertimentos: [12]
    C major, Hob.XVIII:1 (1756?)
    D major, Hob.XVIII:2 (1767)
    F major, Hob.XVIII:6 (1766)
    F major, Hob.XVIII:3 (1771)
    G major, Hob.XVIII:4 (1781)
    D major, Hob.XVIII:11 (1784)
    C major, Hob.XIV:11 (1760)
    C major, Hob.XIV:10 (1764-67)
    G major, Hob.XIV:4 (1764)
    C major, Hob.XIV:3 (1771)
    C major, Hob.XIV:7 (1767)
    F major, Hob.XIV:9 (1767)
    C major, Hob.XIV:8 (1768-72)
    E flat major, Hob.XIV:1 (1766)
    F major, Hob.XIV:2 (1767-71)

For Keyboard Duet

Variations in F major: Master and Scholar, Hob.XVIIa:1

[12]   As listed in New Grove, 1980. Additional Concertos, attributed to Haydn, are also listed, *Haydn*, p. 387.

Finale
from *Sonata in E flat*, Hob.XVI:52

a) ad libitum

Born in Salzburg, Austria,
January 27, 1756
Died in Vienna, Austria,
December 5, 1791,
Age 35 years

Wolfgang Amadeo Mozart

Historical Sketch

The earliest compositions attributed to Mozart appeared in his father Leopold's writing in the *Nannerl Notebook* of 1759 which Leopold compiled and named for Mozart's older sister. It contains material from contemporary composers arranged progressively for her instruction. Between 1761 and 1763, Leopold Mozart added Wolfgang's first works to the collection. As the only intellectual at the Salzburg court chapel for many years, Leopold held a unique place among his musical contemporaries. He composed many symphonies, masses, chamber works, keyboard sonatas, and theoretical works. Among the latter was his famous *Violinschule,* published in 1756, the year Wolfgang was born. It ranks in importance with C.P.E. Bach's *Treatise on the Art of Clavier Playing* of 1753.

Leopold was an ambitious man who saw nothing wrong in showing off Wolfgang's exceptional talents to the public and using every possible occasion to advance his own reputation and livelihood. Exploitation and opportunism certainly entered his management of Wolfgang and Nannerl's early years. However, his incessant advice which continued through letters into Wolfgang's later years did not alter Wolfgang's high spirits, affection, eagerness to learn, independence of musical thought, or charming irresponsibility which kept him impecunious most of his life.

The strength of Mozart's genius, choosing and discarding influences as he saw fit, made him the most universal composer the Western world has known. He was supreme in every form of musical expression, and he used every tool of composition with perfection.

At 5, Mozart made his first public appearance at Salzburg University. The next two years saw performances before the Elector of Bavaria, Empress Maria Theresa, and the court of Salzburg. On the strength of Mozart's dazzling success at improvising, his father decided to storm Paris with visits to every important musical center on the way. There were concerts in Munich, Augsburg, Mainz, Frankfurt, and Brussels before the Mozarts reached Paris. In Paris, young Mozart played before Louix XV at Versailles and published his first works, 2 pairs of *Sonatas* for keyboard and violin. He also met Baron Friedrich Melchior Grimm, of literary fame *(Correspondence Littéraire)*, who was later a helpful friend. After five months in Paris, Mozart and his father went to London where they stayed for over a year. While there, Mozart played for King George III. He met Johann Christian (the *London*) Bach with whom he improvised on the harpsichord. At this time, 1764-5, he composed his first symphonies. For the next five years, Mozart's travels took him back to Paris briefly, to Vienna where he composed the *Singspiel, Bastien und Bastienne,* and to Salzburg where his *opera buffa, La finta simplice,* was performed. He was made an honorary Konzertmeister to the Salzburg court.

In 1770, Mozart's father took him to Italy where he was still considered a child prodigy and drew an admiring and gift-giving public. Mozart wrote his first *String Quartet K.80/73f* outside Milan and successfully produced his opera, *Mitridate, Rè di Ponto,* which had 22 performances. In Rome, he performed the remarkable feat of memorizing Allegri's *Miserere* after one hearing at the Sistine Chapel. Mozart returned to Salzburg and composed there until the end of 1773 with short visits to Italy. This was a fertile period in which he wrote 12 *Symphonies, 8 Divertimentos,* a new opera, *Lucio Silla,* string quartets, and the solo motet, *Exsultate, jubilate.*

By the end of 1773, Leopold Mozart looked toward better financial prospects for his son. His own finances were stable because of his employment at the Salzburg court under Archbishop Hieronymus and the gifts he received on tour. Father and son spent the following year in Vienna. Wolfgang composed with growing variety and intellectual maturity a series of works which included 6 *String Quartets,* the first *Piano Concerto K.175,* and two additional *Concertos,* one for two violins and orchestra and one for bassoon and orchestra. Mozart returned to Salzburg in 1775 and stayed for the next two years until he asked for release from the Archbishop's service. He filled the two years with an incredible number of new works, the opera *La finta gardiniera* (publ. complete in 1978), the earliest surviving piano *Sonatas,* five violin *Concertos,* and four piano *Concertos.*

Between 1777 and 1781 Mozart traveled to Mannheim, Paris, Salzburg, and Munich. His mother accompanied him, as his father was unable to leave Salzburg. In Mannheim, aside from his musical obligations, he fell in love with 16 year old Aloysia Weber, already a recognized singer, whose family were acquainted with his parents.

Letters about the attachment went back and forth between Mozart and his father, reflecting Mozart's gossipy frivolity and his father's disapproval.

Mozart and his mother continued to Paris where Frau Mozart became critically ill. She died unexpectedly, and Mozart left Paris at his father's request to return to Salzburg by way of Munich. During the next four years, Mozart was appointed as salaried court organist at Salzburg and produced a chain of compositions which number 5 important piano *Sonatas, K. 309, 310, 311, 331, and 332.* In 1781, he moved to Vienna with the Archbishop's establishment. He was relegated to the position of servant and grew increasingly resentful. At the end of the year, he won a permanent release from Hieronymus and moved to the house of his Mannheim friends, the Webers. Aloysia was now married, but he fell in love with the third daughter, Constanze. The following year, he received his father's consent to marry Constanze. The ceremony took place at St. Stephen's Cathedral in Vienna where Mozart lived between travels until his death.

He was contented with his marriage but was unable to get away from lasting financial troubles. Nannerl analyzed his situation correctly when she said that Mozart was incapable of managing his own affairs and Constanze was unable to help him. Leopold Mozart's death in 1787 ended a certain stabilizing element in Mozart's affairs, even though Mozart published in that year a number of works for ready money and was appointed to the post of Court Kammermusicus.

The crowning achievement of Mozart's career came during the last five years of his life when he produced four operatic masterpieces,[1] and his three most celebrated symphonies.[2] A few months before his death, while completing *The Magic Flute,* he began his final work, the *Requiem.*[3] He fell ill and became obsessed with the premonition that he was writing the mass for his own death. The cause of death was registered as military fever, later as rheumatic inflammatory fever. There were posthumous rumors that he was poisoned, but there is no evidence to support the theory. He was buried in a mass grave, in the custom of the day, at St. Mark's churchyard outside Vienna.

Style

Bach and Handel brought the Baroque era to its close, while Haydn and Mozart created and defined the new Classical Era. Each set of composers shared characteristics of the particular musical span but wrote with unmistakable individuality. A study of Bach's contrapuntal style by the side of Handel's operatic and choral methods gives a clear profile of each composer. With Haydn and Mozart, surface differences are harder

---

[1]   *The Marriage of Figaro,* 1786; *Don Giovanni,* 1787; *Cosi fan Tutte,* 1790; *The Magic Flute,* 1791.

[2]   The *Jupiter,* the *G Minor* and *E flat Major,* all completed in the space of six weeks in the year 1788.

[3]   A stranger came to Mozart to commission the *Mass* but refused to give information about himself. He was later identified as the steward of Count Franz von Walsegg who intended to have the *Requiem* performed as his own composition.

to find because both composers used contrapuntal texture freely, added supple melodies which were not an outgrowth of counterpoint, and developed true harmonic feeling. But in general, it was Haydn who defined the method and Mozart who expanded it.

Contrast of themes and variety of key relationships were among the foundations of the sonata form of the Classical Era. Haydn exemplified these ideals. Mozart not only incorporated them but pushed the developing form of the piano sonata and piano concerto to the limits of pure Classicism where Beethoven's further innovations waited. The perfection and variety of Mozart's art are expressed in melodies of exceptional beauty, harmonic progressions which include free use of discord, and lilting rhythms. The piano works embody these characteristics as they do the drama and emotion of the operas, symphonies, and string quartets. Mozart's remark that melody is the essence of music is borne out by his own gift for melodic flow, unequalled except possibly by Schubert. Like Chopin, he enriches his scores with serpentine melodies and decorative, expressive chromaticism. Additionally, his delicate, shimmering effects bring to mind Debussy's delight in intrinsic sound quality.

The startling harmonies of Beethoven were yet to appear, but Mozart's occasional arresting dissonances remind listeners that Mozart also was creating emotional impact through unexpected harmonic modulation and resolution. He achieves architectural balance by making each motif indispensable to the grand design. His many masterpieces among the *Sonatas* and *Concertos* illustrate development over Haydn's in length, complexity of harmony, and variety of key relationship.

Compositions

Mozart's leading piano solo works include *Sonatas, Fantasies, Rondos,* and *Variations.* There are in addition twenty-five *Concertos* for solo piano and orchestra as well as numerous *Duets.* These works ran the course of Mozart's creative life.

In 1774-75, Mozart composed six *Sonatas* (K.279-284) which he performed frequently on a grand tour of Mannheim and Paris in 1777-78. The first five show influences of Haydn and Johann Christian Bach but already incorporate the flowing imagination, melodic grace, and originality of structure which characterize the later *Sonatas.* The sixth *Sonata in D major K.284,* so-called Dürnitz, is the culmination of this group.

Sonata in D major K.284 (1775)

In this *Sonata,* for the first time, Mozart wrote a true *Theme and Variations* as an entire last movement. The *Variations* possess chromaticism, full-bodied sound, and the brightness of concerto style, meeting the request of Baron Dürnitz for a work of difficulty and virtuosity.

To supplement the first six *Sonatas*, Mozart created a fresh repertoire while on tour in Mannheim and Paris with seven new *Sonatas*. The first two, *Sonata in C major K.309* and *Sonata in D major K.311*, are called the *Mannheim Sonatas* because of their completion in that city. Mozart considered them among his most difficult to that point.

Sonata in C major K.309 (1777)

Mozart wrote this *Sonata* for Mademoiselle Rose, the daughter of Capellmeister Cannabich, orchestral conductor at Mannheim. The first movement has rhythmic verve, the second, lyric poetry, and the last, subtle expressiveness. Mozart wanted to make the second movement *Andante* "exactly like Mademoiselle Rose herself, a pretty and charming young girl of thirteen."

Sonata in D major K.311 (1777)

The second Mannheim *Sonata* is conceived in a more extended virtuoso style than the preceding C major.

The five Paris *Sonatas* of 1777-78, *K.310, 330, 331, 332,* and *333,* show expansion and intensification of personal feeling leading to the later *Concertos*.

Sonata in A minor K.310 (1778)

For Mozart, the key of A minor was one of hopelessness. This mood pervades the *Sonata* with darkness; even the *Presto* lives in shadow. Mozart wrote it in the aftermath of his mother's sudden death.

Sonata in C major K.330 (1778)

The *Sonata in C major,* lighter than the preceding *Sonata* in relative minor, represents for Alfred Einstein[4] one of Mozart's most loveable compositions.

Sonata in A major K.331 (1778)

The famous *alla turca Rondo* overbalances this *Sonata* with its irresistible drive. However the personality of the first movement is strong, unusual in its construction as *Theme* and *Variations*. The entire *Sonata* displays tonal beauty.

---

4 Einstein, *Mozart – His Character and His Work,* Oxford University Press, London, New York, Toronto, 1945; eighth printing, 1977.

Sonata in F major K.332[5] and Sonata in B flat major K.333 (both 1778)

Both *Sonatas* are intimate works showing Mozart's skill as contrapuntalist in shaping counterpoint to the flexibility of incredibly free melodies.

Between the *Paris Sonatas* and the last three *Sonatas* published posthumously, *K.545, 570,* and *576,* two *Sonatas* appeared among the growing number of *Piano Concertos* much in demand, the great *Sonata in C minor K.457* and the *Sonata in F K.533.*

Sonata in C minor K. 457 (1784)

The *Sonata K.457* preceded by a Fantaisie K.475 is undeniably a great work of art, prophetic of the direction to be taken by piano music and an absorbing composition in its own right. The elements of tragedy and tenderness are predominant, alternated and contrasted. The *Fantaisie,* written a year later but appended to the *Sonata* by Mozart, is sharply drawn, in startling contrast to the composer's accustomed gracefulness.

Sonata in F K.533 (1788/1786)

The first two movements of the *Sonata in F* were finished in 1788. The third movement was a revised version of the *Rondo K.494* of 1786. The slow movement is remarkable for its chromatic and dissonant harmonies and complex rhythmic structure.

The last three *sonatas* contain the two *"Little Sonatas"* in *C major K.545* and *B flat major K.570,* and the very last *Sonata in D major K.576.*

Sonata in C major K. 545 (1778)

The well-known "Little Sonata for Beginners," *K.545,* was obviously written for early learners in the "easy" key of C major. Its humorous *Rondo* would delight students of any age.

Sonata in B flat major K.570 (1789)

The "Little Sonata" in B flat uses counterpoint with wit.

Sonata in D major K.576 (1789)

The opening theme of the concluding *Sonata in D* suggests the brightness of a trumpet call. Woven throughout is deft counterpoint recalling not Johann Christian but his father, Johann Sebastian Bach.

[5]   Recent research now shows that this *Sonata* was probably written somewhat later in Munich or Vienna between 1781 and 1783. It is one of Mozart's most popular works.

Apart from the *Sonatas* are splendid individual works including the following:

Three Fantasies

The *Fantasy in C minor K.396* (1782) suggests improvisation; that in *D minor K.397* (1782) prophesies romanticism; the last in *C minor K.475* (1785) appears with the *Sonata in C minor K.457*.

The *Fantasy and Fugue in C major K.394* is like a preliminary study for the great *C minor Fantasy K.475*. Its date, 1782.

Rondos (3)

Of these, the *D major Rondo K.485* (1786) uses the theme from the *Rondo* of the *Clavier Quartet in G minor K.478*. The *A minor K.511* (1787) alternates major with minor and shows a depth of emotion not usually associated with rondo style.

Adagio in B minor K.540 (1788)

This is a despairing work, perfect in its large proportions.

The *Variations,* in sixteen sets, are unimportant to the development of the form, but excellent as study works. Mozart emphasizes melodic development of themes drawn mainly from operatic arias of the day. *Ah, vous dirai-je, Maman K.265* (1776) exemplifies Mozart's "disarming simplicity." As *Twinkle, Twinkle, Little Star,* the melody brings a smile. *Unser dummer Pöbel Meint K.455,* (1784), from a melody of Gluck, appears occasionally in concert performances.

Mozart was eleven when he wrote the first four *Concertos* for solo piano; he wrote the last one in the year he died. Representing some of his greatest writing, they occupied him during his entire career. With them he felt he attained his musical ideals of emotional contrast, at the same time striking a balance between solo and orchestra new to concerto form. He said himself that they were "written for all kinds of ears, not just for the long ones." Although Mozart performed them publicly, only four were printed during his lifetime.

Concerto in E flat K.271 (1777) No. 9

For Mlle. Jeunehomme

At twenty-one, with the *E flat Concerto,* Mozart achieved his concerto ideals of expressive contrast, symphonic orchestration, and close relation between solo and orchestra. An unusual *Finale* features a menuet with four variations.

Between February 1784 and December 1786, Mozart reached a high point in instrumental composition, producing 12 exceptional piano *Concertos* in succession, *K.449, 450, 451, 453, 456, 459, 466, 467, 482, 488, 491, 503.* These were followed in 1788 and 1791 by the ''Coronation'' *Concerto in D K.537* and the final *Concerto in B flat K.595.*

Concerto in G major K.453 (1784) *No. 17*

For Barbara Ployer

Of the Concertos written before the summer of 1784, the *G major* is the finest. Its light touches of joy and sadness add sophisticated charm.

Concerto in D minor K.466 (1785) *No. 20*

The *Concerto K.466* marks the first Mozart wrote in a minor key. The challenge of minor mode with its innate drama and passion inspired Beethoven to write cadenzas for the work. Alfred Einstein feels that this *Concerto* with its strong contrasts of anguish and tranquility established Mozart as a forerunner of Beethoven.

Concerto in C minor K.491 (1786) *No. 24*

The *Concerto in C minor,* like the *D minor K.466,* is also a great, dark work with vivid orchestration, reaching symphonic proportions. Beethoven is associated with this *Concerto,* publicly admiring it and paying homage in his own *Concerto* of the same key *Op. 37.*

Concerto in C major K.503 (1786) *No. 25*

The *C major Concerto* marks the last of the twelve written in the period 1784-86. The Triumphal March theme of the first movement suggests victory over the turmoil of the two minor key *Concertos* preceding it. Constant variation in the roles of solo and orchestra combined with extreme modulation points to the new direction of Mozart's thought.

Concerto in D major K.537 Coronation (1788) *No. 26*

Mozart composed the *D major Concerto* for the Coronation of King Leopold II. The structure is simple and the melodies appealing. Mozart's virtuosity (the original solo part was written as a sketch for his own performance) gave the work immediate attraction.

Concerto in B flat major K.595 (1791) No. 27

Mozart completed the Concerto in B flat major, the last, the year of his death. It may be considered his farewell to the piano. Alfred Einstein writes:[6] "It is so perfect that the question of style becomes meaningless. The very act of parting from life achieves immortality."

There is also a *Concerto for Two Pianos* and one for *Three Pianos,* as well as a *Sonata* and a *Fugue* in *Duo* form.

Concerto for Two Pianos in E flat K.365 (1779)

Mozart wrote the *Concerto for Two Pianos* for himself and his sister, Nannerl, after his return from Mannheim and Paris in early 1779. It involves spirited play between the two soloists with a mixture of light and shadow turning finally to joy.

Concerto for Three Pianos in F major K.242 (1776)

For Countess Antonia Lodron and her daughters

Of the complete piano *Concertos,* only the one for *Three Pianos* is below the highest standard.

Sonata for Two Pianos in D major K.448 (1781)

The forceful *Sonata in D major* is a very fine work, a staple of two-piano repertoire.

Fugue for Two Pianos in C minor K.426 (1783)

Striking harmonic dissonance is a surprising feature of the *Fugue.* Mozart later arranged it for string quartet and preceded it by an *Adagio.* The theme is of Baroque origin.

For piano *Duet* there are five *Sonatas,* outstanding among them the one in *F major K.497* (1786); *Fugue in C minor K.401; Andante and Variations in G K.501; Adagio and Allegro in F minor K.594;* and *Fantasie in F minor K.608.*[7]

Editions:

Identification of compositions by opus and number came after the time of Haydn

---

6   Einstein, Alfred, Ibid., p. 315
7   Originally for a mechanical organ.

and Mozart. Mozart's numerous works have their own classification, the Köchel catalogue. Dr. Ludwig Köchel, a learned musician as well as naturalist, botanist, and mineralogist, undertook the assembling of a chronological thematic index of all Mozart's works. Köchel's initial and a following number identify each composition.

K

See: Chronologisch thematisches Verzeichnis sämtlicher Tonwerke Wolfgang Amade Mozarts, ed. L. von Köchel (Leipzig 1862; 2/1905 ed. P. Graf von Waldersee; 3/1937 ed. A. Einstein; 6/1964 ed. F. Geigling etc.).

Selected Works for Keyboard

Sonata in C, K.279 (1775)

Sonata in F, K.280 (1775)

Sonata in B flat, K.281 (1775)

Sonata in E flat, K.282 (1775)

Sonata in G, K.283 (1775)

Sonata in D, K.284 (1775)

Sonata in C, K.309 (1777)

Sonata in A minor, K.310 (1778)

Sonata in D, K.311 (1777)

Sonata in C, K.330 (1778)

Sonata in A, K.331 (1778)

Sonata in F, K.332 (1778)

Sonata in B flat, K.333 (1778)

Sonata in C minor, K.457 (1784) (published with *Fantasia*, K.475)

Sonata in F, K.533 (1788)

Sonata in C, K.545 (1788)

Sonata in B flat, K.570 (1789)

Sonata in D, K.576 (1789)

Fantasy in C minor, K.396 (1782)

Fantasy in D minor, K.397 (1782)

Fantasy in C minor, K.475 (1785)

16 sets of *Variations:* K.24 (1766); K.25 (1766); K.54 (1788); K.179 (1774); K.180 (1773); K.264 (1778) *(Lison dormait);* K.265 (1778) *(Ah vous dirai-je, maman);* K.352 (1781); K.353 (1778); K.354 (1778) *(Je suis Lindor);* K.398 (1783); K.455 (1784) *(Unser dummer Pobel meint);* K.460 (1784); K.500 (1786); K.573 (1789); K.613 (1791)

Miscellaneous pieces for piano[8]

6 *Minuets* (including the well-known one in D, K.355)
Fantasy and Fugue in C major, K.394
3 *Rondos:* K.485 in D; K.494 in F; K.511 in A minor
Unfinished *Suite* in the Handelian style, K.399
Fugue in G minor, K.401
Allegro in B flat, K.3
Allegro of a Sonata in G minor, K.312
Allegro and *Andante in F* and *B flat*, K.533
Andantino in E flat, K.236
Adagio in B minor, K.540
Gigue in G, K.574
36 *Cadenzas* to 14 of the *Piano Concertos*, K.624

For Piano and Orchestra

Concertos for solo piano and orchestra:[9] K.37, 39, 40, 41 (adaptations and arrangements from other composers)
Concerto No. 5 in D, K.175 (1773)
Concerto No. 6 in B flat, K.238 (1776)
Concerto No. 8 in C, K.246 (1776)
Concerto No. 9 in E flat, K.271 (1777)
Concerto No. 11 in F, K.413 (1782-83)
Concerto No. 12 in A, K.414 (1782)
Concerto No. 13 in C, K.415 (1782-83)
Concerto No. 14 in E flat, K.449 (1784)
Concerto No. 15 in B flat, K.450 (1784)
Concerto No. 16 in D, K.451 (1784)
Concerto No. 17 in G, K.453 (1784)
Concerto No. 18 in B flat, K.456 (1784)
Concerto No. 19 in F, K.459 (1784)
Concerto No. 20 in D minor, K.466 (1785)
Concerto No. 21 in C, K.467 (1785)
Concerto No. 22 in E flat, K.482 (1785)
Concerto No. 23 in A, K.488 (1786)
Concerto No. 24 in C minor, K.491 (1786)

[8] For other miscellaneous solo keyboard works, see New Grove 1980 under *Mozart*, p. 745.
[9] Twenty five *Concertos* are listed here; a total number of 27 is reached by the inclusion of K.242 and K.365 – Concertos for 3 pianos and 2 pianos respectively and listed as *Nos.* 7 and 10.

Concerto No. 25 in C, K.503 (1786)
Concerto No. 26 in D, K.537 (1788)
Concerto No. 27 in B flat, K.595 (1791)
Rondos for piano and orchestra, K.382 in D (for K.175) (1782) and K.386 in A (1782)
Concerto for three pianos in F, K. 242 (1776) No. 7
Concerto for two pianos in E flat, K.365 (1779) No. 10

For Piano Duo

Fugue for Two Pianos in C minor, K.426 (1783)
Sonata for Two Pianos in D, K.448 (1781)

For Piano Duet

Sonata in C (19d) (1765)
Sonata in D, K.381 (1772)
Sonata in B flat, K.358 (1774)
Fugue in C minor, K.401 (1782)
Sonata in F, K.497 (1786)
Andante and Variations in G, K.501 (1786)
Sonata in C, K.521 (1787)
Adagio and Allegro in F minor, K.594 (1790)
Fantasie in F minor, K.608 (1791)

Rondo Alla Turca
from *Sonata in A major* K.331

a) Always begin the embellishment on the beat.

b)

c) Play the bass with the c sharp in the right hand, accent it strongly, and so proceed throughout the entire theme.

a) Den Vorschlag immer mit dem Takttheil beginnen.

c) Der. Bass muss mit dem ois der rechten Hand gleichzeitig eintreten und sehr markirt gespielt werden, auf gleiche Weise durch den ganzen Satz.

Baptized in Bonn, Germany,
December 17, 1770

Died in Vienna, Austria,
March 26, 1827,
Age 57 years

Ludwig van Beethoven

Historical Sketch

Beethoven's genius survived an abnormal childhood ruled by a despotic father. Johann Beethoven demanded hours of daily piano playing from his son and often waked him in the middle of the night for further practice. The only softening influence in the home was provided by Beethoven's gentle and affectionate mother. At 11, after lessons with various undistinguished teachers, Beethoven came in contact with the organist and pianist Christian Neefe, a thorough musician and enlightened teacher. Requiring Beethoven to study Bach's *Well Tempered Clavier,* Neefe laid the musical foundation which enabled Beethoven to win the admiration of later Viennese audiences. At 13, Beethoven became harpsichordist in the Court Theatre Orchestra. The following nine years saw his mother's death, his father's decline, and his own assumption of family responsibility. His father's influence disappeared, and he was able to transform youthful misery into an enduring crusade for freedom and self-respect. His active musical life included appointment as violist in the Bonn Court Chapel and Court Theatre. Here he associated with established musicians at the center of Bonn's intellectual and social life.

Count Waldstein, an influential member of royalty and Beethoven's life-long friend, was decisive in Beethoven's moving to Vienna in 1792. At 22, Beethoven was already a recognized virtuoso pianist whose ability Mozart prophesied would bring Beethoven world recognition. Beethoven arranged to take lessons with the elderly Haydn. But his uncompromising ideas kept him from accepting Haydn's method of teaching, and the lessons generally were not successful.

Except for Haydn and Mozart, few musicians at the start of Beethoven's career acknowledged his genius as a composer. His often violent expression of emotion was unlike anything previously composed; his novel ideas coupled with fierce independence of temperament cut him off from immediate public acceptance.

A few years after his arrival in Vienna, he began to appear in concerts as a composer-virtuoso, and in 1796 his 3 *Sonatas* of *Op. 2* (dedicated to Haydn) were published commercially. His integrity made him a favorite among families of nobility whose names appeared frequently in his dedications, Count Waldstein, the von Bruenings, Prince Lichnowsky, and the Archduke Rudolph. Rudolph became his greatest patron and in 1809 signed an agreement to make annual payments to Beethoven provided he lived in Vienna. Beethoven left Rudolph an overwhelming legacy of dedications which include Opp. 58, 73, 81a, 96, 97, 106, 111, 133, and 134.[1]

When he was 30, Beethoven began his greatest compositions. This period also marked the onset of deafness which in time became complete. As he himself revealed in the Heiligenstadt Testament,[2] he accepted the tragedy and continued composing with undiminished vitality.[3]

Beethoven's favorite instrument, the piano, was the inspiration for one of music's most profound collections, the *Thirty-Two Piano Sonatas*. The *Sonatas* divide into three groups following the course of Beethoven's deafness and consequent stylistic changes: the first group reflected rules established by Haydn and Mozart; the second showed the fully developed drama of his maturity; the last exhibited the rare beauty and detachment of spiritual isolation.

Beethoven's death was precipitated by a chill caught while travelling with his nephew, Karl. Jaundice and dropsy returned, aggravated by cirrhosis of the liver, and Beethoven spent the winter months of 1826-27 in unsuccessful convalescence. As the spring of 1827 approached, he corrected proofs of the *Ninth Symphony* and the *String Quartet* of *Op. 127*, fully aware of the progress of his fatal illness. It was estimated that 10,000 people attended his funeral and burial in the Währing Cemetery. His remains were moved twice, in 1863, and finally in 1888 to the Central Cemetery in Vienna where Beethoven and Schubert now lie side by side.

---

[1]   These represent the *4th* and *5th Piano Concertos, Piano Sonata* "Les Adieux," *Sonata in G for violin and piano, Archduke Trio, Hammerklavier Sonata* for piano, *Piano Sonata in C minor*, "Grosse Fugue" for string quartet Op. 133, and the same work arranged by Beethoven for piano duet Op. 134.

[2]   Beethoven's "spiritual will" written to his brothers in 1802 in which he renounced the idea of suicide for continuing creativity.

[3]   The *Violin Concerto*, songs (incl. "Ah perfido"), the opera *Fidelio, Missa solemnis*, the 16 *String Quartets*, and the 9 *Symphonies* attest to the extensive range and penetration of Beethoven's creativity.

Style

A facet of Beethoven's greatness was the translation of idealism into music with daring musical innovations which depicted struggle and exalted beauty. Its finest pianistic expression came in the *Sonatas* which show the entire development of his genius up to the last *String Quartets*.[4] Consistently superior in architecture, emotional range, and innovation without repetition, Beethoven's *Sonatas* surpassed all previous works in this form.

The ways Beethoven developed the *Sonata* were complex. He explored the smallest segment of each theme, producing an endless variety of musical ideas. He employed contrast of key, a cornerstone of sonata form, in surprising and unconventional ways, and introduced an irregular number of movements as needed for expressiveness – two, three, or four. At the end of movements he expanded a familiar closing device, the *Coda,* which in his hands became a further commentary on preceding material or the introduction of an entirely new thought.

Beethoven's general technical means were varied and original. He used massed chords as melodic phrases and produced unprecedented power by adding the damper pedal to chordal sound and to the accumulated force of rapid, widespread figures. He frequently interrupted these fortissimo passages with sudden pianissimos to create tension and drama.

At the time Beethoven wrote, a new technique of notation was in the making which he helped to define. He indicated expression, color, and accent through abbreviations which do not obscure the score. Among them:

>, a simple accent for added pressure without the intensity of a *sforzando*

sf, *sforzando,* increased weight in lyrical phrases or striking contrast in loud passages

sfz, *sforzato,* added strength to all notes of a given section

fp, *fortepiano,* an abrupt accent immediately followed by a soft sound

rfz, *rinforzando,* singing stress in gentle context

pp, *pianissimo,* very softly; expectant stillness

dolce, lyrical inner feeling

esp, *espressivo,* ardent, outward feeling

In forging new sounds and styles, Beethoven used the pedal creatively and added specific indications for its use. His pedal marks will be found when a veiled quality is needed; when notes of a pedal point, chord or arpeggio are to be sustained; and when a sound is played against surrounding notes.

---

[4]   The last *Sonata, Op. III,* appeared in 1822 while the last *Quartets, Op. 127, 130, 131, 132, 133* ("Grosse Fuge"), and *135* (all between 1824-26) continued Beethoven's incomparable progression toward musical completeness.

Compositions

The three periods in which Beethoven's *Sonatas* are commonly grouped are defined by the dates: 1795-1800, 1800-1814, and 1816-1822.[5] The works of the first period *(Opus 2 to 22)* follow rules of the sonata as developed by Haydn and Mozart. They contain the only traces among Beethoven's *Sonatas* of virtuoso display for its own sake, but as in the *Pathétique* of *Op. 13,* they foreshadow the inner drama of the later periods.

Sonata Op. 13 in C minor (Pathétique) (1798)

Dedicated to Count Carl Lichnowsky

The *Pathétique Sonata,* written four years before the Heiligenstadt Testament, expresses Beethoven's awareness of advancing deafness. Beethoven's own description, *Pathétique,* apples to the *Sonata* from the passionate slow *Introduction* of the first movement *Allegro,* through the "sad and glowing"[6] *Adagio,* to the restless *Rondo Finale.* The turmoil of the two outer movements is expressed physically by dynamic accents and compressed phrases.

The great second period *(Op. 26 to 90)* contains the bulk of the *Sonatas,* among them *Opp. 27 No. 2, 31 No. 2, 53, 57, and 81a.*[7]

Sonata Op. 27 No. 2 quasi una fantasia in C minor (Moonlight) (1801)

Dedicated to Jiulietta Guicciardi

The appellation *Moonlight* was added to the *Sonata* well after Beethoven's death by the poet-critic Rellstab. But the connotations of moonlight do not express the depth of feeling of the *Sonata* which suggests yet another outburst against the finality of deafness. Never before had music described such intensity of grief and revolt. Between the measured passion of the first movement and the unbroken assault of the last lies the *Allegretto* which Liszt called "a flower between two abysses."

Sonata Op. 31 No. 2 in D minor (Tempest) (1802)

Beethoven often played the *D minor Sonata* in salons of Viennese nobility and considered it his best work of this period. Characteristic extremes of tumult and poesy are

---

[5] Divisions made by von Lenz in "Beethoven et ses trois Styles," St. Petersburg, 1852.
[6] Marek, George R., *Beethoven – Biography of a Genius,* Funk and Wagnalls, New York, 1969.
[7] The two *Sonatas, Op. 49 No. 1* and *Op. 49 No. 2,* were written during the years of the first period, but their opus numbers fall within the second. They are called the *Little Sonatas* because of their simplicity and brevity.

combined with new perfection. The first movement brings together the dynamic and emotional freedom of a *Fantasy*. The *Adagio,* with its broad B flat melody and overtones of orchestral color, lies close to the *Second Symphony.* The *Allegretto Finale* which Czerny calls "galloping" closes the *Sonata* with the dash of a *moto perpetuo.*

Sonata Op. 53 in C (Waldstein) (1804)

Dedicated to Count Carl von Waldstein

The genial warmth of the *Waldstein Sonata* is not found in the other great *Sonatas* of this period. The orchestral first movement contains one of Beethoven's favorite devices of starting a repeated figure pianissimo and working it to a climax. The last movement *Rondo* is preceded by an *Adagio* introduction which takes the place of a slow movement. Its joyousness suggests a village fete accompanied by merry songs.

Sonata Op. 57 in F minor (Appassionata) (1804)

Dedicated to Count Franz von Brunswick

The *F minor Sonata* is dedicated to the brother of Therese von Brunswick, possibly Beethoven's "Immortal Beloved" (or one of them).[8] Perhaps significantly, because of the dedication, the entire *Sonata* seems to sing a "great hymn of passion."[9]

Extremes of mood which characterize the first movement change to peaceful beauty in the 4 *Variations* of the second movement *Andante.* The *Finale* returns to the desperation of the first movement with added savagery in the final *Coda.*

Sonata Op. 81a in E flat (Farewell, Absence, and Return) (1809)

Dedicated to Archduke Rudolph

When Napoleon invaded Vienna in 1809, the entire imperial family fled. The Empress was accompanied by Archduke Rudolph for whom Beethoven wrote this *Sonata.* It details their parting, the sadness of Rudolph's absence, and the joy of his return. It is one of the few cases where Beethoven wrote and followed a specific *programme.*

In the extraordinary third period *(Opp. 101, 106, 109, 110, and 111)* Beethoven reached complete spiritual ascendancy over his deafness. The works of the last years have a force and vision prophesying the Romantic era to follow. Each *Sonata* seems the ultimate of its kind.

[8]   Speculation continues as to the identity of the "true" Immortal Beloved. Probability now points to Antonie Brentano (b. 1780).

[9]   Leichtentritt, Hugo, *Analytical Notes* published on the occasion of Artur Schnabel's *Series of Seven Recitals of the 32 Sonatas of Beethoven,* New York, 1936.

Sonata Op. 101 in A (1816)

Dedicated to Baroness Dorothea Ertmann

In *Sonata Op. 101,* Beethoven experimented with cyclic construction and the relaxed expansiveness which foreshadowed large Romantic forms. The development section of the *Finale* is made up entirely of a fugue, an unusual feature seen also in the first movement of the following *Hammerklavier Sonata.*

Sonata Op. 106 in B flat (Hammerklavier) (1818)

Dedicated to Archduke Rudolph

Using a personal key symbolism (B flat, luminous energy,)[10] Beethoven conceived this work in titanic, symphonic style. It contains skillful, powerful fugal writing; its hurdles are a continuing challenge to listener and performer.

Sonata Op. 109 in E (1820)

Dedicated to Maximiliane Brentano

The *Sonata Op. 109* is constructed in two unorthodox movements on the lines of a Fantasy. Variety of mood and tempo mark the first movement from tender lyricism to the final energetic *Prestissimo.* The second movement weaves 6 Variations from a song-like theme. The changing expression of the Variations places this set among Beethoven's finest.

Sonata Op. 110 in A flat (1821)

In the *A flat Sonata,* Beethoven's mighty spirit reached the extreme limits of expressiveness possible within sonata form. A favorite device of the last period, fugal theme and treatment, ends the work in a temporary shift from the spiritual sphere of the last *Sonatas* to the human exuberance of robust self-confidence.

Sonata Op. 111 in C minor (1822)

Dedicated to Archduke Rudolph

Like *Op. 109,* the *C minor* of *Op. 111* is written in two movements, showing again the irreconcilable extremes with which Beethoven lived and worked, like Dante's Inferno and Paradiso. The second movement *Arietta* with its Variations lends the entire work a spiritual vision for all succeeding composers. The ultimate *Sonata,* it is a fitting close to Beethoven's unchallenged accomplishment.

[10]   Suggested by the pianist-scholar, Alfred Brendel.

Like the *Sonata* and *Concerto,* the ever popular form of *Theme and Variations* reached perfection in Beethoven's hands. The form has various methods of treatment, among them harmonic, melodic, and rhythmic. Of these, Beethoven chose in general the harmonic. His most celebrated, among many lesser sets,[11] are: the *15 Variations and Fugue on a Theme from the Eroica Symphony in E flat Op. 35* (1802) dedicated to Count Moritz Lichnowsky; *32 Variations on an Original Theme in C Minor WoO 80* (1806); and *33 Variations on a waltz by Diabelli in C Op. 120* (1823) dedicated to Antonie von Brentano.

---

33 Variations on a Waltz (Diabelli) Op. 120 (1823)

The composer and publisher, Diabelli, applied to all the leading composers in Austria to write among them 50 *Variations* on a theme of his own. Beethoven alone wrote 33 which were published in the first volume; a second volume brought out the desired 50 by miscellaneous writers, including the young virtuoso Liszt. Beethoven's contribution shows all possible varieties of musical expression from highest sentiment to broadest humor.

Apart from the *Sonatas* and *Variations* are smaller individual works characteristic of Beethoven's wide range of creative ideas: the lyrical *Für Elise WoO 59* (1810); a large scale *Andante favori in F WoO 57* (1804), a remnant of work on *Sonata Op. 53; Fantasy in G minor Op. 77* (1809); *Polonaise in C Op. 89* (1814); *7 Bagatelles Op. 33*[12] (1799-1802), *11 Bagatelles Op. 119* (1820-22), and *6 Bagatelles Op. 126* (1823); Gypsy rondo, *Rage over the Lost Penny Op. 129* (1795), published posthumously; *Ländler* and *Contredanses.*

The following five piano *Concertos* are Beethoven's major contributions to concerto form:[13] *No. 1 in C Op. 15* dedicated to Princess Odescalchi; *No. 2 in B flat Op. 19* dedicated to Charles Nikl;[14] *No. 3 in C minor Op. 37* dedicated to Louis Ferdinand of Prussia; *No. 4 in G Op. 58* dedicated to Archduke Rudolph; and *No. 5 in E flat Op. 73,* also to Archduke Rudolph. The *Fourth* and *Fifth* reach to the future in dramatic and expressive freedom.

Concerto No. 4 in G Op. 58 (1805-6)

Dedicated to Archduke Rudolph

The opening bars of the *Fourth Concerto* are given to the solo piano without orchestral introduction. The slow movement becomes a dialogue between piano and orchestra where the piano retains its gentleness to overcome the orchestra's recurring threats. After this reconciliation, the *Concerto* closes in a rollicking *Finale.*

[11]   Simpler works, good for study. See listing of *Variations* at the end of this chapter.

[12]   Among the *Bagatelles* there are those suitable for the growing pianist.

[13]   With the possible exception of the *Second.*

[14]   The *Second Concerto* was actually written two years earlier than the *First,* revised by Beethoven three years after his writing it and given the designation of *Second.*

Concerto No. 5 in E flat (Emperor) Op. 73 (1809)

Dedicated to Archduke Rudolph

The vast dimensions of the *Emperor Concerto* make it one of the most heroic in the repertoire. Conceived in broad lines, it is more direct and dramatic than the introspective *Fourth*. Its depth and power were unequalled until the piano *Concertos* of Brahms.

Beethoven arranged his *Concerto in D Op. 61 for Violin and Orchestra* (1806) as a *Concerto for Piano and Orchestra* (1807), a version rarely performed.

Works in *duet* form, seldom heard, include the *Sonata in D Op. 6* (1796); *3 Marches Op. 45* (1803); and *Grand Fugue* (arr. by B. from *String Quartet Op. 133,* 1826).

Editions:

L. van Beethoven Werke: Vollständige kritisch durchgesehene überall berechtigte Ausgabe   (Leipzig 1862-5; 1888)   GA

L. van Beethoven Werke: Sämtliche Werke ed. W. Hess (Wiesbaden 1959-71) HS

L. van Beethoven Werke: neue Ausgabe sämtlicher Werke ed. J. Schmidt-Gorg (Munich and Duisberg, 1961)   NA

Das Werk Beethovens: Kinsky, George (1882-1951), catalog section "Werke ohne Opuszahl" (works without opus numbers) provides "WoO" numbers   WoO

Selected Works for Piano

Three Sonatas Op. 2: *No. 1 in F minor* (1793-95) No. 1; *No. 2 in A* (1794-95) No. 2; *No. 3 in C* (1794-95) No. 3

Grand Sonata, Op. 7: *E flat* (1796-97) No. 4

Three Sonatas, Op. 10: *No. 1 in C minor* (1795-97) No. 5; *No. 2 in F* (1796-97) No. 6; *No. 3 in D* (1797-98) No. 7

Grand Sonata pathétique, Op. 13: *C minor* (1797-98) No. 8

Two Sonatas, Op. 14: *No. 1 in E* (1798) No. 9; *No. 2 in G* (1799) No. 10

Grand Sonata in B flat, Op. 22 (1800) No. 11

Grand Sonata in A flat, Op. 26 (1800-01) No. 12

Two Sonatas, Op. 27: *No. 1 Sonata quasi una fantasia in E flat* (1800-01) No. 13; *No. 2 Sonata quasi una fantasia in C sharp minor* (Moonlight) (1801) No. 14

Grand Sonata in D (Pastoral), Op. 28 (1801) No. 15

Three Sonatas, Op. 31: *No. 1 in G* (1802) No. 16; *No. 2 in D minor* (1802) (Tempest) No. 17; *No. 3 in E flat* (1802) No. 18

7 Bagatelles, Op. 33 (1801-02)

6 Variations, Op. 34 (1802)

15 Variations with a Fugue on theme from Prometheus, E flat, Op. 35 (1802) (Eroica)

2 Preludes, Op. 39 (through all 12 major keys) (1789)

Two Easy Sonatas, Op. 49: *No. 1 in G minor* (1797) No. 19; *No. 2 in G* (1795-96) No. 20

2 Rondos in C and G, Op. 51 (1796-97; 1798)

Grand Sonata, Op. 53 (Waldstein) (1804) No. 21

Sonata in F, Op. 54 (1804) No. 22

Sonata in F minor, Op. 57 (Appassionata) (1804-05) No. 23

6 Variations in D, Op. 76 (1809)

Fantasia in G minor/B flat, Op. 77 (1809)

Sonata in F sharp, Op. 78 (1809) No. 24

Sonatina in G, Op. 79 (1809), No. 25

Sonata, Les Adiex, l'Absence, et le Retour, Op. 81a, E flat (1809-10) No. 26

Polonaise in C, Op.. 89 (1814)

Sonata in E minor, Op. 90 (1814) No. 27

Sonata in A, Op. 101 (1816) No. 28

Grand Sonata in B flat, Op. 106 (Hammerklavier) (1817-18) No. 29

Sonata in E, Op. 109 (1820) No. 30

Sonata in A flat, Op. 110 (1821-22) No. 31

Sonata in C minor, Op. 111 (1821-22) No. 32

11 Bagatelles, Op. 119 (1820-22)

33 Variations on a Waltz, Op. 120 (Diabelli) (1819; 1822-23)

6 Bagatelles, Op. 126 (1823-24)

Rondo a Capriccio, Rage over a lost penny vented in a caprice, Op. 129 (1795)

Works Without Opus [15]

Three Sonatas, WoO 47: *E flat, F minor,* and *D* (These *Sonatas* and the *Dressler Variations* my first works, LVB) (1783?)

Sonata in C, WoO 51 (Completed by Ries) (1797-8?)

Rondo, Allegretto, WoO 49 (1783?) (in A)

Minuet in E flat, WoO 82 (before 1805)

Prelude in F minor, WoO 55 (before 1805)

6 Minuets, WoO 10 (1795?)

7 Ländler, WoO 11 (1798?)

6 Ländler, WoO 15 (1801-2)

Andante favori, WoO 57 (said to have been intended for *Op. 53, Waldstein*) (1803)

Bagatelle, Für Elise, WoO 59 (1808, 1810)

10 Cadenzas to the *Concertos in C, B flat, C minor, G,* and *D* (arrangement of Violin Concerto). Also 2 to Mozart's *Concerto in D minor for Piano.*

9 Variations on a March by Dressler, WoO 63 (1782)

---

[15] For a complete listing, see New Grove on Beethoven.

24 *Variations,* WoO 65 (1790-1) (in D)

13 *Variations,* WoO 66 (1792) (in A)

9 *Variations,* WoO 69 (1795) (in A)

6 *Variations,* WoO 70 (1795) (in G)

12 *Variations,* WoO 68 (1795) (in C)

12 *Variations* on a Russian dance, WoO 71 (1796-97)

6 *Variations,* WoO 76 (1799) (in F)

8 *Variations,* WoO 72 (1795?) (in C)

10 *Variations,* WoO 73 (1799) (in B flat)

7 *Variations,* WoO 75 (1799) (in F)

7 *Variations on God Save the King in C,* WoO 78 (1802-3)

5 *Variations on Rule, Brittania in D,* WoO 79 (1803)

32 *Variations in C minor,* WoO 80 (1806)

For Piano and Orchestra

Concerto No. 1 in C, Op. 15 (really the second) (1795; 1800)

Concerto No. 2 in B flat, Op. 19 (really the first) (begun before 1793, revised 1794-95, 1798)

Concerto No. 3 in C minor, Op. 37 (1800; 1803)

Concerto No. 4 in G, Op. 58 (1805-06; 1807)

Concerto for Piano and Orchestra arr. by Beethoven from the *Violin Concerto,* Op. 61 (1806; 1807)

Concerto No. 5 in E flat, Op. 73 (Emperor) (1809; 1811)

For Piano Duet

Sonata for 4 Hands in D, Op. 6 (1796-97)

Three Grand Marches for 4 hands in C, E flat, D, Op. 45 (1803?)

Grand Fugue, Op. 134 (Op. 133) Arr. by Beethoven for 4 hands (1826)

Variations on a Theme of Count Waldstein, WoO 67 4 hands (in C) (1792)

Lied with 6 Variations on a melody to Goethe's Ich denke dein, WoO 74 (4 hands in D) (c. 1800).

First Movement
   from *Sonata (Pathétique) Op. 13*

Grave.

Attacca subito l' Allegro:

Allegro di molto e con brio.

Tempo I.

Allegro molto e con brio.

4 | ROMANTICISM

"Classical" composers of the 18th Century certainly showed "Romantic" qualities, but in the 19th Century, *Romanticism* itself came to full bloom. Placing emphasis on sentiment over precise form, and instinct over reason, Romanticism soon became a powerful force. Rousseau expressed the whole concept of Romanticism in his statement, "I am different from all men I have seen. If I am not better, at least I am different."

The Romantic period in European music includes roughly the years 1800 to 1910.[1] It is a particularly rich era for the pianist because it expanded significantly the range of the piano and produced a large part of the pianist's repertoire. Passing through intense emotional "storm and stress,"[2] composers of this period explored such diverse fields as the supernatural, the chivalrous past, interaction of man with nature, national identity through indigenous folk music, and the "Artist as Hero."

Beethoven's late *Sonatas* foreshadowed the Romantic school by changing the length and altering the classical content of movements: the *Sonatas* grew longer or shorter as required by emotional content; slow movements replaced traditional quick movements; sets of variations took the place of closing *rondos* or *allegros* in sonata form. Schubert combined the growing freedom in the air about him with an innate feeling for extended melody. He built his last *Sonatas* into personal statements of irregular and "heavenly" length. Von Weber is the third composer who may be considered a part of

---

[1] The dates have some flexibility; New Grove 1980 uses 1790-1920, while the Oxford Dictionary of Music (1980) suggests 1830-1900.

[2] Reminiscent of "Sturm and Drang," the intense emotionalism which originally affected German music and literature, roughly 1760-80.

this first phase of Romanticism. His *Konzerstück* for piano and orchestra established the "Artist as Hero," a role the concerto performer would play in the coming years.

In the wake of these pioneers, the middle period of Romanticism brought to piano repertoire the compositions of Mendelssohn, Schumann, Chopin, and Liszt. Interaction among musicians, writers, poets, and artists flourished with these composers[3] and remained a trait throughout the Romantic years. Following their lead, Franck, Brahms, Tchaikovsky, Grieg, and MacDowell continued to develop Romanticism's special qualities of freedom within changing forms. The last phase of Romanticism involved composers more occupied with symphonic forms and opera than the piano—Wagner, Verdi, Bruckner, Dvorák, Elgar, Puccini, Mahler, R. Strauss, and Sibelius.

It was the hallmark of Romantic composers to push tonal (as opposed to later atonal) harmony as far as possible without bringing down the structure. They did this through the use of altered notes, unrelated chords, modulations to any and all keys, extreme chromaticism, irregular phrase lengths, and irregular rhythms. In terms of genre, they created three new forms: the *Symphonic Poem* for orchestra; the *Art Song* for voice and piano; and the *Character Piece* for piano solo. With special significance for the pianist, the *Character Piece* uses the Romantic ardor and color of longer works to create a short, intimate musical profile. It crops up in the short piano works of all the Romantic composers from Mendelssohn *(Songs without Words)* to MacDowell *(Sea Pieces)* and shows its influence well into the 20th Century with the *Preludes* of Debussy and collections of short pieces of Bartók.

Thus the Romantic period has left a legacy of personal awareness which continues to influence some composers in every generation. Its popularity changes with the fashion of the times. But its qualities which reflect the human condition will never be truly out of style.

---

[3] Berlioz (1803-69) was a potent influence on Romanticism although not a piano composer.

Born in Vienna, Austria,
January 31, 1797

Died in Vienna, Austria,
November 19, 1828,
Age 31 years

Franz Peter Schubert

Historical Sketch

    Franz Schubert's family was financially modest, his mother in domestic service before marriage and his father a small town school master and amateur cellist. His father's musical talents, like those of the town's choir master, were at young Schubert's disposal. But Schubert's musical knowledge was intuitive, and he needed little teaching.

    At eleven, Schubert competed successfully for entrance into the Imperial Choir School at Lichtenthal. The Convict, as the school was called, gave him his only formal musical training. He left the Convict at sixteen but continued to study with the celebrated musician, Salieri, who was also an acquaintance of Haydn, Mozart, and Beethoven. The following year he was teaching in his father's school. Here he began to write the songs *(Lieder)* which estabished a genre of unequaled descriptiveness where interdependence of melody and accompaniment enriched the form to the level of chamber music. As expressions of pianistic art, the accompaniments to the songs provide a rewarding study in themselves. Successive Romantic composers such as Mendelssohn, Schumann, Brahms, and Hugo Wolf expanded Lieder form with individual vividness, but none surpassed the perfection of Schubert's balance between words and music.

Schubert left Lichtenthal for Vienna at nineteen (1816) to try for the first time to live by music. He did not succeed financially and often had no funds except those supplied by friends. His gift for friendship created a circle of devoted and helpful admirers including Spaun from Lichtenthal days, Schober, and the operatic baritone, Vogel. Naturally carefree and desperately poor all his life, Schubert nevertheless wrote music continually. The year 1816 alone saw the composition of over 200 songs, and the following year, four major *Sonatas*. [1] These compositions stand at the beginning of a seemingly endless chain of compositions which write a biography in themselves. By the year 1817, Schubert showed the characteristics which marked his mature style – harmonic daring, exuberant melody, spontaneous modulation, and delight in stretching out new rhythmic and melodic ideas.

Unfortunately, in this period of music history, a composer's fame rested on his ability to perform. Schubert was not a virtuoso, and except for the songs and duets played at private "Schubertiads" his works were rarely presented. His musical circle did not include influential members of the nobility who could secure public performances as they had for Beethoven. In fact, Beethoven, who was also living in Vienna, was hardly aware of Schubert. Contrary to legend, Schubert did not visit Beethoven on his death bed but followed closely the reports on Beethoven's illness.

By 1822, Schubert's compositions included the *Unfinished Symphony in B minor* and the *Wanderer Fantasy*. The following year, five years before his death, Schubert fell ill from the onset of syphilis. However by 1825, there was a steady growth in the reputation of his songs presented by concert singer Vogel. The publishing houses of Artaria, Diabelli, and Schott began to take an interest in his work. He composed constantly, and except for two terms as music master to the Esterházy family remained close to Vienna.

Ill though he was from 1823 on, he produced the *Schöne Müllerin* song cycle and for piano the 8 *Impromptus* and 3 major *Sonatas*. [2] A few months before his death in 1828, he wrote the 3 greatest of all the piano *Sonatas*[3] and made final corrections in the *Winterreise* song cycle.

Although numerous press notices began to appear late in Schubert's life concerning publication and performances of the songs, interest did not last long. Three decades of neglect followed his death. It was not until 1860, when Romanticism was firmly established, that his works were finally known.

Schubert asked to be buried near Beethoven: and so he was, first in the Währing Cemetery and later in the Central Cemetery of Vienna. The words inscribed on Schubert's monument speak a universal regret:

"Music has here entombed a rich treasure,
But still fairer hopes."

---

[1]　*A minor D.537; E flat major D.568; B major D.575; E minor D.566* with *Finale D.506.*
[2]　*Reliquie D.840; A minor D.845; D major D.850.*
[3]　*C minor D.958; A major D.959; B flat major D.960.*

Style

Schubert was a man of extreme sensitivity who wrote under the shadow of Beethoven. "Who can do anything after Beethoven?" he was supposed to have asked. Brahms also felt Beethoven's strength and the contrasting weakness in structural development of Beethoven's successors. If Brahms at the distance of seventy years felt the exhilaration of Beethoven's power, Schubert living in the same generation may have felt it oppressive.[4] Schubert's genius however was altogether different; lyrical rather than formal, it developed without methodical training. Schubert used his gift spontaneously and felt little need to reinforce it with studied knowledge of musical construction.

With Schubert, harmony and rhythm were subservient to the grace and individuality of melody. Harmonies involved unexpected, frequent modulations and quick changes between major and minor. Accompaniment figures provided a foundation of sound, often built on the idea of orchestral tremolos. The form of theme and variations appeared frequently in place of a true development section, spinning out melody through thematic transformation.

Characteristics of orchestral and vocal tone-quality influenced Schubert's piano style. The last three *Sonatas* for example can be thought of in terms of string sound, while individual melodies, particularly in slow movements, have a close relation to the lyricism of *lieder*. And again, avoiding the percussive attack unpleasantly common in piano technique, Schubert used accents as an orchestral change of instrumentation or a singer's increase of vocal intensity.

Schubert's own small hands and short fingers favored a technique of repeated figures and chords which built passages of driving power. He excelled also in another kind of virtuosity which foreshadowed the lyricism of Schumann and Chopin — that of lyric poetry. The control of nuance, mood, and subtle coloring through long passages required a technique of its own; here Schubert was supreme.

Compositions

The piano compositions fall into the two main periods of 1812 to 1818, and 1819 to Schubert's death in 1828. The first includes *Sonatas* (some incomplete), *Dances, Variations,* and slow movements (Adagio, Andante, etc.), while the second contains the major *Sonatas,* the *Wanderer Fantasy, Moments Musicals, Impromptus, Dances,* and the finest of the four-hand works.

Of the piano compositions in extended form, the *Sonatas* are the most numerous,

[4]   For another opinion, the pianist-scholar, Alfred Brendel, suggests that Schubert worshipped Beethoven and was not overwhelmed by his greatness, accepting their differences of temperament, mentality, and background. Brendel, Alfred, *Musical Thoughts and Afterthoughts,* Princeton, 1976, p. 31.

forming a constant stream throughout Schubert's creative life. Philip Radcliffe[5] suggests that Schubert chose this form because of its basic compatibility with melodic contrast. Like Haydn, Schubert shows in the *Sonatas* every side of his personality, "delighting in travels through remote keys, sampling the emotional countryside."[6] There are references to Beethoven as well, sometimes in rhythmic patterns, melodic intervals, or phrase shapes. And there are foreshadowings of Brahms in the unexpected birth of one theme from another against new harmonic backgrounds. But the core of spontaneity, inventiveness, directness, and power remains unshakeably Schubert's from beginning to end.

Sonatas

The two earliest *Sonatas* of 1815 (*D.157* and *D.279*) were not complete, but in 1816, the most attractive of the early *Sonatas* appeared, that in *E major D.459,* not only complete but containing an extra *Scherzo.* Because of the additional movement, it was originally titled *5 Klavierstücke,* suggesting that certain movements of the 5 could stand alone as "pieces." In 1817, three *Sonatas* appeared, more mature than the preceding *E major.* Here, in *D.537, D.568,* and *D.575,* Schubert introduced sudden and remarkable variety.

Sonata in A minor Op. post. 164 (1817) D.537

The strong first movement looks ahead in dramatic moments to the two later and greater *Sonatas* in the same key of A minor (*D.784* and *D.845*). The mixture of different phrase lengths which worked well for the songs is effective here, giving a strong feeling of expectation through asymmetry.

Sonata in E flat Op. post. 122 (1817) D.568

Schubert brought to this *Sonata* the unity of light charm and Viennese geniality. It is melodious, graceful, flowing, and emotionally more relaxed than the first *Sonata* of this group.

Sonata in B Op. post. 147 (1817) D.575

The mood of the *A minor D.537* returns to this *Sonata* in the aggressive first movement opening with its dotted note rhythms and varying phrase lengths. Abrupt modulations give continuing restlessness to the *Andante* and *Finale.*

Between the early *Sonatas* of 1817 and the established *Sonatas* of 1823-26, came the following work which Philip Radcliffe feels is one of the most compact and appealing

---

[5]   Radcliffe, Philip, *Schubert Piano Sonatas,* British Broadcasting Corp., London, 1967.
[6]   Ibid.

of all the *Sonatas*. It opened Schubert's second period of piano composition that would end only with his death.

Sonata in A major Op. post. 120 (1819) D.664

The lively, happy themes of the *A major Sonata* have their lyrical counterpart in the *Trout Quintet* (for piano and strings) which Schubert wrote in the same year and in the same key.

Five major *Sonatas* appeared between 1823 and 1826 leading to the final three which Schubert wrote in the last months of his life.

Sonata in A minor Op. post 143 (1823) D.784

The key of A minor drew from Schubert the same qualities of power, suspense, drama, and tragedy that C minor inspired in Mozart and Beethoven. Bleak octaves open the first movement and appear again in the *Andante* in an unsettling rhythmic figure. The *Finale*, like the first movement, is stark and biting.

Sonata in C major (1825) ("Reliquie") D.840

The unfinished *C major Sonata* is orchestral in spaciousness. In the year preceding this work, Schubert was concerned with chamber music (the *Octet* and 2 *String Quartets*) and produced only the *Grand Duo in C for piano Duet*. The *Sonata in C major* with its sombre C minor *Andante* marked his return to piano composition uninterrupted until his death.

Sonata in A minor Op. 42 (1825) D.845

Dedicated to Archduke Rudolph

The *A minor Sonata,* one of the most rewarding to perform, suggests Beethoven in the cumulative power of its first movement coda. The second movement, *Theme with Variations,* contains strong harmonic clashes in remote keys which Schubert contrasts with serene, visionary passages found again in the last three *Sonatas*. In the third movement, the rhythmic drive of the outer sections surrounds the gentle, barcarolle melody of the *Trio*. The *Rondo Finale* ends in two final chords identical to the close of the first movement.

Sonata in D Op. 53 (1825) D.850

Dedicated to Karl Maria von Bocklet

The only *Sonata* Schubert wrote for a virtuoso pianist, the *D major* shows once again Schubert's genius in contrasting mood and tempo to produce an inspired kind of unity.

The first movement's opening and closing vigor suggests Beethoven. The second movement contains many unusual modulations which vary the beautiful main theme, while the third movement *Scherzo* has a quiet *Trio* again made up of remarkable modulations. The fourth movement *Rondo Finale* introduces a Viennese Beergarden atmosphere of charm and happiness which for all its lightness Alfred Einstein calls the "crown of the *Sonata*".

Sonata in G Op. 78 (1826) D.894

Dedicated to Josef, Edler von Spaun

This *Sonata,* sometimes called the *Fantasy Sonata,* was published as *Fantaisie, Andante, Menuet et Allegretto.* It is one of Schubert's most poetic works with sustained expression seen also in such songs as "Du bist die Ruh" and "Abendrot." Its intimate, almost ethereal, quality looks ahead to the last works.

Schubert's last three *Sonatas,* written in September of 1828, needed the passage of time for proper recognition; as late as 1927, critical views were cool, perhaps because of what Philip Radcliffe calls their "slow moving time scale." However, they have won overdue appreciation through the efforts of performers like Arthur Schnabel, and at last have a fixed place in the repertoire. Although ill when he composed them, Schubert nevertheless played selected movements at the house of a friend, Dr. Ignaz Menz. He intended to dedicate them to Hummel, but the publisher Diabelli, after Schubert's, and Hummel's, death, dedicated them to Robert Schumann in 1838.

Sonata in C minor (1828) D.958

The Sonata in C minor, stormy and foreboding, reflects what Joseph Kerman calls Beethoven's "C minor mood" as seen in the *Pathétique Sonata.* In spite of the *Ländler Trio* of the *Menuet,* it expresses Schubert's darker qualities. It culminates in a large *Finale* built on modulations through the most remote keys.

Sonata in A (1828) D.959

The movements of the *A major Sonata* combine miraculously to give a picture of Schubert's musical personality, a composite of an infinite variety of mood contrasted with flowing lyricism. Schubert runs the course of poetic drama from an unusual *Scherzo* with suggestions of pizzicato to an equally surprising *Andantino* which contains an elemental outburst unique in all the *Sonatas.*

Sonata in B flat (1828) D.960

The last *Sonata* reaches a level of spirituality akin to Beethoven's last *Sonatas.* Coinciding with vitality and even playfulness are profundity and serenity which lie beyond analysis. Schubert's farewell to the piano remains as mysterious as the *Sonata's* distant modulations.

Wanderer Fantasy in C Op. 15 (1822) *D.760*

Dedicated to Emanuel Karl, Edler von Liebenberg

Virtuoso character and cyclical unity of its four movements (thematic transformation of *The Wanderer* song motif) place the *Wanderer Fantasy* apart from the *Sonatas*. It is a complex piano solo which stands near the beginning of Schubert's second period of composition. Surpassing Schubert's own technique, brilliant passage work and massed chords approach the qualities of a concerto.

Aside from the *Sonatas* and the *Wanderer Fantasy*, there are many compositions in smaller form including *Moments Musicals, Impromptus, Klavierstücke, Waltzes, Ländler, Ecossaises,* and *German Dances.* Schubert's extraordinary genius bursts from every page where spontaneity creates intimacy, and thematic or structural development is not desired or required.

Moments Musicals Op. 94 (1823-27) *D.780*

The six *Moments Musicals* show restraint and finish and make one of the most delightful sets of musical miniatures in piano literature.

Four Impromptus Op. 90 (1827) *D.899*

The *Op. 90 Impromptus* reach a high level of beauty and expressiveness. Their moods range from nocturne-like mysticism to broad powerful statement.

Four Impromptus Op. 142 (1827-28) *D.935*

Of the *Op. 142 Impromptus, No. 1 in F minor* contrasts the main theme with unusual episodes containing major-minor alternations; *No. 2 in A flat* is a favorite, simple and direct; *No. 3 in B flat* provides a fine example of variation form while *No. 4 in F minor* with its striking coda is an impressive virtuoso work.

Klavierstücke (3 Piano Pieces) (1828) *D.946*

The 3 *Klavierstücke,* written shortly before the last 3 *Sonatas,* are characteristic of Schubert's uncanny ability to shift mood through unexpected key changes. Philip Radcliffe considers the set one of the most individual of Schubert's piano works.

Waltzes, Ländler, Ecossaises, German Dances

Schubert wrote dances throughout his life, producing an enormous number, several of which Liszt transcribed in his *Soirées de Vienne*. Many are short, some not more than a few lines long. An excellent set of *Ecossaises,* perhaps more related to Vienna than Scotland, is that of *D.781.*

There are no works for piano and orchestra[7] or for two pianos among Schubert's compositions. His fondness for piano ensemble confined itself to many exceptionally fine duets.[8] The *Sonata (Grand Duo) in C Op. 140* (1824) *D.812,* and the *Marches Militaires* (1818) *D.733* are well known, as are the great *Fantasy in F minor Op. 103* (1828) *D.940,* and the *Rondo in A Op. 107* (1828) *D.951.*

Editions:

F. Schuberts Werke: kritisch durchgesehene Gesamtausgabe, ed. E. Mandyczewski, J. Brahms (Leipzig 1884-97/ revised 1964-69)   SW

F. Schubert: Neue Ausgabe sämtliche Werke, ed. W. Dürr, A. Feil, C. Landon (Kassel 1964)   NSA

F. Schubert: thematisches Verzeichnis seiner Werke in Chronologischer Folge von Otto Deutsch (Kassel 1978)   D

Note: Otto E. Deutsch, foremost authority on Schubertian biography and bibliography, compiled a Thematic Index originally in 1950 which includes more than 1200 of Schubert's documents.

Opus numbers used before Deutsch have little to do with the actual order of composition.

Selected Works for Piano

Sonata in E (D.154) D.157 (1815)
Sonata in C, D.279 (1815) (3 movements only)
Sonata in E, D.459 (1816) (publ. as 5 Klavierstücke)
Sonata in A minor, Op. 164, D.537 (1817)
Sonata in A flat, D.557 (1817)
Sonata in E minor, D.566 and D.506 (1817)

[7]   Liszt wrote an arrangement for piano and orchestra of the *Wanderer Fantasy D.760* as well as an arrangement of the same work for two pianos.
[8]   The *duets* furnish a wealth of material for the early as well as the mature pianist.

Sonata in D flat, D.567 (1817)

Sonata in E flat, Op. 122 D.568 (1817)

Sonata in F sharp minor, D.571 (1817) (unfinished)

Sonata in B, Op. 147, D.575 (1817)

Sonata in C, D.613 (1818) (unfinished)

Sonata in F minor, D.655 (1818) (unfinished)

Sonata in C sharp minor, D.625 (1819) (unfinished)

Sonata in A, Opus 120, D.664 (1819)

Sonata in E minor, D.769a (1823) (unfinished)

Sonata in A minor, Opus 143, D.784 (1823)

Sonata in C, D.840 (1825) (movements 3 and 4 unfinished, "Reliquie")

Sonata in A minor, Opus 42, D.845 (1825)

Sonata in D, Opus 53 (D.604) D.850 (1825)

Sonata in G, D.894 (1826) (published as Fantaisie, Andante, Menuet et Allegretto)

Sonata in C minor, D.958 (1828)

Sonata in A major, D.959 (1828)

Sonata in B flat, D.960 (1828)

Miscellaneous Works

Andante in C, D.29 (1812)

10 *Variations in F*, D.156 (1815)

Variations on a Theme by A Hüttenbrenner, D.576 (1817)

2 *Scherzi: No. 1 in D*, D.570; *No. 2 in B flat and D flat*, D.593 (1817)

March in E, D.606 (1818)

Adagio in E, D.612 (1818)

Variations on a Waltz by Diabelli, D.718 (1821)

Fantasy (The Wanderer), Op. 15, D.760 (1822)

Moments Musicals, Op. 94, D.780 (1823-28)

Allegretto in C minor, D.915 (1827)

4 *Impromptus*, Op. 90, D.899 (1827)

4 *Impromptus*, Op. 142, D.935 (1827-8)

3 *Klavierstücke in E flat*, D.946, No. 2 (1828)

Dances for Piano

Misc. Deutsche Tänze, Ländler und Waltzer, D.135, 139, 354, 370, 679, 680, 681, 841

Ecossaisses, D.145, 158, 299, 421, 511, 529, 643, 697, 734, 735, 781, 782, 783, 816, 977

12 *Grätzer Waltzer*, Op. 91, D.924 (1827)

12 *Valses nobles*, Op. 50, D.969 (1826)

Many other sets of German *Dances, Ländler*, etc.

For Piano Duet

Many *Marches, Variations, Overtures, Polonaises, Fantasies, Ländler, Divertissements*
Rondo in D, Op. 138, D.608 (1818)
Sonata in B flat, Op. 30, D.617 (1818)
Sonata in C (Grand Duo), Op. 140, D.812 (1824)
Andantino varié in B minor on French motives[9] D.823 (1825)
3 *Marches Militaries,* D.733 (1818)
2 Characteristic *Marches,* Op.121, D.886 (1826)
Fantasy in F minor, Op.103, D.940 (1828)
Lebenstürme in A minor, Op. 144, D.947 (1828)
Rondo in A, Op.107, D.951 (1828)
Fugue in E minor, Op. 152, D.952 (1828)

[9]   Also 1) Marche brilliante; 2) Andantino (above); and 3) Rondeau brillant.

Moments Musicals Op. 94 No. 1, 2, 3 D.780

Born in Hamburg, Germany,
February 3, 1809

Died in Leipzig, Germany,
November 4, 1847,
Age 38 years

Felix Mendelssohn-Bartholdy

Historical Sketch

Felix Mendelssohn[1] was one of the very few great composers whose professional life was unusually happy and prosperous. He was born into a gifted, wealthy family which appreciated music and encouraged its talented members.[2] Frau Mendelssohn was a pianist, her husband a lover of music, and both Felix and his favorite sister, Fanny, were pianists and composers. Felix Mendelssohn's talents combined with personal charm and integrity to bring him early and enthusiastic recognition. His gifts as pianist, violinist, composer, and conductor were accompanied by distinguished contributions as teacher, organist, musicologist, professional water colorist, and linguist.

Along with frequent visits to foreign countries, the Mendelssohn family moved in 1825 from Hamburg to Berlin. Mendelssohn brought with him his earliest piano compositions dating from 1821 and 1822: the *Sonata in G minor Op. 105* (publ. posthumously) and the *Concerto in A minor.* The Mendelssohn house was noted for its Sunday morning concerts, at which Felix, now sixteen, played and conducted his own

---

[1]   Mendelssohn adopted the name Bartholdy from his mother's side of the family as an outward indication of the family's Christian conversion.

[2]   Moses Mendelssohn, the philosopher, was the grandfather of Felix.

compositions. He studied with Zelter and Moscheles, gaining wide reputation as a concert pianist. At seventeen, he wrote his first masterpiece, the incidental orchestral music to Shakespeare's *A Midsummer Night's Dream.*

One of Mendelssohn's early contributions to music was the "discovery" of Bach after many years of neglect. As conductor and performer, Mendelssohn introduced many of Bach's forgotten compositions to a new public. At twenty, he conducted the *St. Matthew Passion,*[3] first of a succession of memorial concerts of Bach's long disregarded treasury of music. Mendelssohn's uncompromising performance ideals made these concerts and his personal tours successful and popular. As conductor and pianist, he visited England, France, Italy, and Switzerland, composing as he travelled. The years of 1829-35 saw the first sketches of the *Scotch Symphony* and the *G minor Piano Concerto Op. 25.* A few years later at Düsseldorf, he conducted a series of Handel oratorio performances, including the *Messiah.* In this way, he "popularized" Handel's choral works for the German musical public as he had Bach's. The year 1829 also marked Mendelssohn's composition of the first book of the *Songs Without Words* for solo piano which he continued to produce during the rest of his life.

At twenty-six, from 1835-40, Mendelssohn settled in Leipzig as conductor of the Gewandhaus symphony concerts. He improved standards of orchestral performance and campaigned for a challenging repertoire. He turned to neglected 18th Century works as well as contemporary composers, including in his programs the *Suites* of Bach, *Symphonies* of Mozart and Beethoven, and various compositions of Liszt. He engaged Clara Schumann as soloist twenty-one times and supported Liszt's special concerts where more virtuoso musicians including Anton Rubinstein, Joachim, and Jenny Lind were introduced. And it was Mendelssohn who gave the premier performance of Schubert's *C major Symphony* (the Great) in 1839.

More travel followed as Mendelssohn's fame increased. His popularity in England was reminiscent of Handel's and was unrivaled by any musician during his lifetime. However, Mendelssohn always maintained ties with the city of Leipzig and in 1843 opened the Leipzig Conservatory. While director, he added prestige to the musical scene by engaging as teachers Ferdinand David, Clara and Robert Schumann, and Moscheles.

By 1846, Mendelssohn's health could not stand the strain of his many activities of revising, conducting, composing, and performing. When he returned to Germany from a London tour in May, 1847, he received the news of his sister Fanny's sudden death. He was unable to recover from the shock of losing his most respected musical advisor and confidante, and he composed his last *String Quartet in F minor Op. 80* as a "Requiem for Fanny." He lived six months longer in quiet despair and died from a series of strokes.

---

[3]   This performance took place in Berlin at the Singakadamie March 11, 1829, with another performance ten days later. Again, on April 4, 1841, twelve years after the first performance, Mendelssohn presented the *St. Matthew Passion* at the close of the Leipzig musical season.

Style

When Beethoven enlarged and broke through the classical molds of Haydn and Mozart, he gave Romanticism its first stirrings; Schubert added to its development in subordinating form to feeling. Succeeding composers abandoned classical restraint in style and content, until Romanticism was ripe for variety of individual expression. Although Mendelssohn grew up surrounded by Romantic influence, he retained certain classical features as a bridge to his own brand of Romanticism. His stylistic grace and purity, different from the intricacies of fellow Romantic artists, were reminiscent of his classic predecessors. In orderliness and precision he was compared to Bach and Mozart. On the other hand, his lyrical style, seen at its best in the *Songs Without Words,* was thoroughly Romantic. Similarly, the airy and sentimental works, and those in small forms, were all immediate forerunners of the condensed Romantic patterns of Schumann, Chopin, Liszt, Brahms, and Grieg.

Mendelssohn's sunny nature was evident in his piano writing; it was consistent with his feeling that the function of music was to give pleasure, not to express intense personal emotion. In contrast to the usual association of minor harmony with emotional stress, his fondness for minor keys did not imply sadness. His music flowed without apparent effort, unattended by great upheavals of the soul. It conformed to a standard of polish and perfection which admitted few startling passages. Accompaniment figures followed unvaried patterns and did little more than furnish harmonic background.

Opinions of Mendelssohn's greatness have varied with the years. He was a man of high principle and generous spirit, widely influential during his lifetime and unique in music history for his rediscovery of Bach's music. Certainly his orchestral, choral, and chamber works are a lasting contribution to musical literature. But critics are justifiably disappointed in the piano compositions, for with certain exceptions they do not share the drama, forceful ideas and high order of creative genius of the larger works. Nevertheless, if accepted for themselves, they express to perfection Mendelssohn's particular delicacy and fantasy.

Compositions

Among Mendelssohn's compositions is the large collection of *Songs Without Words (Lieder ohne Wörte),* which are characteristic of Mendelssohn's piano style. The intimate, lyric quality expressed in these short works reappears in subsequent compositions as Mendelssohn's signature. Melodic and graceful, they were enormously popular during his lifetime. The forty-eight *Songs* were published in eight books of six each. They are comparable to Grieg's *Lyrical Pieces,* small, descriptive works written over many years. The *Songs* do not attempt to portray vast themes and searching emotion but are delightful, spontaneous tone-pictures. Many of them are playable by pianists of all ages.

Actually, the cult of the small form began with Beethoven in his *Bagatelles*. The essence of this style is to accomplish much with little, and almost every Romantic composer tried his hand at it. Mendelssohn was one of the most successful. His own vigor in performance of the *Songs* brought out their vividness and clarity of form, denying the criticism of frequent blandness.

Songs Without Words[4]

Book I Op. 19 (1829-30)

No. 3 *Hunting Song;* horn calls in octaves ring out above a six-eight rhythm.

No. 5 *Restlessness;* an agitated chromatic *moto perpetuo* ranges from F sharp minor to F sharp major.

Book II Op. 30 (1834) (Dedicated to Elisa von Woringen)

No. 10 *The Wanderer;* an *agitato con fuoco* with octaves and chords gives the wanderer no rest.

No. 12 *Venetian Boat Song No. 2;* the *Boat Song* introduces a welcome note of tranquility while retaining a delicate rocking motion in the bass.

Book III Op. 38 (1836-37)

No. 15 *The Poet's Harp;* running sixteenth notes, *presto* and *molto vivace,* give *The Poet's Harp* a virtuoso character.

No. 18 *Duetto;* the two voices of the duet are surrounded by serpentine sixteenth notes in triplets.

Book IV Op. 53 (1839-41) (Dedicated to Sophy Horsley)

No. 23 *Folk Song;* the allusion in this *Folk Song* is to a patriotic anthem sung with brief interludes stanza by stanza. Additional voices join to make a mighty chorus. A modified coda repeats the interlude in a quiet ending.

No. 24 *The Flight* (also called *Song in A*); Eric Werner[5] calls this the crown of the *Songs Without Words.* Highly original, feverish, and sharply dissonant, it has stimulated composers from Liszt to Bartók.

Book V Op. 62 (1842-44) (Dedicated to Clara Schumann)

No. 27 *Funeral March;* the *March* was orchestrated by Moscheles and played at Mendelssohn's funeral.

[4]　The titles of the *Songs* are those listed in Schirmer's Edition.
[5]　Werner, Erich, *Mendelssohn,* Collier-Macmillan Ltd., London, 1936

No. 30 *Spring Song;* the *Spring Song* is probably the most beautiful of the collection, with a delicate detached accompaniment figure.

Book VI Op. 67 (1843-45) (Dedicated to Sophie Rosen)

No. 32 *Lost Illusions;* the charm of *Lost Illusions* lies in a song-like melody set to a *staccato sempre* accompaniment.

No. 34 *Spinning Song;* in *Spinning Song* one can almost see thread vibrate in a breathless *moto   perpetuo.*

Book VII Op. 85 (1834-45) (Posthumous, first publ. 1851)

No. 38 *The Adieu; the Adieu* is impassioned and leaves the listener in suspense with the mystery of the last chord.

No. 39 *Delirium;* again in a *moto perpetuo,* Mendelssohn takes his listeners into a tempest of repeated chords, sharp accents, and dynamic contrasts.

Book VIII Op. 102 (1842-45) (Posthumous, first publ. 1868)

No. 43 *Homeless;* Mendelssohn marks the tempo *un poco agitato* and uses a minor key and syncopated accompaniment to describe the tension of sorrow.

No. 47 *The Joyous Peasant;* in another vein altogether, *The Joyous Peasant* dances, runs, and laughs.

The works in sonata form comprise the early *Sonata in G minor Op. 105* (1821), *Sonata in E Op. 6* (1826), *Sonata in B flat Op. 106* (1827),[6] and the later (1833) very fine *Fantasy in F sharp minor Op. 28* (also called *Scotch Sonata*).

Fantasy in F Sharp minor Op. 28 (1833)

Dedicated to Ignaz Moscheles

The *Fantasy,* in three movements (Andante, Allegro, Presto), contains the best of Mendelssohn's vitality and lyricism. However, the outer movements overshadow the second movement *Allegro* and create a possible problem of artistic balance in performance.

By unity of elfin character rather than title or opus, the following works belong within the same group. They are characterized by a touch of the supernatural, of enchanted forests and moonlit revelry.

Rondo capriccioso Op. 14 (1824)

Mendelssohn composed the *Rondo capriccioso in E* in the same spirit and period as the

---

6   The opus numbers are misleading as to date of composition.

Overture to *A Midsummer Night's Dream*. The simple beauty of the introductory *Andante* is followed by the *Rondo*'s airy sparkle. Mendelssohn's particular lightness, speed, and dexterity as seen in the *Rondo* have influenced many succeeding composers.

Seven Characteristic Pieces Op. 7 (1827)

Dedicated to Ludwig Berger

Smooth counterpoint and witty scherzos suggest the influence of Bach and Scarlatti.

Three Caprices in A minor, E, and B flat minor Op. 33 (1833-35)

Dedicated to Karl Klingemann

The *Caprices* resemble fast sonata movements. The third is the most successful because of the beauty of its slow introduction.

Scherzo a capriccio in F sharp minor (for the Pianists' Album, 1835-6)

Like the *Rondo capriccioso,* the *Scherzo a capriccio* lives within a fairy tale.

In the *6 Preludes and Fugues Op. 35* (1832-36), Mendelssohn combined polyphonic tradition with free piano style. His homage to Bach skillfully avoided imitation or academic mannerisms, and the results are impressive. The *Preludes* are predominantly romantic; the *Fugues* follow contrapuntal rule with fresh themes and pianistic figures. The first *Prelude* and *Fugue* are among the most important.

Prelude and Fugue No. 1 in E minor-major Op. 35

The *Prelude* underscores breadth of form and idea. Its theme is sustained by a fluid, resonant accompaniment typical of Mendelssohn's fondness for continuous, fast-moving figures. The *Fugue* is structurally outstanding. A dramatic crescendo near the end culminates in an imposing chorale which in turn leads to a serene close.

Mendelssohn wrote his finest piano composition, *Variations sérieuses Op. 54* (1841) when he was less than twenty-seven years old. It was his answer to the many shallow sets of variations popular in the 1800's.

Variations sérieuses Op. 54 (1841)

This work holds a significant place in the development of variation form. Seventeen *Variations* are introduced by an eloquent, chromatic theme *(Andante sostenuto)* which casts aside charm and light heartedness and anticipates Brahms in richness of basic material. In a master stroke, Mendelssohn contrasts the technical virtuosity of the climax with an unexpectedly quiet final coda. Eric Werner[7] suggests that the *Variations,* by their excellence, stand on a lonely height above Mendelssohn's other piano compositions.

Mendelssohn's works for solo piano and orchestra comprise the very early *Concerto in A minor* of 1822; *Capriccio brilliant in B minor Op. 22* (1825-6); the two mature *Concertos, No. 1 in G minor Op. 25* (1831) and *No. 2 in D minor Op. 40* (1837); *Rondo* (or *Capriccio*) *brilliant in E flat Op. 29* (1834) dedicated to Ignaz Moscheles and often played by him; and *Serenade and Allegro gioioso in B minor Op. 43* (1838). There are in addition two *Concertos for Two Pianos and Orchestra in E* and *A flat,* unpublished for many years. The first of these was written in 1823 when Mendelssohn was 14, the second the following year. The second shows growth in mastery of form with a strong *Finale* and good orchestration.

Concerto No. 1 in G minor Op. 25 (1831)

Dedicated to Delphine von Schauroth

Mendelssohn wrote this *Concerto* at twenty-two while travelling in Italy. It shares the same creative period as the *Italian Symphony.* Its joyousness prompted Schumann to call it a "fleeting, carefree gift." The three movements, *Molto Allegro, Andante* and *Presto,* reflect sound structure and interesting cyclic ideas. The slow movement is a type of *Song Without Words,* fresh and graceful. The outside movements provide virtuoso display.

Among the *Duets* are *Variations in B flat Op. 83a* (1841) (arrangement from pf. solo of *Op. 83*); *Allegro brilliant in A Op. 92* (1841); and without Opus number, *Duo concertant* (1833) (Variations written jointly with Moscheles on the March in Weber's *"Preciosa"*) dedicated to Baroness O. von Goethe.

Editions:

F. Mendelssohn-Bartholdy: Werke: kritisch durchgesehene Ausgabe, ed. J. Rietz (Leipzig 1874-7)   R

Leipziger Ausgabe der Werke Felix Mendelssohn Bartholdy, ed. Internationale Felix Mendelssohn Gesellschaft (Leipzig 1960)   L

There is as yet no definitive catalogue of M.'s work as a whole, but Briefkopf and Härtel (Leipzig) lists 121 works with opus numbers.

[7]   *Op. cit.,* p. 360

Selected Works for Piano[8]

Capriccio in F sharp minor, Op. 5 (1825)

Sonata in E, Op. 6 (1826)

Seven Characteristic Pieces, Op. 7 (1827)

Rondo Capriccioso in E, Op. 14 (1824)

Fantasie in E, on the Irish Air, "The Last Rose of Summer", Op. 15 (1827)

Three Fantasies (or Caprices) in A minor, E minor, E, Op. 16 (1829)

Six Songs Without Words, Bk. I, Op. 19 (1829-30)

Fantasie in F sharp minor (Sonate ecossaise), Op. 28 (1833)

Six Songs Without Words, Bk. II, Op. 30 (1834)

Three Caprices in A minor, E, B flat minor, Op. 33 (1833-35)

Etude in F minor (no opus) (1836)

Six Preludes and Fugues, Op. 35 (1832-36)

Gondellied in A (no opus) (1837)

Six Songs Without Words, Bk. III, Op. 38 (1836-37)

Andante cantabile and Presto agitato in B (no opus) (1838)

Six Songs Without Words, Bk. IV, Op. 53 (1839-41)

Variations sérieuses in D minor, Op. 54 (1841)

Prelude (1841) and Fugue (1827) in E minor

Six Songs Without Words, Bk. V, Op. 62 (1842-44)

Six Songs Without Words, Bk. VI, Op. 67 (1843-45)

Six Kinderstücke, Op. 72 (known in England as "Christmas Pieces") (1842)

Variations in E flat, Op. 82 (1841)

Variations in B flat, Op. 83 (1841)

Six Songs Without Words, Bk. VII, Op. 85 (1834-45)

Six Songs Without Words, Bk. VIII, Op. 102 (1842-45)

Three Preludes and Three Studies, Op. 104a (1836)

Sonata in G minor, Op. 105 (1821, publ. post.)

Sonata in B flat, Op. 106 (1827)

Album-blatt, Song Without Words in E minor, Op. 117 (1837)

Capriccio in E, Op. 118 (1837)

Perpetuum mobile in C, Op. 119 (1873)

Scherzo in B minor (no opus) (1829)

Scherzo a capriccio in F sharp minor (no opus) (1835-36)

2 Clavierstücke in B flat and G minor (no opus) (1860)

[8]   The reader is directed to the New Grove Dictionary (1980) for a complete listing of numerous smaller works without opus number and very early works.

For Piano and Orchestra

Concerto in A minor (1822)
Capriccio brilliant in B minor, Op. 22 (1825-26; 1831)
Rondo (or Capriccio) brilliant in E flat, Op. 29 (1834)
Concerto in G minor, No. 1, Op. 25 (1831; 1832)
Concerto in D minor for Piano and Orchestra No. 2, Op. 40 (1837)
Serenade and Allegro gioioso in B minor, Op. 43 (1838)

For Piano Duo

Variations on the March in Weber's Preciosa, jointly composed by Mendelssohn and Moscheles (1833)

For Piano Duet

Variations in B flat, Op. 83a (arr. from pf. solo) (1841)
Allegro brilliant in A, Op. 92 (1841)

Spring Song
from *Songs Without Words* Op.62 No.6

Allegretto grazioso (♩= 88)

Born in Zwickau, Saxony,
June 8, 1810
Died in Endenich, Germany,
July 29, 1856,
Age 46 years

Robert Schumann

Historical Sketch

One of the romantic stories of musical literature is woven around Robert Schumann and his wife, Clara. Their love survived the bitter disapproval of Clara's father, Professor Friedrich Wieck, who forced Schumann to carry the questions of marriage to a court of law. During the long, distraught courtship, Schumann poured into composition the passion and uncertainty of a man in love; Clara, a celebrated concert pianist, performed his music widely as new works appeared. The course of their stormy engagement,[1] marriage, and family life, and Schumann's early death while insane, reflected the extremes of the Romantic Age.

To fulfill his parents' wish, Schumann at 18 began to work toward a law degree, first at the University of Leipzig and a year later at Heidelberg. But piano study and composition were a stronger influence, and with a reprieve from legal studies, Schumann turned to music.[2] While still a student at Heidelberg in 1829, he had writ-

---

[1]   In 1836, there was a serious break between Clara and Robert. It was brought about by Professor Wieck, but both Clara and her father had doubts about Robert's financial responsibility. Clara returned Robert's letters and asked for hers. However, in the following year, they were reconciled, and Clara formally pledged herself to Robert. Three years later they were married.

[2]   Schumann did not receive any degree until 1840 when the University of Jena granted a Ph.D. without thesis or examination because of his reputation as composer, writer, and editor.

ten four songs whose musical material he used almost unchanged in the later *Piano Sonatas Op. 11* and *22* as well as the *Intermezzo Op. 4 No. 4.* He said of himself at this time that he was "neither a connoisseur of harmony and thoroughbass nor a contrapuntist, but purely and simply guided by nature." He made arrangements to study with the celebrated teacher, Friedrich Wieck in Leipzig. With Wieck for piano and Heinrich Dorn for thoroughbass, he hoped to "get on with the proper study of composition." The "proper study" produced in 1820 the *Abegg Variations* which he published as *Op. 1.* He was further stimulated by studying in the same year the *Là ci darem Variations for Piano and Orchestra* of his new idol, Chopin.

With his earliest compositions, Schumann introduced the emotional extremes of two imaginary figures, really two sides of himself, which would appear often in his musical and literary future. He personified these extremes as Florestan the impetuous lover and Eusebius the gentle dreamer. Additional descriptive titles were suggested by the writings of contemporary English and German Romantics, among them Lord Byron, Heine, and Richter. By 1832, Schumann was having serious trouble with the fingers of the right hand[3] and realized it meant the end of a possible virtuoso career. He turned to composition with renewed vigor and set about learning score reading and instrumentation. One of several incomplete works of this period was a single symphonic movement which was performed at a concert in Zwickau on the same program as Beethoven's *Seventh Symphony.* Of the piano pieces, he completed both the *Toccata,* later *Op. 7,* and *Papillons Op. 2.*

In 1834, Schumann helped to found an important musical periodical, the *Neue Leipziger Zeitschrift für Musik.* The following year, at 25, he took over as editor. Embracing the work of young composers, he instigated spirited controversies among musicians over the relative merits of conservatism and modernism. He defended such composers as Chopin and Brahms and called this group the *Hosts of David* in opposition to the *Philistines.* Schumann lifted this famous struggle from the pages of the Journal to the final climax of *Carnaval* where the *Hosts of David* continue to triumph in their famous march against the Philistines.

By 1836, Robert and Clara were in love. Schumann turned again to piano composition and within the next four years produced a body of important keyboard works from *Op. 11* through *Op. 32.* In 1840, Schumann at last was able to marry Clara. With marriage, his compositions embraced the new direction of song, so much so that 1840 has been dubbed the *Year of Song.* Three cycles attest to the creativity of that remarkable year, *Liederkreis Op. 24, Frauenliebe und leben Op. 42,* and *Dichterliebe Op. 48.* The following year he began to concentrate on orchestral and chamber music and produced the *Spring Symphony* (first performed by Mendelssohn in the Leipzig Gewandhaus), the first movement of the *Piano Concerto in A minor,* three *String Quartets* (dedicated to Mendelssohn), and the *Piano Quintet in E flat, Piano Quartet in E flat,* and sketches of the *Andante and Variations* for two pianos.

During the course of his life, Schumann suffered from recurring sleeplessness, depression, and fear of insanity. In 1843 he was in a critical state of instability which he

---

[3] Possibly from experiments with a mechanical device aimed at strengthening the fingers, or possibly from medication for another problem.

hoped to relieve by moving from Leipzig to Dresden. He was able to compose again and in 1844 accompanied Clara on her concert tour to Russia. In 1847 he held a short conducting term in Düsseldorf. Five years later he suffered a possible stroke and another illness described as a rheumatic attack. In 1853-54, he entered his last creative period when he wrote the *3 Sonatas for the Young Op. 118, Kinderball Op. 130,* and *Opp. 124, 126, 133,* and *134.*

From 1854 until his death two years later, Schumann stayed in a private asylum in Endenich near Bonn, writing occasional letters and music sketches. Clara and Johannes Brahms were with him when he died.

Style

New ideas and their application to music were ever present in Schumann's mind. He expanded musical possibilities by portraying characters and events found in the literature of the period, and he surrounded his piano writing with open quotations and fragmentary allusions to Beethoven, to Clara, to the Marseillaise, to his own compositions, etc. Mysterious clues written into the music never lost their fascination for Schumann, nor have they for the listener.

Schumann's piano music is generally composed of separate pieces loosely joined by a main idea, usually a literary one, as in *Papillons, Carnaval, Phantasiestücke,* and *Kreisleriana.* These are descriptive pieces built on small, carefully modelled phrases that are well suited to reflect sudden emotional contrasts and quick changing harmonies. They also incorporate Schumann's fondness for the strong rhythmic impetus of bravura leaps of chords and octaves. In a more subtle way, cross rhythms, syncopations and deliberately misplaced accents give even the reflective moods a pulsation not felt again so strongly until the appearance of the *Capricci* and *Intermezzi* of Brahms.

Schumann's earliest surviving works are songs which show his basic trend toward lyricism. He treated melody as having value in itself, not merely as a piece of structural material in the context of classical sonata form. He adapted melodic line to variation form and successfully created the illusion of large works through drawn-out reworking of the original theme. His melodic bent was not the Italianate style[4] of Chopin and Liszt but rather the simple *lied* associated with four line verse stanzas.

A year before their marriage, Clara Schumann wrote in her journal "...it would be best if he composed for orchestra; his imagination cannot find sufficient scope on the piano[5] ... His bulk of compositions are all orchestral in feeling." Undoubtedly, orchestral feeling was an underlying influence in Schumann's piano writing as seen in chordal thickness characteristic of full orchestra and polyphonic inner melodies suggesting individual orchestral instruments. Nevertheless, while orchestral influence remained strong throughout Schumann's career, it did not overwhelm his pianistic

---

[4]   i.e., floating melodies operatically inspired and embellished.

[5]   Two years later, in 1841, Schumann *was* in his chamber music and orchestral "period."

idiom which involved arpeggio figures, repeated chords, octaves, and scale passages. As Schumann continued to write, he developed unique and arresting ideas which could be expressed only through pianistic sound and the resources of the pedals.

Compositions

With strong ideas of pianistic expression, i.e., richness of partwriting, harmonic variety, free use of the pedals, and prevailing lyricism, Schumann at twenty began a chain of composition which would occupy him for the next ten years and produce the majority of his major piano works.

Abegg Variations Op. 1 (1830)

Dedicated to Meta Abegg of Mannheim

Characteristic of Schumann's use of titles having literary or concrete application, the notation of the Theme represents the proper name seen in the dedication.

Papillons Op. 2 (12 pieces) (1829-31)

Dedicated to Therese, Rosalie and Emilie Schumann (the composer's sisters-in-law)

At a masked ball, two brothers aspire to win the same young woman. During the evening, they exchange masks to discover the girl's true love. The chosen one is deliriously happy, while the rejected suitor angrily tries to stop the dancing. The clock strikes six. The dancers vanish. The musical allusions in *Papillons* are to earlier waltzes and four hand polonaises in imitation of Schubert.

Davidsbündlertänze Op. 6 (1837)

Dedicated to Walther von Goethe

The *Davidsbündlertänze*, subtitled *18 characteristic pieces,* were the first compositions to appear after the 1837 reconciliation between Robert and Clara which erased doubts about their contemplated marriage.

Toccata Op. 7 (1829-1832)

Dedicated to Ludwig Schunke 0

The Toccata had an interesting metamorphosis from its original Op. 6 (later occupied by the Davidsbündlertänze) to Op. 7. The original key was D major, subsequently changed to C major, and the temporary title of "Étude fantastique en doubles-sons" gave way to the final "Toccata."

Carnaval Op. 9 (21 pieces) (1833-35)

Dedicated to Carl Lipinski

Préambule	Chiarina
Pierrot	Chopin
Arlequin	Estrella
Valse noble	Reconnaissance
Eusebius	Pantalon et Colombine
Florestan	Valse allemande
Coquette	Intermezzo: Paganini
Réplique	Aveu
Sphinxes	Promenade
Papillons	Pause
A.S.C.H.-S.C.H.A.	Marche des "Davisbündler" contre les Philistins

Carnaval represents a collection of various personalities at a masquarade. Each piece is built on the letters ASCH,[6] which spell the name of the town of Ernestine von Fricken, Schumann's youthful love. Festive confusion surrounds a crowd dressed in glamorous disguises, fantastic as they dance by moonlight. Pierrot and Harlequin join the revels as do Chopin and Paganini and two new visitors, Florestan and Eusebius. The musical imagery of *Carnaval* made it a public favorite during Schumann's lifetime through Clara's interpretation. It ends with the famous *March of the Davidsbündler against the Philistines.* The *March's* second theme is an old students' song repeated from the *Finale* of *Papillons.*

Phantasiestücke Op. 12 (8 pieces) (1837)

Dedicated to Anna Robena Laidlaw

Des Abends	In der Nacht
Aufschwung	Fabel
Warum?	Traumes Wirren
Grillen	Ende vom Lied

The *Fantasy Pieces* are portraits of the emotions. *Aufschwung* (Soaring), second in the collection, is a musical description of energetic and revitalizing joy.

Études symphoniques Op. 13 (1834-37)

Dedicated to William Sterndale Bennett

The *Études symphoniques,* written in variations form, belong among the greatest in

---

6   A, S or ES (E flat), C, H (B).

piano literature. As does *Carnaval,* they have an association with the family of von Fricken. It was the Baron, father of Ernestine, the lady love in *Carnaval,* who wrote the theme. The style is clearly orchestral; the variety, nobility, and tonal beauty of the variations suggest counterparts in orchestral richness.

Kinderscenen Op. 15 (13 pieces) (1838)

About strange Lands and People	Dreaming (Träumerei)
Curious Story	By the Fireside
Catch me if you can	The Knight of the Hobby-Horse
Entreating Child	Almost too serious
Contentedness	Frightening
Important Event	Child falling asleep
	The Poet speaks

The *Scenes from Childhood* are more mature and complex than the later *Album for the Young Op. 68.* They portray childhood emotions and situations as seen by the adult in retrospect. Reflections between youth and maturity bring this work its particular charm. *Child falling asleep* is a delicate sound picture of the mysterious half-sleep which precedes sleep, while *Träumerei* (Dreaming) may be chracterized as "Such stuff as dreams are made on..."

Kreisleriana Op. 16 (8 Fantasies) (1838)

Dedicated to Fr. Chopin

The literary inspiration for *Kreisleriana* was a character from the writing of E.T.A. Hoffman. The description of the character, Johannes Kreisler, whose counterpart in real life was a half-mad pianist, furnishes some of the most lyrical and capricious music in piano literature. Schumann considered this work his finest for piano solo. He wrote to Clara, "Play my Kreisleriana often. A positive wild love is in some of the movements, and your life and mine, and the way you look." And again, "Even to myself my music now seems wonderfully intricate in spite of its simplicity; its eloquence comes straight from the heart."

Phantasie in C Op. 17 (1836-38)

Dedicated to Liszt (orig. Clara Wieck)

With the exception of the *Concerto for Piano and Orchestra Op. 54,* the *Phantasie in C* shows Schumann at his most powerful. The angularity of the first movement suggests ancient glory, originally inscribed *Ruins* and marked *Sempre fantasticamente ed appassionatemente;* the second movement brings vigorous associations of final victory, originally inscribed *Trimphal Arch;* the third evokes the human soul, originally inscribed *The Starry Crown*. Schumann wrote the *Phantasie* as part of Liszt's project to raise funds for a monument to Beethoven.

Arabesque Op. 18 (1839)

Dedicated to Frau Majorin F. Serre

This graceful rondo, which stands apart from any collection, has become a favorite for its ornamental tracery and simple beauty.

Between *Arabesque Op. 18* and *Album for the Young Op. 68* are several collections of varying importance, among them: *Blumenstück in D flat Op. 19* (1839); *Humoreske in B flat Op. 20* (1838); *8 Novelletten Op. 21* (1838); *Sonata No. 2 in G minor Op. 22* (1833-38); *4 Nachtstücke Op. 23* (1839); *Faschingsschwank aus Wien: Fantaisiebilder Op. 26* (1839-40); *3 Romances Op. 28* (1839); *4 Clavierstücke Op. 32* (1838-39).

Album for the Young Op. 68 (43 pieces) (1848)

Melody
Soldiers' March
Ditty
Choral
Bagatelle
The poor Orphan
Hunting Song
The wild Horseman
Folk-song
The merry Farmer
Sicilienne
Knight Rupert
Maying
Little Study
Spring Song
First Loss
Roaming in the morning
The Reaper's Song
Little Romance
Rustic Song
* * *
Roundelay
The Rider's Story
Harvest Song
Echoes from the Theatre
* * *
Little Song in Canon-form
In Memoriam (of Mendelssohn)
The Strange Man
* * *
War Song
Sheherazade
Vintage-time
Theme
Mignon
Italian Sailors' Song
Sailors' Song
Winter-time I
Winter-time II
Little Fugue
Norse Song
Figured Choral
New Year's Eve

By deliberately putting *Album for the Young* within technical reach of young players, Schumann declared his affinity for children's hopes and despairs and joined their quick pleasure in story telling.

Following *Op. 68* are individual pieces and additional collections including *4 Fugues Op. 72* (1845); *Waldscenen Op. 82* (1848-49); *Bunte Blätter Op. 99* (1838-49); *3 Piano Sonatas for the Young Op. 118* (1853); *Albumblätter Op. 124* (1832); *Sieben Clavierstücke in Fughettenform Op. 126* (1853); and *Gesänge der Fruhe* (5 pieces) *Op. 133* (1853).

Although contemporary with the great early works from *Carnaval* to the *C major Phantasie*, Schumann's three *Sonatas, Op. 11 in F sharp minor* (1832-35), *Op. 14 in F minor* (1835-36), and *Op. 22 in G minor* (1833-38) are less successful than the other extended piano works. Their form loses a measure of strength and unity through irregular structure but they deserve study and a wider performance than they receive.

The single *Concerto in A minor* is the finest of Schumann's works for piano and orchestra, which also include *Introduction and Allegro Appassionato in G Op. 92* (1849) and *Concert-Allegro with Introduction in D minor Op. 134* (1853).

Concerto in A Minor Op. 54 (1841-45) (introduced by Clara Schumann)

This is the flower and climax of Schumann's long list of piano compositions. It was written after Schumann had finished most of the important piano works, as he turned to vocal, chamber, and instrumental writing. He composed it over a period of four years with several revisions. It stands as one of the supreme examples of concerto form where Schumann emerges as master both of piano and orchestra.

In the field of *Piano Duo* compositions, Schumann wrote the appealing and original *Andante and Variations Op. 46* (1843) dedicated to Harriet Parish. Debussy also arranged for 2 pianos Schumann's 6 *Etudes* in the form of a canon Op. 56 (1845) originally for pedal-piano.[7]

In *Duet* form, Schumann composed 8 *Polonaises* (1828), 6 *Impromptus Op. 66* (1848), 12 *Clavierstücke für kleine und grosse Kinder Op. 85* (1849), 9 *Ball-Scenen Op. 109* (1851), and 6 *Kinderball Op. 130* (1853).

Edition:

R. Schumann: Werke, ed. C. Schumann, J. Brahms and others (Leipzig 1881-93)

SW

---

[7]   In the pedal-piano (Pédalier, Pedalklavier) a pedal keyboard was attached to the piano capable of activating the piano's hammers. In another version, the pedal-piano was placed underneath the piano and played independently (made by Pleyel, Wolff and Co. in Paris). The pedal-piano, unlike the pedal-harpsichord and pedal-clavichord, was not used as a practice instrument for organists but as an extension of the piano's possibilities. Mozart had one made for himself in 1785, and Joseph Brodmann made others in Vienna in 1815. Schumann, Alkan, and Gounod are among the few composers who wrote works specifically for the pedal-piano.

Selected Works for Piano[8]

Variations on the name Abegg, Op. 1 (1829-30)

Papillons, 12 pieces, Op. 2 (1829-31)

6 *Studies after Paganini's Caprices,* Op. 3 (1832)

Intermezzi, 6 pieces, Op. 4 (1832)

Impromptus (Variations) on a theme of Clara Wieck, Op. 5 (1833)

Davidsbündlertänze, 18 pieces, Op. 6 (1837)

Toccata, Op. 7 (1829-32)

Allegro, Op. 8 (1831)

Carnaval, 21 pieces, Op. 9 (1833-35)

6 *Studies after Paganini's Caprices,* Op. 10 (Set II) (1833)

Sonata in F sharp minor, Op. 11 (1832-35)

Phantasiestücke, 8 pieces, Op. 12 (1837)

Études en forme de variations (Études symphoniques), Op. 13 (1834-37)

Sonata in F minor, Op. 14 (1835-36) (Concert sans Orchestre)

Kinderscenen, 13 pieces, Op. 15 (1838)

Kreisleriana, 8 pieces, Op. 16 (1838)

Fantasia in C, Op. 17 (1836-38) (Phantasie)

Arabeske, Op. 18 (1838)

Blumenstück in D flat, Op. 19 (1839)

Humoreske in B flat, Op. 20 (1838)

Novelletten, 8 pieces, Op. 21 (1838)

Sonata in G minor, Op. 22 (1833-38)

Nachtstücke, 4 pieces, Op. 23 (1839)

Faschingsschwank aus Wien, Op. 26 (1839-40)

3 *Romances,* B flat minor, F sharp, B, Op. 28 (1839)

Scherzo, Gigue, Romanza and *Fughetta,* Op. 32 (1838-39)

6 *Etudes* in the form of a canon for pedal-piano, Op. 56 (1845)

4 *Sketches* for pedal piano, Op. 58 (1845)

6 *Fugues* on the name *Bach,* for piano or organ, Op. 60 (1845)

Album for the Young, 43 pieces, Op. 68 (1848)

4 *Fugues,* D minor, D minor, F minor, F, Op. 72 (1845)

4 *Marches,* E flat, G minor, B flat, E flat, Op. 76 (1849)

Waldscenen, 9 pieces, Op. 82 (1848-49)

Bunte Blätter, 14 pieces, Op. 99 (1838-49)

3 *Fantasiestücke,* C minor, A flat, C minor, Op. 111 (1851)

3 *Piano Sonatas for the Young,* G, D, C, Op. 118 (1853)

---

[8]   Numerous pieces are listed without opus number in the complete catalogue. See New Grove Dictionary 1980.

Albumblätter, 20 pieces, Op. 124 (1854)
Sieben Klavierstücke in Fughettenform, Op. 126 (1853)
5 *Gesänge der Frühe,* Op. 133 (1853)

For Piano and Orchestra

Concerto in A minor, Op. 54 (1st movement, 1841; final movements, 1845)
Introduction and Allegro Appassionato in G, Op. 92 (1849)
Concert-Allegro with Introduction in D minor, Op. 134 (1853)

For Piano Duo

Andante and Variations in B flat, Op. 46 (1843)

For Piano Duet

8 *Polonaises,* no opus (1828)
6 *Impromptus,* "Bilder aus Osten," Op. 66 (1848)
12 *Clavierstücke für kleine und grosse Kinder,* Op. 85 (1849)
9 *Ballscenen,* Op. 109 (1851)
6 *Kinderball,* Op. 130 (1853)

Préambule and *Pierrot*
from *Carnaval* Op. 9

Der Name eines Städtchens in Böhmen, in dem eine Freundin des Komponisten lebte.
*) A. S. C. H. *The name of a small town in Bohemia where a lady who was a friend of the composer lived.*
Le nom d'une petite ville en Bohème qu' habitait une amie du Maitre.

Born in Zelazowa Wola, Poland,
March 1, 1810
Died in Paris,
October 17, 1849,
Age 39 years

Frédéric François Chopin

Historical Sketch

Chopin was half French by birth, but by nature and temperament he was passionately Polish. His French father adopted the cultural traditions of Poland, became a professor at the Warsaw Lyceum, and married a well educated Polish woman who personified the ardent individuality of her countrymen. Chopin's musical roots remained in Poland with a life-long national loyalty in which musical inspiration and patriotism merged. Although he spent many years in Paris, his music never acquired a "French" flavor.

Chopin's musical development was orderly and rapid. From 1823-26, he studied in high school and also took lessons with Elsner, director of the Warsaw Conservatory. He received a solid academic foundation as well as the early musical discipline of learning Bach and the Viennese Classical composers. On graduation from high school, he entered the Warsaw Conservatory. Outstanding for his talent and natural grace, he became a favorite in the salons of Warsaw aristocracy. Early compositions appeared including the *Rondo Op. 5* (1826), *Là ci darem Variations Op. 2* (1827), *Sonata in C minor Op. 4* (1828), *Fantasia on Polish Airs Op. 13* (1828), and *Krakowiak Rondo Op. 14* (1828). In 1829, he graduated with distinction from the Conservatory. His skilled virtuosity at nineteen assured his reputation as concert pianist and interpreter of his own compositions.

On a short tour to Vienna shortly after graduation, Chopin featured the *Op. 2 Variations* and *Krakowiak Rondo.* Returning to Warsaw in 1830, he finished the two *Concertos in E minor Op. 11* and *F minor Op. 21.* With these compositions and the *Polonaise in E flat Op. 22, G minor Ballade,* and *B minor Scherzo,* he left again for Vienna.[1] Eight months later, after concerts in Breslau, Dresden, Prague, Munich, and Stuttgart, Chopin left Vienna for Paris. On the way, he learned that Warsaw had been captured by the Russians. Unable to return to Poland, he became an exile for the rest of his life.

Chopin settled in Paris. He became a notable figure within a few months through the success of his first concert on February 26, 1832. He had formulated strong ideas of pianistic technique as shown in the *Op. 10 Etudes* and was determined to create a new world of musical sound and structure. The Rothschilds became his patrons, introduced him to French society and contributed to his financial security. Among his distinguished musical admirers were Liszt, Berlioz, Mendelssohn, Schumann and the operatic composers Bellini and Meyerbeer. His early friendship with Liszt cooled; he disliked Berlioz but respected his music; he was not enthusiastic about Mendelssohn's music but was sympathetic to his personality; and finally, he had little respect for Schumann in spite of Schumann's early allusion to him, "Hats off gentlemen, a genius." With Clara Schumann's performance of his music, however, it was a different story; he was impressed with her intuitive grasp and deftness.

Although he was not robust enough for a virtuoso career and appeared in only some thirty public performances,[2] Chopin developed a compelling musical image and had considerable income from giving lessons to young women of society and from the ready sale of his compositions. He was sought after by writers and artists in the great salons of 19th Century Paris where the intellects of the day exchanged compliments, insults, and ideas. The stimulating atmosphere was congenial to Chopin's temperament, and he produced a series of new works including the *Boléro Op. 19, Allegro de concert Op. 46,* and the second set of *Etudes Op. 25.* The public accepted him, and serious artists played his works in concert.

In 1837, Chopin began a liaison of nine years with the writer George Sand. The affair brought energy and excitement to his musical imagination in spite of a steady deterioration of his health. Tuberculosis had overshadowed a large portion of his life, but on the island of Majorca, a temporary refuge for Chopin and Sand, he was able to complete the 24 *Preludes.* For the next eight years, he divided his life between Paris and Sand's estate at Nohant, completing a formidable number of works.[3]

---

[1]   It was the second departure for Vienna that gave rise to the legend of the goblet of Polish earth. According to the erroneous story, told by Chopin's biographer, Karaskowski, Elsner presented this goblet to Chopin as a treasure. Some Polish earth *was* later scattered on Chopin's grave in Paris, but it did not come from this source.

[2]   His active years of public performance numbered about four.

[3]   The *Sonata in B flat minor Op. 35, Ballade in F Op. 38, Scherzo in C sharp minor Op. 39, Tarantelle Op. 43, Fantasy in F minor Op. 49, Ballade in F minor Op. 52, Berceuse Op. 57, Sonata in B minor Op. 58, Barcarolle Op. 60, Polonaise Fantasie Op. 61,* and individual *Polonaises, Impromptus, Waltzes, Nocturnes,* and *Mazurkas.*

When Sand broke off the relationship in 1846, Chopin was no longer able to compose. He sent his last compositions, 4 *Mazurkas Op. 67,* 5 *Waltzes Opp. 69 and 70,* and 3 *Polonaises Op. 71* to the publisher before the final separation, and they were brought out in 1855, posthumously. The 1848 revolution which broke out in Paris forced Chopin to go to Scotland with his pupil Jane Stirling (who also saved many copies of Chopin's music with his own notations). His health was at such a desperate stage that he was able to appear only occasionally at small private gatherings. He returned to Paris in the fall of 1848, a year before his death. He was an invalid, unable to compose or teach. He is buried in the Père-Lachaise Cemetery.

Style

In the early half of the 19th Century, the piano was developing into an instrument of a different sound quality from the essential clarity of Mozart's, Beethoven's, and Schubert's pianos. The Romantic ideals of increased resonance and dynamic extremes demanded a wider tonal range, and piano manufacturers began to produce more versatile instruments. Heavier construction favored larger sound, but on the other hand, hammers now covered with additional felt produced a more seductive tone. The French pianos of Pleyel and Érard in the 1830's combined brilliance and mellowness and were the instruments of Chopin's choice. Although he could achieve a striking tone, Chopin in general preferred the subtlety possible within smaller acoustical bounds. With few exceptions,[4] Chopin wrote exclusively for the piano. Showing penetrating knowledge of hand physiology and keyboard resources, he composed at the piano and captured pianistic effects from experiments and innovations of the moment.

Conscious of the unifying power of melody, Chopin remarked that pianists should hear all the leading singers of the day. Because of his affinity for vocal art, Chopin found the lyricism of contemporary Italian opera congenial to his style. His abundant melodies also recalled Schubert's gift for continuously singable lines. He added the further development of chromaticism as an integral part of the melody and separated it from the function of ornamentation.

A great harmonic innovator of his century, Chopin expanded chromatic harmony and its accompanying dissonance into areas previously unknown. Remote modulations, successions of unresolved diminished 7ths, passages with no clear harmonic base all pointed to the further explorations of Wagner, Franck, Fauré, and Debussy.

Chopin seemed at his happiest with small forms (mazurkas, nocturnes, etudes, waltzes, etc.) which reflected a procedure natural to him of statement, departure (or development), and return. This treatment was equally effective in the larger structures of the polonaise.

[4] Orchestral accompaniments for the piano works with orchestra, *Trio Op. 8, Sonata for Piano and Violoncello Op. 65, Polonaise in C* for the same instruments, and songs.

Rhythmically, the *Waltzes, Mazurkas,* and *Polonaises,* with typical dance patterns, conform to Chopin's fondness for repeating characteristic rhythms. By contrast, the works in free form, *Fantasies, Scherzos, Etudes, Preludes* and *Ballades* display rhythmic sophistication and variety.

The *Concertos* and *Sonatas* show greater strength through the ingenuity of their musical components rather than through organic form and structural development in a classical sense.

Chopin invented new patterns and sonorities in accompaniments by assigning them importance equal to the melodies they support. Both elements combine to create a compelling flow of sound which often ranges from one end of the keyboard to the other. In freedom of motion and contrast of bass with a widely spaced treble, Chopin was a forerunner of Brahms.

Rubato, first explored by Chopin, is one of the outstanding characteristics of his style. It appears in connection with phrases decorated by quick running notes, often chromatic. The word *rubato* or *robbed* indicates a certain freedom of tempo in the melodic line. Contrary to the assumption that robbed time must be paid back, that a ritardando must be compensated by an accelerando, or that rhythm may be abandoned entirely, Chopin gave the following definition of rubato:

"The singing hand may deviate from strict time, but the accompanying hand must keep time."

He added:

"Fancy a tree with its branches swayed by the wind–the stem is the steady time, the waving leaves are the melodic inflections."

Chopin's musical bequests enlarged the artistic horizon of his own and succeeding generations. They rest primarily on his gift for melody, adventurous harmonic modulation, instinctive balance of length with form and content, and high order of craftsmanship. These bequests combined an understanding of the physical and emotional characteristics of the instrument which produced a piano repertoire unequalled by any composer of the Romantic period.

Compositions

Chopin's works in short form include *Mazurkas, Nocturnes, Etudes, Waltzes, Scherzi, Ballades, Polonaises,* and *Preludes.*[5] The *Mazurkas, Nocturnes, Waltzes,* and *Polonaises* were published in groups through the years, each addition representative of some

---

[5]   Descriptive titles for many of the short works were added by publishers. The few added by Chopin appear in the New Grove 1980 Catalogue of complete works.

aspect of Chopin's musical growth.[6] There are also single masterpieces: among them, *Fantasie in F minor, Berceuse, Barcarolle,* the two *Sonatas in B flat minor* and *B minor,* and the two *Concertos in E minor* and *F minor.* Almost without exception these works bear Chopin's arresting, original mark and represent unique advances in piano literature.

The *Mazurka* was a Polish dance originally, but Chopin expanded its content as he did with every short form. Among the first musical nationalists, Chopin had an early interest in Polish folk music. The *Mazurkas* (61),[7] in contrast to the dramatic expansiveness of the *Polonaises,* show a quieter, more condensed variety possible in their smaller form. Later nationalist composers like Grieg, Dvořák, Albeniz, Falla, Bartók, and the Russians developed Chopin's lead in incorporating authentic folk songs into Western music. The *Mazurkas,* basically ternary,[8] are divided into three types, 1) fast, 2) slow and melancholy, and 3) intermediate tempo and mood. Characteristics are triplets in the melody, accent generally on the third beat, use of the scale's sharpened fourth, and modal and chromatic passages. *Mazurka Op. 33 No. 2 in D* suggests a "Chopin" *Waltz; Op. 50 No. 3* incorporates the developing *Coda* as part of the structure.

The *Nocturnes* (21),[9] pieces associated with the romantic implications of night, follow a style which Chopin took from the Irish composer, John Field. Chopin developed it into an expressive and well-balanced art form which incorporated power as well as delicacy. The *Nocturne Op. 9 No. 3 in B* foreshadowed the shape and content of Chopin's future Nocturnes; *Op. 15 No. 2 in F sharp* is one of the best known and most often played; *Op. 55 No. 2 in E flat* is among the most beautiful in the collection.

The *Twelve Etudes* of *Op. 10* and the *Twelve* of *Op. 25* are among Chopin's great contributions to piano literature. They are studies which present specific technical problems. Before Chopin, *Etudes* were largely functional; Chopin's creative solutions raised his *Etudes* to masterpieces. Each work serves as a study in technique but also has a particular beauty of sound and mood. The *Etudes* remain among the most varied and distinguished written.

Twelve Etudes Op. 10 (1829-32)

Dedicated to Franz Liszt

Chopin began these *Etudes* at nineteen and finished them two years later in Paris. The third and twelfth *Etudes* in particular portray the depth of Chopin's patriotism.

---

[6]   Given the consistently high quality of Chopin's works, it is hard to speak of works superior to others except in rare cases. Rather it is a matter of personal preference and emotional or intellectual attachment. Exploring them, the student will find many within his or her range.

[7]   Including posthumous *Mazurkas* and those without opus numbers.

[8]   i.e., in three-part form.

[9]   Including posthumous *Nocturnes* and those without opus numbers.

Etude No. 3 in E
_____

Once while playing this *Etude,* Chopin is supposed to have sighed, "Oh, my native land" One of his favorites, it is also one of the most beautiful.

Etude No. 12 in C minor (called the *Revolutionary*)
_____

Expressing overwhelming power, Chopin wrote the *Revolutionary Etude* after the fall of Warsaw. Right hand octaves play a tragic, distraught melody over the surging rise and fall of the left hand.

Twelve Etudes Op. 25 (1832-36)
_____

Dedicated to Countess d'Agoult

Chopin's dedication of the *Op. 25 Etudes* pays homage to Liszt's companion of many years, the Countess d'Agoult. The first and ninth *Etudes (Aeolian Harp* and *Butterfly)* have lightness and grace, while the eleventh *(Winter Wind)* suggests the psychological tempest present also in *Op. 10 No. 12 (Revolutionary).*

Although not profound works in the sense of the *Sonatas,* the *Waltzes*[10] are graceful and polished. Built on ternary form, they are simpler harmonically than Chopin's other compositions and project an immediate charm. Three particularly attractive *Waltzes* may be mentioned: *Op. 64 No. 1 in D flat (Minute); Op. 69 No. 1 in A flat (l'Adieu); No. 133* (no. Op. number) *in E flat (Sostenuto).*

The four *Scherzi* are works of major proportion, popular as concert works, while the four *Ballades* are fine examples of climax building. The form and poetry of the *Scherzi* and *Ballades* match the best in Chopin's writing. They are rewarding to study and gratifying to perform, continuously fresh and inventive.

Scherzo in B minor Op. 20 (1831-32)
_____

Dedicated to T. Albrecht

Scherzo in B flat minor Op. 31 (1837)
_____

Dedicated to Adele de Fürstenstein

Scherzo in C sharp minor Op. 39 (1839)
_____

Dedicated to Adolph Gutmann

10   Including posthumous *Waltzes* and those without opus numbers.

Scherzo in E Op. 54 (1842)

Dedicated to Clotilde de Caraman

Ballade in G minor Op. 23 (1831-35)

Dedicated to Baron von Stockhausen

Ballade in F Op. 38 (1836-39)

Dedicated to Schumann

Ballade in A flat Op. 47 (1840-41)

Dedicated to Pauline de Noailles

Ballade in F minor Op. 52 (1842)

Dedicated to Baroness Rothschild

The *Polonaise,* originally a national ceremonial dance in Poland, was slow, austere and aristocratic. Chopin, with ever-present nationalistic spirit, took this typically Polish expression and built stirring works that transformed the original dance. He retained characteristics of the form, i.e., repetition of theme and rhythmic content, and built them into heroic proportions. Among the *Polonaises* (16, including the *Polonaise Fantaisie)* which represent dramatic statements of Chopin's nationalism are *Op. 26 No. 2 in E flat minor (Revolt* or *Siberian)* (1834-35); *Op. 40 No. 1 in A (Militaire)* (1838); and *Op. 53 in A flat (Heroic)* (1842). The *Polonaise-Fantaisie Op. 61* (1845-46) is the last of Chopin's major compositions for piano solo. According to Alan Walker, it is an unqualified masterpiece. Difficult to project, its ideas are striking, pointing to new harmonic and textural developments which Chopin did not live to explore.

The twenty-four *Preludes Op. 28* (1836-39) dedicated to Pleyel (French edition) and Kessler (German edition) were written in Majorca after Chopin's collapse from tuberculosis. They explore all the major and minor keys with constant variety of technical means and emotional message. They are strong as individual works but also go well in a cycle; their vividness is unsurpassed by any of Chopin's other writing. In general they are short, many not more than a page long. Among the most familiar are *No. 4 in E minor* (played at Chopin's funeral), *No. 15 in D* (called the *Raindrop), No. 16 in B flat minor* (Anton Rubinstein's favorite), and *No. 20 in C minor* (known to every piano student).

Chopin wrote three *Sonatas* of which the first in *C minor Op. 4* (1828), offered posthumously for publication in 1851, is a rarely heard youthful work. The latter two, *Op. 35 in B flat minor* and *Op. 58 in B minor,* are masterworks.

Sonata in B flat minor Op. 35 (1839)

The *Sonata in B flat* minor is one of Chopin's finest works. In its four movements, Chopin bent and changed the content of sonata form to fit the single mood of tragedy.

The violence of the first two movements and quality of doom of the third movement *Funeral March* led one critic to call the *Funeral March* a "Poem of Death." It is one of the most famous in musical literature, a fitting tribute to Chopin's own cortège. The short *Finale,* like the "whirling away of withered leaves over a fresh grave," is a foreboding rush of notes divided in unison between the hands. The movement ends with the harsh finality of two unprepared fortissimo chords.

Sonata in B minor Op. 58 (1844)

Dedicated to Countess de Perthuis

The *B minor Sonata Op. 58* appeared five years after the *B flat minor Op. 35.* It is the only work Chopin composed during the entire year of 1844. Although not as overtly powerful or compact as *Op. 35,* it nevertheless involves complex harmonic development and continuous inspiration. The third movement *Largo,* based on a broad, tranquil theme, provides contrast between the first two movements and the virtuoso *Finale.* The fireworks of the *Finale* exemplify Chopin's respect for virtuosity which speaks with clarity, rhythmic control, and contrast.

Individual works in free form which show unfailing distinction and a high order of creative energy are the *Fantaisie in F minor Op. 49* (1840), *Berceuse in D flat Op. 57,* and *Barcarolle in F sharp Op. 60* (1845-46). The *Fantaisie* is one of Chopin's finest compositions, with wide range of emotion and great individuality of theme. It ranks with the two major *Sonatas.* The *Berceuse* occupies a high point in Chopin's writing because of its extreme chromaticism. The *Barcarolle* requires exceptional technique as well as poetic insight to do justice to its heroic concept. Additional single works in short form are the 3 *Impromptus, Op. 29 in A flat* (1837), *Op. 36 in F sharp* (1839), and *Op. 51 in G flat* (1842); the *Fantaisie-Impromptu in C sharp minor Op. 66* (1835); *Boléro in C Op. 19* (1833); *Tarantelle in A flat Op. 43* (1841); and 3 *Rondos, Op. 1 in C minor* (1825), *Op. 5, à la Mazur* (1826), and *Op. 16 in E flat* (1832).

The two *Concertos for Piano and Orchestra, Op. 11 in E minor* and *Op. 21 in F minor* show immaturity of orchestration, as Chopin did not think orchestrally or even seek to develop a specialized knowledge of orchestration. However, the solo parts are filled with fresh turns of phrase and melody. They contain beautiful music, especially in the slow movements.

Concerto in E minor Op. 11 (1830) (called No. 1)

Dedicated to Kalkbrenner

The *E minor Concerto* was written after the *F minor* Concerto which bears the later Opus number. It is a virtuoso piece with an outstanding *Romanze.*

Concerto in F minor Op. 21 (1829) (called No. 2)

Dedicated to Delphine Potocka

The first movement of the *F minor Concerto* is less extended than the lengthy first movement of the *E minor Concerto*. The *Finale,* in mazurka rhythm, is particularly attractive.

Additional but less important works for *Piano and Orchestra* are: *Variations on Là ci darem* from Mozart's *Don Giovanni Op. 2* (1827); *Fantasy on Polish Airs Op. 13* (1828); *Krakowiak,* concert rondo *Op. 14* (1828); and *Grande Polonaise in E flat Op. 22* (1831). The *Andante Spianato* (1834) for piano solo, given the same *Op. 22,* was appended to the preceding *Grande Polonaise* on publication.

Chopin's only work for *Piano Duo* is the *Rondo in C Op. 73* (1828), originally for piano solo. There also is a single work for *Piano Duet,* the *Variations in F* (1826) dedicated to Titus Woyciechowski.

Editions:

F. F. Chopin: Dziela wszystkie (Complete Works), ed. I. J. Paderewski (Warsaw and Krakow, 1949-61)   P

M. J. E. Brown: Chopin: an Index of his Works in Chronological Order (London, 1960, rev. 2/1972)   B

Note: Editions suffered from interference of editors. First serious effort at a scholarly edition was by Oxford University Press 1932, ed. Edouard Ganche (he used pupil Jane Stirling's copies).

Only complete edition published 1937-66 by Chopin Institute in Warsaw and Polskie Wydawnictwo Muzyczne in Krakow–20 volumes. Not all Western sources available in putting it together.

Best available though not yet complete edition is Ewald Zimmerman's, published by Henle Verlag in Munich.

Selected Works for Piano

Rondo in C minor, Op. 1 (1825)
Sonata in C minor, Op. 4 (1828)
Rondo à la Mazur, Op. 5 (1826)
Four Mazurkas, Op. 6 (1830)
Five Mazurkas, Op. 7 (1831)
Three Nocturnes, Op. 9 (1830-31)

Twelve Etudes, Op. 10 (publ. 1833)

Variations brilliantes on a rondo from Halévy's "Ludovic", Op. 12 (1833)

Three Nocturnes, Op. 15 (publ. 1833)

Rondo in E flat, Op. 16 (1832)

Four Mazurkas, Op. 17 (1832-33)

Waltz in E flat, Op. 18 (1831)

Boléro, Op. 19 (1833)

Scherzo in B minor, Op. 20 (1831-32)

Ballade in G minor, Op. 23 (1831-35)

Four Mazurkas, Op. 24 (1834-35)

Twelve Etudes, Op. 25 (publ. 1837)

Two Polonaises, Op. 26 (1834-35)

Two Nocturnes, Op. 27 (1836)

Twenty-four Preludes, Op. 28 (1836-39)

Impromptu in A flat, Op. 29 (1837)

Four Mazurkas, Op. 30 (1836-37)

Scherzo in B flat minor, Op. 31 (1837)

Two Nocturnes, Op. 32 (1836-37)

Four Mazurkas, Op. 33 (1837-38)

Three Waltzes, Op. 34 (publ. 1838)

Sonata in B flat minor, Op. 35 (1839)

Impromptu in F sharp, Op. 36 (1839)

Two Nocturnes, Op. 37 (publ. 1840)

Ballade in F, Op. 38 (1836-39)

Scherzo in C sharp minor, Op. 39 (1839)

Two Polonaises, Op. 40 (publ. 1840)

Four Mazurkas, Op. 41 (publ. 1840)

Waltz in A flat, Op. 42 (1840)

Tarantelle, Op. 43 (1841)

Polonaise in F sharp minor, Op. 44 (1840-41)

Prelude in C sharp minor, Op. 45 (1841)

Allegro de Concert, Op. 46 (1832-41 incl. material originally intended for a 3rd piano concerto)

Ballade in A flat, Op. 47 (1840-41)

Two Nocturnes, Op. 48 (1841)

Fantasie in F minor, Op. 49 (1841)

Three Mazurkas, Op. 50 (1842)

Impromptu in G flat, Op. 51 (1842)

Ballade in F minor, Op. 52 (1842)

Polonaise in A flat, Op. 53 (1842)

Scherzo in E, Op. 54 (1842)

Two Nocturnes, Op. 55 (1843)
Three Mazurkas, Op. 56 (1843)
Berceuse, Op. 57 (1843-44)
Sonata in B minor, Op. 58 (1844)
Three Mazurkas, Op. 59 (1845)
Barcarolle, Op. 60 (1845-46)
Polonaise-Fantasie, Op. 61 (1845-56)
Two Nocturnes, Op. 62 (1846)
Three Mazurkas, Op. 63 (1846)
Three Waltzes, Op. 64 (1846-47)
Fantaisie-Impromptu, Op. 66 (1835)
Four Mazurkas, Op. 67 (publ. 1855)
Four Mazurkas, Op. 68 (1849)
Two Waltzes, Op. 69 (publ. 1855)
Three Waltzes, Op. 70 (publ. 1855)
Three Polonaises, Op. 71 (publ. 1855)
Nocturne in E minor, Op. 72 (1827); *Marche funèbre in C minor, Op. 72 (1829)*; *Three Écossaises, Op. 72 (1826)*

Certain *Mazurkas, Polonaises, Waltzes, Variations,* and *Etudes* not given opus numbers are identified in New Grove, 1980 by catalogue number.

For Piano and Orchestra

Variations, Là ci darem, Op. 2 (1827)
Concerto No. 1 in E minor, Op. 11 (1830)
Fantasy on Polish Airs, Op. 13 (1828)
Concert Rondo on Polish Airs, Krakowiak, Op. 14 (1828)
Concerto No. 2 in F minor, Op. 21 (1829)
Grande Polonaise in E flat with Andante Spianato, Op. 22 (1831)

For Piano Duo

Rondo in C, Op. 73 (1828)

For Piano Duet

Introduction, Theme and Variations in F (no opus) (1826)

Etude in E major Op.10 No.3

*Born in Raiding, Hungary,
October 22, 1811*

*Died in Bayreuth, Germany,
July 31, 1886,
Age 75 years*

Franz Liszt

Historical Sketch

Franz Liszt was born into a milieu of musical performance through his father's position as steward on the Esterházy estate and as cellist in the court orchestra there. The Esterházy family had played an important part in music history, notably in the case of Haydn, before Liszt was born. Through the years, the family supported music, subsidized orchestras, and engaged composers and performers who were among the finest of the day.

When Liszt was 10 years old, the Esterházys and local Hungarian families financed his piano study in Vienna. As with Haydn, Mozart, Beethoven, and Schubert, Vienna in Liszt's youth was one of Europe's important music centers. At 11, Liszt gave his first public concert and at 12, his first concert tour of Europe including the German cities of Munich and Stuttgart. After the tour, he settled in Paris where his playing was a sensational success. He performed some of his own compositions in Paris, and soon London, and set the stage for his beginnings as a serious composer. His definitive work in 1826 was the original version of the *Transcendental Etudes*.

At 19, Liszt met Berlioz, the first of the three musicians who were to exert an indelible influence on his style. Berlioz, composer of the *Fantastic Symphony*,[1] stirred in

[1] Filled with supernatural ideas, this symphony was a nightmare of strange shapes and noises in which the hero dreamed he was executed.

Liszt a diabolical streak through daring and bizarre harmonic innovations. The other two were Paganini, a phenomenal violin virtuoso spoken of as the devil himself, who inspired Liszt's awesome ranges of pianistic bravura, and Chopin who countered diabolism and excessive virtuosity with grace and poetry. Liszt absorbed these influences into his own natural expression to create works that extended through the years from heroic fire to religious meditation to startling bleakness. By 1830, Liszt was on the threshold of his career and within four years established himself as a serious and original composer with works which included *La Campanella, Harmonies poétiques et religieuses,*[2] *De Profundis for Piano and Orchestra,*[3] and the set of 3 *Apparitions.*

In his early twenties, Liszt eloped to Switzerland and Italy with Countess d'Agoult (better known by her literary name of Daniel Stern), a friend of Chopin and George Sand. The liaison inspired sketches of the *1st Book of Années de pèlerinage* (Switzerland), completion of the *2nd book* (Italy), as well as first versions of the *Paganini Etudes, 12 Transcendental Etudes,* and *Todentanz for Piano and Orchestra.* In 1838, a daughter, Cosima, was born who was later to become the wife of Richard Wagner.[4] Six years after Cosima's birth, Liszt and the Countess separated.

At the height of his career as a concert pianist, Liszt retired to Weimar in 1846 to conduct occasional concerts of the court orchestra. Two years later, he was appointed as full time conductor, a post he held for the next twelve years. He began a new liaison with Princess Carolyne Sayn-Wittgenstein who was a strong influence on his creative drive. During these years of 1848-60, with the Princess's encouragement, Liszt wrote or revised many of his major works, including 15 *Hungarian Rhapsodies,* the single *Sonata in B minor,* the two *Concertos for Piano and Orchestra in E flat* and *A,* 3 *Études de Concert,* the later set of *Harmonies poétiques et religieuses,* 1st *Mephisto Waltz,* 3 *Liebesträume,* and the *Grosses Konzertsolo* arranged for piano and orchestra, and for two pianos as the *Concerto pathétique.*

In the field of symphonic music, Liszt invented and developed a short form called the *Symphonic Poem.*[5] As conductor of the Weimar orchestra, he introduced his own compositions as well as those of younger musicians. Wagner, Schumann, Berlioz, Verdi, and Donizetti owed performances of their works to him. Although he discovered or befriended nearly every musical figure of the day, Liszt fell somewhat out of favor in Weimar because of his leadership of the New German School of "futurists" who emphasized the cause of new music. Both Brahms and Joachim signed petitions against the New School, and in 1860 Liszt chose to leave Weimar for Rome.

---

[2]   In this case, a *single* piece, the name of which Liszt gave between 1845-52 to a *set* of pieces including *Bénédiction de Dieu dans la Solitude, Pensée des Morts, Cantique,* and *Funérailles.*

[3]   The unfinished ms. is in the Liszt Museum. 5691.

[4]   Cosima's first husband was the distinguished musician (pianist and conductor) Hans von Bülow.

[5]   Liszt's *Symphonic Poem* is a musical narrative with several themes which appear in disguise throughout the composition in a recurring treatment called *Cyclic. Cyclic form,* as later enriched by César Franck, states one theme as the foundation of a work and builds the entire structure on *transformations* of it. Liszt composed 13 *Symphonic Poems,* among them *Les Préludes, Prometheus, Tasso,* and *Mazeppa.*

In Rome, Liszt concerned himself with religious music and wrote the 2 *Legends of St. François d'Assise* and *St. François de Paul, A la Chapelle Sixtine,* and the *Variations Weinen, Klagen, Sorgen, Zagen.* In 1865, he took the four minor orders of the Catholic Church and became an honorary Abbe although not a priest. For the next twenty years, he divided his time among the cities of Rome, Weimar, and Budapest, playing, composing, and teaching. The incredible list of composers, performers, and pupils who surrounded him contained such distinguished names as Albeniz, Debussy, Saint-Saëns, Fauré, Anton Rubinstein, Frederic Lamond, Moritz Rosenthal, Sophie Menter, von Sauer, and d'Albert—each one an individual who has left a lasting mark on music.

The compositions of Liszt's later years showed new extremes of style and structure, harmonic innovations, and finally, a disturbing austerity and desolation. Typical of this time in his life were the two *Concert Studies, Waldesrauschen* and *Gnomenreigen, Rhapsodie espagnole, Jeux d'eau à la Villa d'Este* (from *3rd Book* of *Années de pèlerinage),* and 3rd *Mephisto Waltz.*

In 1886, at 75, Liszt completed his final concert tour in Luxembourg. He then travelled to Bayreuth for performances of Wagner's *Parsifal* and *Tristan* which he endorsed as visionary forms of music drama built on provocative new ideals. In Bayreuth he was taken ill with pneumonia and died ten days later.

Style

Liszt's strength of vision lasted a lifetime, giving his style power and originality. Like Mendelssohn and Schumann, he was influenced by arts other than music—literature and painting. He came close to realizing his dream that music should embody the world through his all inclusive contributions as conductor, composer, arranger, and pianist. His restless intellect explored the possibilities of freeing form from its association with Classical structures. This led to his successful use of thematic transformation where he invented his own forms and developed a harmony of extreme chromaticism to support them, a harmony which he pushed beyond the limits of recognized key relationships. He outstripped the evolving ideas of Romanticism by ingenious combinations unique to his own style—the lyricism of Italian cantilena, Mendelssohnian lightness and playfulness, the violence of unrestrained orchestral sound, and nationalist rhythmic drive.

As pianist, Liszt was generally accepted as the greatest of his time. Called the "virtuoso of virtuosi," he developed piano technique to the limits of physical possibility. His "transcendental technique" explored every resource of the piano and pushed on to orchestral effects which he sometimes indicated by the use of three staves. He demanded equal strength of both hands for all kinds of playing—octaves (his unusually long fingers played 10ths as easily as 8vas), chords, repeated notes, and trills at a speed never before approached, using extreme parts of the keyboard with freedom and flexibility.

Liszt's virtuosity proceeded along Chopin's technical lines but translated Chopin's more intimate style into concert hall distinctiveness. Using a high piano seat, with his forearms sloping toward his hands, he achieved great force. The pianist Arthur Friedheim said that to the end Liszt was without equal in the production of powerful sound and overwhelming climaxes. It was true of Liszt, but not always his followers, that beauty of sound was present even in loud passages. Like Chopin, Liszt turned the hand's basic weakness (the third and fourth finger side) into a means for producing beautiful tonal quality. As with other romantics, he enhanced pure sound by using the sustaining pedal freely to liberate the hands and blend dynamics.

The pianist-scholar, Alfred Brendel,[6] has called Liszt one of the most amazing revolutionaries in music history, with daring harmony, lyrical freshness, inimitable keyboard sounds, and unsurpassed technique. Mr. Brendel suggests we are all of Liszt's line—that he created the type to which we aspire: the universal performer of grand stature.

Compositions

Liszt's works[7] fall into three classes: *transcriptions and arrangements; program music; absolute music.* The bulk lies in the first group, transcriptons and arrangements, based on operatic, vocal (single songs) and instrumental works by himself and other composers, including Mozart, Beethoven, Schubert, Schumann, Chopin, Mendelssohn, and Wagner.

While some of the *transcriptions* intensify the original musical idea, there is rarely enough enhancement or originality to make them more than historically interesting. Exceptions are the *Transcendental Etudes after Paganini,* the famous *Liebestraum,* the Schubert *Soirées de Vienne,* and the *Mephisto Waltzes.*

Transcendental Etudes after Paganini R.3a (1838)

Dedicated to Clara Schumann

These are 6 studies which include *Tremolo study in G minor, Octave study in D flat,* the famous *La campanella, Arpeggio study in E, La Chasse,* and *Theme and Variations in A minor.* The first version is considered one of the most difficult sets of pieces written for the piano. The second version of 1851 is somewhat simpler.

Liebestraum No. 3 in A flat R.211 (1850)

This perennially affecting piece is the third of three *Notturnos* which Liszt transcribed from his own songs.

---

[6]   Brendel, Alfred, *Musical Thoughts and Afterthoughts,* Princeton, 1976, p. 81

[7]   See paragraph following Selected Works for Piano in this chapter for explanation of *R* and *S* letters.

Soirees de Vienne R.252 (1852)

Dedicated to Simon Lowy

These are delightful caprices founded on waltzes of Schubert.

Mephisto Waltzes

Dedicated to Carl Tausig (No. 1), to Camille Saint-Saëns, and to Marie Jaell (No. 3)

The First Mephisto Waltz appeared originally as Der Tanz in der Dorfschenke R.181 (1859-60). The Second Mephisto Waltz R.182 (1881) and the Third R.38 (1838) are separate compositions which share with the First the inspiration of Faust, one of Liszt's favorite literary figures.

In program music inspired by nature, Liszt created the suggestive, picturesque, lyrical style found in Années de pèlerinage and Harmonies poétiques et religieuses. His later program music, the three Études de Concert, the Transcendental Etudes, the two Concert Studies, and the two Légendes are works of spectacular virtuosity.

Années de pèlerinage (3 volumes) R.10a,b,c,e, (1836-77)

Volume I Switzerland R.10a (1836)

Volume I reflects the purity and freshness of nature in 9 descriptive pieces including Lake Wallenstadt and Au bord d'une source.

Volume II Italy R.10b (1838-89)

Volume II contains allusions to the legacy of the past and to Petrarch in Nos. 4-6 in the Sonnets 47, 104, and 123. The last piece, No. 7, is the evocative Après une lecture de Dante, fantasia quasi sonata.

Supplement to Volume II Venezia e Napoli R.10c (1859)

The Supplement to Volume II suggests the atmosphere of sun and song in Gondoliera, Canzone, and Tarantella.

Volume III R.10e (1877)

Volume III describes in the fourth of 7 pieces the sparkling Jeux d'eaux à la Villa d'Este, an impressionistic work well ahead of its time.

Harmonies poétiques et religieuses R.14 (1845-52)

Dedicated to Princess Sayn-Wittgenstein

This collection of 10 pieces, some revisions from 1834, was suggested in part by poems of Lamartine. At least two in the collection *Bénédiction de Dieu dans la Solitude* and *Funérailes,* are masterworks. *Bénédiction de Dieu,* like the original single piece, *Harmonies poétiques et religieuses,* has overtones of late Beethoven in spiritual self-examination. *Funérailles,* a funeral march of shattering impact, suggests the middle section of Chopin's great *A flat Polonaise.* Its expression of grief relates to victims of the Hungarian revolution of 1848-49.

---

3 Études de Concert R.5 (1848): *No. 1 in A flat; No. 2 in F minor; No. 3 in D flat*

Dedicated to Eduard Liszt

No. 1, called *Lamento,* is a romantic improvisation suggestive of Schumann. *No. 2, La Leggierezza,* is one of Liszt's finest concert studies, while *No. 3, Un sospiro,* is popular for its immediate melodic appeal.

Transcendental Etudes (12) *R.2b* (1851)

Dedicated to Carl Czerny

Liszt revised these *Etudes* over a considerable period of time as he learned, in his works, "to distinguish between proper pianoforte effects and mere dare-devil bravura." They explore the entire range of piano technique. In 1852, titles were added to all but two. Those with titles are *Preludio, Paysage, Mazeppa, Feux follets, Vision, Eroica, Wild Jagd, Ricordanza, Harmonies du soir,* and *Chasse-neige.*

---

2 Concert Studies R.6 (1862): *No. 1 Waldesrauschen; No. 2 Gnomenreigen*

Dedicated to Dionys Pruckner

Waldesrauschen contains one of Liszt's most graceful and shimmering themes; *Gnomenreigen* is a light, staccato scherzo reminiscent of Mendelssohn's *Midsummer Night's Dream.*

Légendes R.17 (1863): *No. 1 St. François d'Assise. La prédication aux oiseaux; No. 2 St. François de Paule marchant sur les flots*

Dedicated to Princess Czartoryska (No. 1) and to Cosima von Bülow (born Liszt) (No. 2)

No. 1, St. François d'Assise preaching to the birds, is strikingly original, without parallel until the Twentieth Century composer Messiaen began to write *his* evocation of bird sounds. Liszt's musical sermon refers to a multitude of wayside birds who would not "fly away until the Saint had given them his blessing." In *Legend No. 2, St. François de*

Paule is challenged to walk on the sea (the Straits of Messina) and does so successfully to the menacing sound of rolling waves.

The *absolute music*,[8] while smaller in quantity than the transcriptions and program music, contains many of Liszt's finest works. These include *6 Consolations, Sonata in B minor, Variations on Weinen, Klagen, Sorgen, Zagen,* and the *Hungarian Rhapsodies.*

Consolations R.12 (1849-50)

The six *Consolations* which take their title from Sainte-Beuve correspond roughly to certain of Chopin's *Nocturnes.* They are charming and original.

Sonata in B minor R. 21 (1852-53)

Dedicated to Robert Schumann

The *Sonata in B minor* is one of the masterpieces of the Nineteenth Century piano literature. It remains Liszt's greatest pianistic creation in which technique serves only to make the work musical and poetic. Cyclical form pioneered by Liszt takes the place here of traditional sonata movements and allows the work to be played without pause. Frequent changes of mood balance the extended structure and give it a cohesion attempted later by Schoenberg in his 12 tone serialism built in part on Liszt's principles of thematic transformation.

Variations on Weinen, Klagen, Sorgen, Zagen R.24 (1862)

Dedicated to Anton Rubinstein

Liszt wrote this composition after the death of an elder daughter, a sister of Cosima's. The *Variations* are built on the passacaglia theme from Bach's *Contata No. 12 (Weinen, Klagen, etc.)* which also appears in the Crucifixus of the *B minor Mass.* Compared with a visit to Purgatory, it utters bitter grief and regret. In one of his most neglected and moving masterpieces, Liszt suggests through advanced use of chromaticism the poignant enormity of human suffering.

Hungarian Rhapsodies R.106 (1840-47; 1852-53; 1885)

Dedicated to numerous people including Count Esterházy, Joseph Joachim, and Hans von Bülow.

The fire and freedom of the 19 *Rhapsodies* are qualities Liszt shared with gypsy musical

---

8   As opposed to "programme" music which tells a story, illustrates action, etc.

style and the spirit of the Magyars.[9] The first 15 appeared between 1851-53 on the basis of pieces in Hungarian style written between 1840-47. The last four are late works of 1885. They possess freedom, strange modulations, dash, and romantic intensity. Bartók felt the *Rhapsodies* were perfect creations of their own kind although he was too much a purist to care for the material used. Of particular interest are the durable *Second Rhapsody,* the *Third, Eighth, Eleventh, Thirteenth, Fourteenth,* and *Fifteenth.* The *Fifteenth* is one of 3 versions of Liszt's *Rakoczy March.*

The works for piano and orchestra include four *Fantasias* and the two *Concertos in E flat and A.*[10]

The *Fantasias* include *Todtentanz R.457* (1849) (a set of *Variations* on the "Dies Irae," dedicated to Hans von Bülow), and *Hungarian Fantasia R.458* (1852), also dedicated to Hans von Bülow. *Todtentanz,* the powerful *Dance of Death,* is based on the Gregorian chant of the *Dies Irae,* while the *Hungarian Fantasia* is another setting of the solo *Hungarian Rhapsody No. 14.*

Concerto No. 1 in E flat (called the *Triangle Concerto) R.455* (completed in 1849; revised in 1853 and 1856)

Dedicated to Henry Litolff

Liszt shocked the critics by using the triangle in the *Scherzo* movement opf the *E flat Concerto;* it marked one of the first important appearances of the triangle as a serious instrument of the orchestra. Although Liszt finished revising the *Concerto* in later life, he sketched it at nineteen. Working through the years, he gave it youthful energy as well as mature craftsmanship. Its "four movements-in-one" form is borrowed from Schubert's *Wanderer Fantasy* with the four sections linked thematically.

Concerto No. 2 in A R.456 (completed in 1839, revised in 1849-61)

Dedicated to Hans von Bronsart

As with the *First Concerto,* Liszt revised the *Second* over a period of more than 20 years. It is considered by some more beautiful than the *First,* its form freer and highly original. Like the *First,* it is built on continuously unfolding cyclic structure. The orchestration is exceptionally good.

---

[9]   There are three areas of so-called "Hungarian Music": gypsy musical style assimilated from melodies of individual native composers, stressing improvisation; folk melodies of the 18th and 19th Centuries, called "urban", derived from the aristocracy and middle class; actual peasant folk songs discovered through research of Bartók and Kodály. Liszt did not use traditional material but applied Gypsy *style* to the *Rhapsodies.*

[10]   Liszt wrote an historically interesting orchestral accompaniment to Schubert's *Wanderer Fantasy in C* listed as *R.459* (1851).

For *Duet,* Liszt wrote 3 original works, little performed today, *Fest polonaise R.296* (1876), *Variations on Chopstick Theme R.297* (1880), and *Notturno (S. identification 256a).* For *Duo* there is but one published work, *Concerto pathétique R.356* (1856) dedicated to I. von Bronsart. The *Concerto pathétique* is an arrangement of *Grosses Konzertsolo* of 1849, also for piano and orchestra c.1850. Liszt made innumerable *duet* and *duo* transcriptions of his own and other composers' works, rarely performed.

Editions:

F. Liszt: Musikalische Werke, ed. F. Busoni, P. Raabe, etc.(Leipzig) 1907-36/R)

                                                                                B

Liszt Society Publications (London, 1950)   LS

F. Liszt: Neue Ausgabe sämtlicher Werke/New Edition of the Complete Works, 1st ser., ed. Z. Gardonyi and others (Kassel and Budapest 1970)   NA

Liszt, Ferencz: H. Searle, Grove 5   S

Franz Liszt: P. Raabe (Stuttgart 1931, rev. 2/1968)   R

Selected Works for Piano

Two complete cataloguing systems deal with Liszt's prodigious musical production, those of Peter Raabe,[11] whose book *Franz Liszt* remains a standard biography, and Humphrey Searle, author of *The Music of Liszt.*[12] The selected works listed below are cross-indexed with the Raabe and Searle numbers. For complete listing of Liszt's piano works and for individual titles within each collection, please see New Grove 1980.

12 *Études d'exécution transcendante,* R.2b and S.139 (1851)
6 *Études d'exécution transcendante d'après Paganini,* R.3a and S.140 (1838)
    Ab Irato, R.4b and S.143 (1852)
3 Études de Concert in A flat, F minor, D flat, R.5 and S.144 (1848)
2 *Concert Studies,* R.6 and S.145 (1862-3): 1. *Waldesrauschen;* 2. *Gnomenreigen* 3 *Apparitions,* R.11 and S.155 (1834)
Album d'un voyageur (3 volumes), R.8 and S.156 (1835-36)
9 *Années de pèlerinage. Premiere Année: Suisse,* R.10a and S.160 (1848-52) (Publ. complete in 1855)

---

[11]   Raabe (1872-1945) was for many years Director of the Liszt Museum at Weimar.
[12]   Dover Publications Inc., New York, 1966

7 *Années de pèlerinage. Deuxieme Année: Italie*, R.10b and S.161 (1837-49) (Publ. 1858.)

3 *Venezia e Napoli*, R.10c and S.162 (1859) (Publ. 1861)

7 *Années de pèlerinage. Troisieme Année*, R.10e and S.163 (1867-77) (Publ. 1883)

Feuilles d'album in A flat and A minor, R.62,64 and S.165,167 (1843)

Ballade No. 2 in B minor, R.16 and S.171 (1853)

6 *Consolations*, R.12 and S.172 (1849-50)

10 *Harmonies poétiques et religieuses*, R.14 and S.173 (1845-52)

Légendes, R.17 and S.175 (1863)[13]

Scherzo and March, R.20 and S.177 (1851)

Sonata in B minor, R.21 and S.178 (1852-53)

Variations on the theme of Bach, basso continuo of the first movement of his cantata *Weinen, Klagen, Sorgen, Zagen*, and of the *Crucifixus* of the *B minor Mass*, R.24 and S.180 (1862)

Hungarian Historical Portraits, R.112 and S.205 (1870)

Trois Caprices--Valses, R.32b and S.214 (based on Waltzes already composed in 1836; 1839; 1842)

4 *Valses Oubliées*, R. 37 and S.215 (1881-85)

Third Mephisto Waltz, R.38 and S.216 (1883)

Mazurka brillante, R. 43 and S.221 (1850)

2 *Polonaises*, R.44 and S.223 (1851): 1. C minor; 2. E

19 *Hungarian Rhapsodies*, R.106 and S.244 (1846-85)

Spanish Rhapsody, R.90 and S.254 (1863)

9 *Soirées de Vienne, Valses caprice d'après Schubert*, R. 252 and S.427 (1852)

A la Chapelle Sixtine, R.114 and S.461 (2 pieces that are transcriptions of the *Miserere* of Allegri and *Ave Verum* of Mozart) (1862)

Der Tanz in der Dorfschenke (1st *Mephisto Waltz*), R.181 and S.514 (1859-60).

2nd *Mephisto Waltz*, R.182 and S.515 (1881)

Fantasy and Fugue on Bach, R.22 and S.529 (1871)

Liebesträume. 3 Notturnos, R.211 and S.541 (1850).

For Piano and Orchestra

Malédiction, R.452 and S.121 (1830; 1840)

Fantasia on themes from Beethoven's Ruins of Athens, R.454 and S.122 (1848; 1852)

Concerto No. 1 in E flat, R.455 and S.124 (1849; 1853; 1856)

Concerto No. 2 in A, R.456 and S.125 (1839; 1849-61)

Todtentanz, R.457 and S.126 (1849; 1859)

Fantasia on Hungarian Folk Tunes, R.458 and S.123 (1852)

Franz Schubert's *Wanderer Fantasy in C*, Op. 15, Symphonic arr., R.459 and S.366 (before 1852)

---

[13]   1. *St. François d'Assise. La prédication aux oiseaux;* 2. *St. François de Paule marchant sur les flots.*

For Piano Duo
_____

Concerto pathétique, R.356 and S.258 (1856)

For Piano Duet
_____

Festpolonaise, R.296 and S. 255 (1876)
Chopsticks, R.297 and S.256 (1880)
Notturno, (no R. number), S.265a (date unknown)

Liebestraum (Notturno) No.3
from 3 *Notturnos* R.211

"O love!"
Poem by F. Freiligrath

O love! O love, so long as e'er thou canst, or dost on love believe;
The time shall come, when thou by graves shalt stand and grieve;
And see that still thy heart doth glow, doth bear and foster love divine,
So long as e'er another heart shall beat in warm response to thine.
And, whoso bares his heart to thee, O, show him love where in thy power,
And make his every hour a joy, nor wound his heart at any hour.
And keep a guard upon thy tongue — an unkind word is quickly said:
Ah me! — no ill was meant — and yet
The other goes and weeps thereat.

Franz Liszt

Poco allegro, con affetto

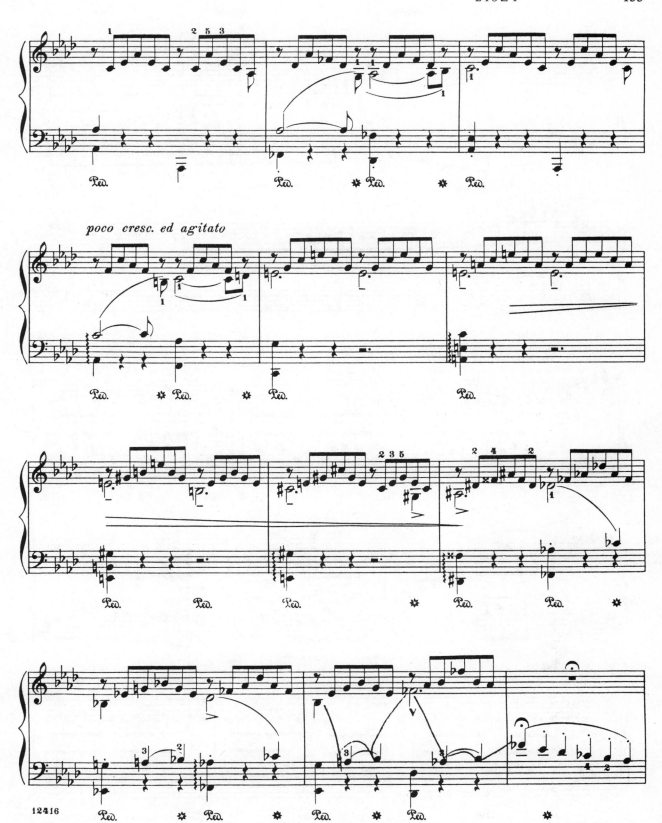

poco cresc. ed agitato

12416

Più animato, con passione

Born in Hamburg, Germany,
May 7, 1833

Died in Vienna, Austria,
April 3, 1897,
Age 64 years

Johannes Brahms

Historical Sketch

Because Brahms combined the principles of Classical construction with the Romantic spirit of Mendelssohn and Schumann, he was considered in his time as heir to the central German heritage. His concern for form carried throughout his life. Except for deepening emotion and growing spirituality, his style was well defined from the beginning.

Brahms's father was a bassoonist and double-bass player in the Hamburg city orchestra. His sturdy farming and artisan stock appeared in his son as robust good health which did much to support Brahms's creative life. Brahms's mother, seventeen years older than her husband, became the idol of her son. Ambitious, bright, and sensitive, she nourished Brahms's musical intellect with her determination. At 7, Brahms studied with Otto Cossel, a musician of some distinction who developed in Brahms an early proficiency as pianist. Six years later in 1846, Brahms began theory training with the highly regarded Marxsen; in 1848 and 1849, he gave his first solo concerts. He worked intensively at composition but also gave lessons and played in dance halls to improve family finances. An important influence came into his life in 1848 when escapees from the Hungarian uprising passed through the port of Hamburg on their way to North

America. Brahms gleaned from them the Hungarian czardas and alla zingarese styles that left on him the stamp of triplet figures and irregular rhythms.

Among those escaping Hungary at this time was the violinist Reményi. In 1853, at 20, Brahms embarked on a tour with Reményi which brought him in contact with the celebrated violinist, Joachim. Joachim in turn introduced Brahms and Reményi to Liszt. Although Brahms admired Liszt personally, he did not fall under Liszt's prestigious spell. Leaving Liszt at Weimar, Brahms met Robert and Clara Schumann in Düsseldorf. Among Brahms's compositions at this time were the early *Scherzo in E flat minor Op. 4* (written in 1851 at 18), the *Sonata in F sharp minor Op. 2* of 1852, the *Sonata in C Op. 1* of 1852-3, and the *Sonata in F minor Op. 5* of 1853. Schumann endorsed these compositions and greeted Brahms as "this young eagle." Schumann felt in Brahms's romanticism a spirit congenial to his own, and in Brahms's classicism a solidity which he himself lacked. The friendship of the three musicians, born of their art, outlived their lifetimes in the music inspired by it. Brahms fell in love with Clara but was loyal to Robert during the years of mental deterioration before Schumann's death.

In 1857, Brahms was appointed court choir and orchestra conductor at Detmold near Hamburg. The following year he completed the *D minor Concerto for Piano and Orchestra Op. 15*. In this period he wrote his first lieder (in folksong style) inspired by his attachment to Agathe von Siebold, and in 1861 he completed the *Variations on a Theme by Handel Op. 24*.

In 1862, Brahms left Hamburg to establish his reputation in Vienna. Here he met Wagner as well as the pianist Carl Tausig who motivated Brahms's second great set of *Variations*, those on a *Theme by Paganini Op. 35* which appeared between 1862-3. With the exception of the *16 Waltzes Op. 39* (1865, also for piano duet), Brahms wrote nothing more for piano solo for 15 years until the *Op. 76* pieces of 1878. Eager to conduct (he had hoped for an appointment to the Hamburg orchestra), he became director of the Vienna Singakadamie. He gave up this post after one season because of administrative difficulties. In the meantime he introduced his piano works to the Viennese public and began to develop a reputation of European standing as pianist and composer.

In 1868, Brahms finished the *German Requiem Op. 45* which he began in 1857. Public acclaim was high, and Brahms was hailed as a "patriot" for the scope and magnificence of the work. Four years later, as a permanent resident of Vienna, Brahms accepted the post of conductor of the orchestra and chorus of the Vienna Gesselschafts-konzerte. However, his abilities as conductor were limited, especially in contrast to von Bulow, Mottl, Muck, and others who were beginning to make conducting their only profession. Brahms gave up conducting in favor of his career as an internationally famous composer with over 60 opus numbers to his credit. In 1873, he wrote another acclaimed work, the *Variations on a Theme by Haydn Op. 56a* which also appeared at the same time in an "original" version for two pianos as *Op. 56b*.

In his early 40's, Brahms began an exceptionally productive era in which he wrote the songs of *Opp. 69-72* inspired by Elizabeth von Herzogenberg, a former pupil and respected life-long friend. This period also produced for piano the *8 Pieces Op. 76, 2 Rhapsodies Op. 79*, the *Second Piano Concerto in B flat Op. 83,* and the single *Violin Concerto.* In 1890, Brahms destroyed everything unusable or incomplete among his works. However, two years later and in the space of little more than a year, he wrote a legacy of 20 pieces for the piano comprising *Opp. 116, 117, 118,* and *119.*

Brahms's final compositions involved the piano as a collaborating instrument with the clarinet. Although Brahms was composing little by 1894, he paid tribute to the clarinetist Richard Mühlfeld with the two *Sonatas for Clarinet and Piano in F minor* and *E flat Op. 120.* These were his last instrumental compositions. Brahms died from cancer of the liver nine months after he became ill. He was buried in Vienna's Central Cemetery with Beethoven and Schubert.

Style

Brahms's admiration for Bach and his skill in interpreting Bach's music are the touchstones of his own polyphony. His technical ideal was polyphonic. As he adapted this style to the piano, he developed a new kind of pianism which conformed to the keyboard but added orchestral independence of voice-leading. Brahms had little regard for pianistic idiom in the sense of Chopin and Liszt; his interest lay in communication of ideas and in the musical rather than idiomatic worth of every phrase. This brought the early criticism that his music was not pianistic.

Brahms appeared also as Beethoven's spiritual successor. Of the romanticists, Brahms alone was able to recreate the universality of Beethoven's music. Structural development and emphasis on form and technique came to perfection with Beethoven. These were subordinated by the romanticists to the mood and message of each composer. But Brahms returned to formal structure and became the most skillful polyphonist after Beethoven. The "tramp of the giant" was close. In addition, Brahms's debt to Schumann must not be overlooked in the more obvious comparison with Bach and Beethoven. He drew from Schumann all that was congenial to his own style: massed chords, cross rhythms, and expressive cohesion of small, descriptive forms. He created works of proportion, logic, and contrast from the simplest melodic or harmonic germ and built simplicity into complexity with economy of motif.

Brahms's harmony is consistently rich, often modal, its thickness contrasted frequently with rugged polyphony. Melodies of beauty and expressiveness, occasionally of folk song character, are instrumental and at the same time song-like. Rhythms are vital, enlarging Schumann's legacy of writing rhythms across the measure for syncopation. Brahms's use of the triplet and his fondness for placing two notes against it are among the most characteristic features of his music. The triplet appears again and again in contrasted settings of mood and tempo. Brahms sought constantly to suggest orchestral timbre, bringing from the piano orchestral fullness. His method for these effects was to use octaves, sixths, and tenths as the basis for powerful thickly scored and widely spaced chords. He gave equal importance to treble and bass, again through wide spacing, and rarely employed passage work for its own sake.

Compositions

Chronologically Brahms's solo piano works fall into two clear divisions: the first from 1851, with the *E flat minor Scherzo Op. 4*, to 1863, with the *Paganini Variations Op. 35*; the second from 1878, with the *8 Pieces* of *Op. 76*, to 1893, with the *4 pieces of Op. 119*. Three general categories make up the complete piano listing – *Sonatas, Variations,* and individual compositions in shorter forms including *Ballades, Capricios, Intermezzi,* and *Rhapsodies.*[1]

The three *Sonatas Opp. 1, 2,* and *5* of 1852-53, the only *Sonatas* Brahms composed for piano solo, were preceded by his first published work, the *Scherzo in E flat minor Op. 4* (1851). The first two *Sonatas* are those which he showed to Schumann at their meeting in Düsseldorf. The third in *F minor* is orchestral in power, one of the finest works of the early years.

Sonata in F minor Op. 5 (1853)

Dedicated to Countess Ida von Hohenthal

The second movement of this *Sonata,* an *Andante,* was inspired by a verse of Sternau evoking a romantic moonlit setting. Schumann said of it that it was "profoundly grasped, living, deep and warm throughout."

In variation form, Brahms produced some of the finest sets since Beethoven. His two masterworks for piano solo, the *Handel* and *Paganini Variations,* are both built on simple themes already treated by their own composers. In Brahms's hands, however, thematic simplicity was the springboard for balanced complexity, inventiveness, vitality, and color. By 1861, Brahms had already written several sets, those on a *Theme of Robert Schumann Op. 9* (1854);[2] on an *Original Theme Op. 21 No. 1* (1856); and on a *Hungarian Song Op. 21 No. 2* (1853). These showed his early assimilation of fanciful and formal elements necessary for major compositions in this style. With them, he set the stage for the monumental *Handel* and *Paganini Variations* written with the concert hall in mind.

Variations and Fugue on a Theme by Handel Op. 24 (1861)

In his survey of Brahms, William Murdoch calls the *Variations,* with their crowning *Fugue,* one of the finest in the whole literature of the piano. Handel wrote the theme for one of his harpsichord *Leçons,* or exercises, and followed it with several unimportant variations. Brahms took the same theme and composed twenty-five variations

[1]   Each genre incorporates certain characteristics although these are flexible: the *Ballades* follow the structure of the literary patterns; the *Capriccios* are generally sparkling and playful; the *Intermezzi* speak with tenderness; the *Rhapsodies* suggest sonata form in the middle sections.
[2]   Whimsically inscribed, "Little Variations on a Theme of His, dedicated to Her," *Him* and *Her* being, of course, Robert and Clara Schumann.

which are among the most imaginative written. In the same vein, Karl Geiringer[3] states, "It is not easy to say which deserves the greater admiration, their (the *Variations*') logical evolution, firm organic structure, profound spirituality, or purely technical effectiveness as piano music."

Variations (Studien) on a Theme by Paganini in A minor Op. 35 (2 sets) (1862-63)

The *Paganini Variations* appeared a year after the *Handel* set. Brahms was probably more successful here even than Liszt in capturing the magic of Paganini's style by giving himself over largely to technical wizardry. The *Paganini Variations* mark the end of Brahms's concern with the titantic technique of his youth; in later works, technical means serve purely musical concepts.

The first compositions under the grouping of individual works in shorter forms are the *4 Ballades* of *Op. 10* (1854). They are an exception to the *Sonatas* and *Variations* (forms which do not appear again in the piano solos) and foreshadow, in spite of their early Opus, the condensed musical statements of *Opp. 76-119*. Among the *4 Ballades:*

Ballade in D minor Op. 10 No. 1 (1854)

This work was inspired by the Scottish ballad *Edward* in which Edward's dying mother cries out his name as that of her murderer. In a climax of terror, she screams a curse on him and dies.[4]

Ballade in D Op. 10 No. 2 (1854)

The second *Ballade* ranks among the finest works of Brahms's youthful period.

With the *8 Piano Pieces* of *Op. 76*, Brahms embarked on the intimate forms which would occupy the remainder of his piano composition. Although hinting at the spirit of Mendelssohn and Schumann, they are essentially Brahms in varying expressions of subtlety and reticence. The *Capriccio No. 2 in B minor* closes with a gradual diminuendo, its final major chord written as two eighth notes to create unexpected suspense. The *Capriccio No. 3 in C,* with varying moods, is intricate and whimsical.

Harking back to the grand scale of the *Sonatas,* the *Two Rhapsodies* of *Op. 79* (1879) are more extended than any of the *Capricci* and *Intermezzi.* Temperamental and dramatic, they could be works of Brahms's youth except for the greater directness and concentration marking his mature years. They project themselves more clearly than the mystical last works of *Op. 118* and *Op. 119.*

---

[3]   Geiringer, Karl, *Brahms, His Life and Work,* second edition, Allan and Unwin, Ltd., London, 1948, pp. 213-14.

[4]   Other versions of the ancient Edward ballad involve Edward as the murderer of his brother or of his father.

Rhapsody No. 1 in B minor

Dedicated to Elisabeth von Herzogenberg

The serene trio section of this *Rhapsody* suggests similar quiet sections in Schubert's *Sonatas*.

Rhapsody No. 2 in G minor

Dedicated to Elisabeth von Herzogenberg

Unexpected dynamic contrasts carry dramatic tension from beginning to end.

For 12 years between the *Rhapsodies* and the remaining works of *Opp. 116, 117, 118, and 119*, Brahms was occupied with symphonic, vocal, and chamber music works. When he returned to the piano it was again in works of small scale.[5]

7 Fantasies Op. 116 (1891-92)

The *Capriccio No. 3 in G minor* contrasts passion with a broad melodic interlude. *Intermezzo No. 4 in E*, originally titled Nocturne, has a freedom of expressiveness associated with improvisation.

3 Intermezzi Op. 117 (1892)

Intermezzo No. 1 in E flat is a tender slumber song based on a folk tune inspired by Herder's lines: "Sleep well, my child, sleep well and gently." The melody is skillfully written into the inner voices which change color with each entrance of the theme. The foreboding minor section is followed by the final quiet entrace of the slumber song. Brahms called it "the lullaby of my griefs."

Intermezzo No. 2 in B flat minor is a forerunner of the mystical overtones felt in the last two sets of *Op. 118* and *Op. 119*.

6 Pieces Op. 118 (1893)

The *Ballade No. 3 in G minor* from this Opus is a popular work. In Brahms's characteristic fashion, heavy chords are tossed dramatically between the hands.

In the *Intermezzo No. 6 in E flat minor*, the essence of Brahms's mysticism suggests the spiritual remoteness of Beethoven's last period.

4 Pieces Op. 119 (1893)

The 4 *Pieces* of *Op. 119* are the last for piano solo. *Intermezzo No. 3* in C is delicately

---

5 With the exception of *Intermezzo Op. 118 No. 6 in E flat minor* and *Rhapsody Op. 119 No. 4 in E flat*.

humorous, in a light-hearted mood unusual for Brahms at this late period of his life.

Rhapsody No. 4 in E flat is in free Rondo form. Its powerful drive is in strong contrast to the three preceding *Intermezzi* of this Opus. It combines the force of the earlier works with the subtlety characteristic of Brahms's maturity.

---

51 Exercises

These studies, published in the same year as *Op. 118* and *Op. 119,* deal with all the essentials of Brahms's particular technical demands. These included finger extension, passage of the thumb, double notes, trills, scales, arpeggios, smoothness of fingering, and variety of touch.

The two *Concertos for Piano and Orchestra in D minor* and *B flat* are symphonic and share the richness of all Brahms's works for orchestra. They represent a development in concerto construction, for Brahms wrote them on a musical level with the symphony. He treated the piano not only as a solo instrument, but also as an instrument of the orchestra, making solo and accompaniment interdependent.

Concerto No. 1 in D minor Op. 15 (1854-58)

The *First Concerto* was originally planned as a symphony, then a sonata for two pianos, finally a concerto. Thickness of orchestral scoring and keyboard writing find their counterpart in the storminess, even defiance, of the first movement; the second movement *Adagio* is quieter and more accepting, possibly a "portrait" of Clara Schumann or a kind of Requiem for Robert. The *Finale,* written later than the first two movements, closes this early *Concerto* with power and exuberance.

After initial success, Brahms performed it in Leipzig to a storm of protest and abuse. The public and critics were not prepared for its unconventional structure and berated Brahms for its lack of pleasing themes. The blending of solo part and orchestra to the exclusion of bravura passages for piano was considered a flouting of musical tradition. Brahms waited over 20 years before writing his *Second Concerto in B flat.*

Concerto No. 2 in B flat Op. 83 (1878-1881)

Dedicated to Eduard Marxsen

The second *Concerto* was Brahms's answer to charges of critics that the first *Concerto* lacked individuality in the solo part. Longer and more elaborate than the first, it rivals the *1st Symphony* in variety of mood. The expansiveness of the first movement gives way to an ardent and driving second movement *Scherzo.* The slow movement opens and closes with a lyrical cello obbligato of serene beauty. The *Rondo Finale* closes the *Concerto* with light scoring and lilting freedom.

For *Piano Duo* Brahms composed the *Sonata in F minor Op. 34b* (published 1872), and dedicated it to Princess Anna of Hesse. Massive and almost outside the bounds of piano sound, it was one version of his *Piano Quintet Op. 34.* The *Variations on a Theme by Haydn,* also called the *St. Antony Variations,* Op. 56b (1873) are a very fine addition to *Piano Duo* repertoire. Opinions vary as to the source of the theme, and in the section on Brahms's complete works in New Grove 1980, the writer of the index states that it is even probable that the *St. Antony Chorale* is not by Haydn. The *Variations* appeared at the same time in orchestral version as *Op. 56a,* one of Brahms's most popular works. A *Piano Duo* arrangement of five *Waltzes* from *Op. 39* is available in Schirmer's edition.

Brahms's *Piano Duets* include *Variations on a Theme by Schumann*[6] *Op. 23* (1861), dedicated to Julie Schumann;[7] the famous *Waltzes Op. 39* (1865), dedicated to Eduard Hanslick; two sets of *Liebeslieder Waltzes Op. 52a* and *65a* (with vocal quartet) (1868-69 and 1874); and twenty-one *Hungarian Dances*[8] (from 1858) in 4 sets.[9] The *Waltzes* are charming and popular, suggesting the Viennese spirit of the earlier waltz-form masters, Schubert and Johann Strauss. Brahms arranged the *Waltzes* as well as the *Hungarian Dances* for piano solo. The *Duets* all fall well within the average pianist's grasp.

Edition:

Johannes Brahms sämtliche Werke, ed. H. Gál and E. Mandyczewsky (Leipzig 1926-27)   BW

Selected Works for Piano

Sonata in C, Op. 1 (1852-53)

Sonata in F sharp minor, Op. 2 (1852)

Scherzo in E flat minor, Op. 4 (1851)

Sonata in F minor, Op. 5 (1853)

Variations on a Theme by Robert Schumann in F sharp minor, Op. 9 (1854)

Ballades, Op. 10 (1854): *No. 1 in D minor* ("Edward"); *No. 2 in D; No. 3 in B minor; No. 4 in B.*

11 *Variations on an Original Theme in D,* Op. 21 No. 1 (1856)

13 *Variations on a Hungarian Song in D,* Op. 21 No. 2 (1853)

25 *Variations on a Theme by Handel in B flat,* Op. 24 (1861)

[6]   Schumann composed the melody shortly before his final illness.

[7]   Robert and Clara's daughter.

[8]   The origin of the *Hungarian Dances* was in Gypsy tunes which Brahms collected after his concert tour with the Hungarian violinist, Reményi. Evidence of Brahms's fondness for Gypsy music appears also in the *Finale* of the *Piano Quartet in G minor Op. 25* (1861).

[9]   Brahms also turned out a set of 6 variation-fantasies on Russian tunes for piano four hands in the early 1850s before his Op. 1. They were designed for home entertainment.

28 *Studies (Variations) on a Theme by Paganini in A minor,* 2 sets, Op. 35 (1862-63)

16 *Waltzes,* Op. 39 (1865)

8 *Pieces,* Op. 76 (1878). Set 1: *No. 1 Capriccio in F sharp minor; No. 2 Capriccio in B minor; No. 3 Intermezzo in A flat; No. 4 Intermezzo in B flat.* Set 2: *No. 5 Capriccio in C sharp minor; No. 6 Intermezzo in A; No. 7 Intermezzo in A minor; No. 8 Capriccio in C.*

2 *Rhapsodies,* Op. 79 (1879): *No. 1 in B minor* and *No. 2 in G minor*

7 *Fantasien,* Op. 116 (1891-92). Set 1: *No. 1 Capriccio in D minor; No. 2 Intermezzo in A minor; No. 3 Capriccio in G minor.* Set 2: *No. 4 Intermezzo in E; No. 5 Intermezzo in E minor; No. 6 Intermezzo in E; No. 7 Capriccio in D minor*

Three Intermezzi, Op. 117 (1892). *No. 1 Intermezzo in E flat; No. 2 Intermezzo in B flat minor; No. 3 Intermezzo in C sharp minor*

Six Pieces, Op. 118 (1893): *No. 1 Intermezzo in A Minor; No. 2 Intermezzo in A; No. 3 Ballade in G minor; No. 4 Intermezzo in F minor; No. 5 Romanze in F; No. 6 Intermezzo in E flat minor*

Four Pieces, Op. 119 (1893): *No. 1 Intermezzo in B minor; No. 2 Intermezzo in E minor; No. 3 Intermezzo in C; No. 4 Rhapsody in E flat.*

Five Studies, (no Opus) (1852-1877): *No. 1 Etude after Chopin in F minor (publ. 1869); No. 2 Rondo after Weber in C (1852); No. 3 Presto after Bach in G minor; No. 4 Presto after Bach in G minor (publ. 1869–2 versions); No. 5 Chaconne of Bach for the left hand in D minor (1877).*

Without Opus

Gavotte in A minor (1854)

Gavotte in A (1855)

2 *Gigues in A minor and B minor* (1855) (publ. 1927)

2 *Sarabandes in A minor and B minor* (1855) (publ. 1917)

Theme and Variations in D minor (1860) (publ. 1927)

Gavotte in A (publ. 1871)

10 *Hungarian Dances* (publ. 1872)

Study for the left hand in E flat (publ. 1927)

51 *Exercises* (publ. 1893)

Cadenzas (publ. 1927)

Piano Concerto in D minor (Bach) (BWV 1052)

Piano Concerto in G (Mozart, K.453, 2 cadenzas)

Piano Concerto in D minor (Mozart, K.466)

Piano Concerto in C minor (Mozart, K.491)

Piano Concerto in G (Beethoven, Op. 58, 2 cadenzas)

Piano Concerto in C minor (Beethoven, Op. 37)

For Piano and Orchestra

Concerto No. 1 in D minor, Op. 15 (1854-58)

Concerto No. 2 in B flat, Op. 83 (1878-81)

For Piano Duo

Sonata in F minor, Op. 34b (publ. in 1872)
Variations on a Theme by Haydn in B flat, Op. 56b (1873)

For Piano Duet

Variations on a Theme by Schumann in E flat, Op. 23 (1861)

16 *Waltzes,* Op. 39 (1865) (also solo version)

18 *Liebeslieder Waltzes,* Op. 52a (1868-69) (arr. from original version for 4 voices, pf. 4 hands)

15 *Neue Liebeslieder Waltzes,* Op. 65a (1874) (arr. from original version for 4 voices, pf. 4 hands)

21 *Hungarian Dances,* 4 sets (no opus) (1852-69).

Ballade Op.10 No.1 (Edward)

5 | UNIQUE CONTRIBUTIONS

Apart from the greatest composers who wrote with range and depth in many musical forms and for many different instruments are four additional writers who made smaller but significant contributions to the piano—Franck, Tchaikovsky, Grieg, and MacDowell. Each of these men presents a unique profile: Franck wrote only three major piano works to support his solid reputation; Tchaikovsky excelled in orchestral writing but created a sweeping and idiomatic *Piano Concerto;* Grieg became one of music's consistent and influential nationalists; MacDowell was the first widely recognized American composer.

Born in Liège, Belgium,
December 10, 1822

Died in Paris,
November 8, 1890,
Age 68 years

César Franck

Historical Sketch

Like many composers, César Franck was also a virtuoso pianist and organist. His mother's background was German; his father's home was located near the German border of the Waloon and Flemish provinces, which in 1830 became the new country of Belgium. The parents settled in Liège (where César was born) and adopted Belgian nationality. When Franck was 8, his father enrolled him in the Liège Conservatory. During the next five years, he received 1st prizes for solfège and piano and studied harmony with Dassoigne, a nephew of the composer Méhul. Franck's boyhood compositions were largely facile transcriptions and operatic fantasies in the fashion of the day. He gave a series of concerts in Liège, Brussels, and Aachen which prompted his father to move the family to Paris in 1835 so that young Franck could study at the renowned Paris Conservatoire. Because of his nationality, he had to wait for two years to be accepted by the Conservatoire, but within a year of his entrance he was awarded 1st prizes in piano and counterpoint, and a 2nd in organ. He won the attention of Meyerbeer, Liszt, Donizetti, and Chopin who subscribed to the publication of his first major composition, *Trois Trios concertants for piano, violin, and cello Op. 1* (1841). The following year he returned to Liège with his family, but in 1844 he went back to Paris for good.

As a young virtuoso, Franck performed music in the popular French style where tunes from current operas were treated to endless, unimportant variations. He soon tired of the musical emptiness of the repertoire and abandoned a career as a pianist. He broke with his family and began to support himself as organist at the little church of Notre Dame de Lorette. His first major choral composition, the oratorio *Ruth,* was poorly received, and except for a symphonic poem *Ce qu'on entend sur la montagne* and an unpublished opera *Le valet de ferme* of 1848, he composed nothing of real importance for ten years. During these years he was appointed organist at St. Jean-St. François du Marais. Here he continued to develop his organ technique and an already extraordinary skill at improvisation. He became a representative of the organ builder, Cavaillé-Coll, and in 1859 inaugurated one of Cavaillé-Coll's finest instruments at the church of Ste. Clothilde. His *Six Pieces* of 1860-62 which Liszt heard at Ste. Clothilde established Franck as a first rank composer for the organ.

For the next ten years, until 1871, Franck was occupied with his duties as organist and as the influential teacher of a growing group of devoted pupils. The original core of this "Bande à Franck" included d'Indy, Duparc, Chausson, Pierné, Ropartz, Holmes, Bordes, Lekeu, and Dukas. In 1868 they formed a society (with Duparc as its early organizer) which was a forerunner of the *Société Nationale de Musique.* Its first concert included Franck's *Trois Trios Op. 1.* In later years the Société was responsible for performances of such important works of Franck as the symphonic poems *Les Éoilides, Le Chasseur maudit* and *Psyché,* and the two works for piano and orchestra *Les Djinns* and *Variations symphoniques.* In 1871, Franck was appointed Professor of Organ at the Paris Conservatoire. There he campaigned against the public fondness for vapid, showy pieces that pushed aside the masterpiece repertoire. His influence on students was far reaching; he helped to form the solid musical language of an entire generation of important French composers.

Between this appointment and 1875, Franck completed another oratorio, *Redemption,* added the famous tenor aria *Panis angelicus* to the 1860 *Mass for 3 voices,* and worked on his crowning oratorio, *The Béautitudes* (which took ten years to complete in 1879). In the fifteen years between 1875 and his death in 1890, Franck composed the *Piano Quintet;* another oratorio *Rebecca;* 4 symphonic poems including *Les Djinns* for piano and orchestra; *Prélude, Chorale and Fugue* for piano; *Variations symphoniques for piano and orchestra; Sonata for piano and violin; Prélude, Aria and Finale* for piano; *Symphony in D minor;* and *String Quartet in D.* Five years before his death, Franck was given the *Légion d'Honneur* and one year later the presidency of the *Société Nationale.* At the time of his death from pleurisy, Franck was at work on the huge project of composing 91 pieces for harmonium (he completed 59) incorporating each major and minor key.

Critics and certain composers like Saint-Saëns bitterly faulted Franck for composing so little – after all, he wrote only a half-dozen or so major works. They also remarked sharply that he was not always adequately prepared for public performances. However, his reputation as a teacher remained secure in the hands of devoted pupils. Six years after Franck's death, they founded the *Schola Cantorum* of Paris, a celebrated institution honoring his memory, which provided the impetus for his ultimate recognition.

Style

Franck's emphasis on musical values built into his style a capacity for innovation; he transcended pianistic limitations to achieve orchestral effects and produced unified contrapuntal forms in the face of Impressionism's growing case for fragmentary and exotic combinations of sound. While his idiom was entirely personal, he was influenced strongly by Bach and Liszt; he combined the architecture of one with the pianistic technique of the other to produce balanced compositions of solidity and drama. Invoked again were Bach's mastery of organ style, insight, and feeling for structure. From Liszt, Franck evolved a modern keyboard technique applicable to classical forms. He showed too that decorative writing with a maximum of bravura could be justified musically.

Congenial to Franck's style was the triptych idea of three movement construction. He also worked in sonata form and used cyclical treatment pioneered by Liszt where variants of the original motifs were introduced in successive movements. His melodies, characteristically chromatic, frequently pivoted around one note, leaving impulsion to the changing (also chromatic) harmonies. In this respect, the influence of Wagner was unmistakable.[1] Sensitive to the particular color of each key, Franck had a fondness for sharps, feeling they gave luminosity and emotional unity. He consistently directed climaxes to fixed exaltation. There were no instances of unresolved conflict.

As we have seen, Franck produced few major keyboard pieces. In other fields of composition he restricted himself in the same way, with but one *Piano Quintet,*[2] *Symphony* (dedicated to Henri Duparc), *Sonata for violin and piano* (transcribed also for *violoncello and piano* and dedicated to Eugene Ysaÿe, and *String Quartet,* dedicated to Léon Réynier). Absorbed by a relentless teaching schedule, he was able to devote only the very early morning hours to creating, or as he said, "thinking." However, within this alloted time, shorter than that of any major composer, he produced in each field an enviable masterwork. In the face of apathy, animosity, and changing styles, Franck remained steadfast to his artistic convictions. Almost alone among the great composers, he consistently translated spirituality in musical terms.

Compositions

Franck's early works from 1842-45 included superficial fantasies and transcriptions of French operas by such composers as Hérold, Auber, and Halévy. Other early compositions showed his interest in construction as the basis of musical style. Among them are 4 *Songs* of Schubert transcribed for piano *Op. 8,* and *Ballade Op. 9,* the latter one of

---

[1]   Franck heard *Tristan and Isolde* in 1874, and the impact became evident in all his subsequent instrumental music.

[2]   The *Piano Quintet in F minor* (1879) came about at the request of the Société Nationale and provided a spring board for the major compositions which followed. It is dedicated to Saint-Saëns.

the best of the early group. Midway between the youthful pieces of 1842-45 and the major ones of 1884-87 appeared *Les Plaintes d'une Poupée* (1865), not prophetic of treasures to come but a mature piece anticipating Debussy's *Children's Corner*. Twenty years later Franck sandwiched between the two big piano triptychs of 1884 and 1886 a companion piece to *Les Plaintes*, the *Danse lente* (1885).

In writing the two large triptychs, *Prélude, Chorale and Fugue* and *Prélude, Aria and Finale*, Franck wanted to add important compositions to the solo piano repertoire and enlarge the forms he used.

Prélude, Chorale and Fugue (1884)

Dedicated to Marie Poitivin

Franck's original intention was to write a *Prélude* and *Fugue* in the style of Bach. His decision to link the *Prélude* and *Fugue* by a *Chorale* which would prepare the entrance of the *Fugue* produced a large and complex work that honored Bach as it captured Franck's exalted mood and cyclical method. His customary program of darkness to light is magnificently set forth in the *Fugue* which triumphs at the close with a theme foreshadowed on the second page of the *Prélude*.

Prélude, Aria and Finale (1886-87)

Dedicated to Mme. Bordes-Pène

The *Prélude, Aria and Finale* is less popular than the *Prélude, Chorale and Fugue* perhaps because there is less internal drama and less varied cyclical development. High points are striking key changes and melodic wealth. Laurence Davies[3] calls it a major sonata in all but name with structure harmonic rather than polyphonic. The rolling bass of the *Finale* may have had its beginnings in the pedal-board of Franck's organ at Ste. Clothilde.

In 1884, Franck wrote the first of two compositions for piano and orchestra, *Les Djinns*.[4] To avoid keyboard display, Franck cast the piano part not as a true concerto, but as a concertante partner of the orchestra. A year later the *Variations symphoniques* appeared, a thoroughly successful combination of piano and orchestra in concerto style. Using two themes, Franck created a set of double variations of wide emotional and technical range which take their place among the finest examples of variation form.

Franck wrote two early duets based on themes of others: *Duo* on *God save the King Op. 4* (1842), and *Duo à quatre mains* on Grétry's *Lucile Op. 17* (1846).

---

[3] Davies, Laurence, *Franck*, J.M. Dent and Sons Ltd. (Master Musician's Series), London, 1973
[4] Based on verse of Victor Hugo depicting devilry vs. forces of good.

Edition:

Thematic catalogue of publ. works in Mohr   M

No works composed after 1863 bear opus numbers

Selected Works for Piano[5]

Éclogue, Op. 3 (1841-42)
Grand Caprice, Op. 5 (1843)
Souvenir d'Aix-la-Chapelle, Op. 7 (1843)
Four songs of Schubert, Op. 8 (1844) (trans. for pf.)
Ballade, Op. 9 (1844)
First Grand Fantasia on Dalayrac's "Guilistan", Op. 11 (1844)
Second Grand Fantasia on Air from Dalayrac's "Guilistan", Op. 12 (1844)
Fantasia, Op. 13 (1844)
Fantasia on two Polish Airs, Op. 15 (1845)
Three Bagatelles (Trois Petits Riens), Op. 16 (1845)
Les Plaintes d'une poupée, M 20 (1865)
Prélude, Chorale and Fugue, M 21 (1884)
Danse lente, M 22 (1885)
Prélude, Aria and Finale, M 23 (1886-87)

For Piano and Orchestra

Les Djinns, symphonic poem, M.45 (1884)
Variations symphoniques, M.46 (1885)

For Piano Duet

God Save the King, Op. 4 (1884)
Gretry's *Lucile,* Op. 17 (1846)

---

[5]   The following works are listed in Franck's catalogue begun by his father, Nicolas-Joseph Franck. They contain the late major compositions and early works of historical interest. A complete listing of juvenilia and unpublished works may be found in New Grove 1980.

Aria
from *Prelude, Aria and Finale*

sempre dolcissimo e legatissimo

Born in Votinsk, Russia,
May 7, 1840
Died in St. Petersburg, Russia,
November 6, 1893,
Age 53 years

Peter Ilyich Tchaikovsky

Historical Sketch

Peter Tchaikovsky studied law and practiced as a clerk in the Ministry of Justice before he began to study music seriously. At twenty-three, he entered the St. Petersburg Conservatory and set about a career devoted exclusively to music.

Active in the Russian musical scene at this time were the famous brothers, Anton and Nicholas Rubinstein. These men were Russia's outstanding musicians, influential teachers, pianists, and composers. Anton, the elder brother, taught Tchaikovsky orchestration at the St. Petersburg Conservatory where Tchaikovsky graduated with honors and a silver medal. Nicholas Rubinstein then invited him to become professor of harmony at the new Conservatory in Moscow, a branch of the St. Petersburg school. Tchaikovsky held the position fifteen years, resigning in 1881. The outlets of the Moscow Conservatory and Nicholas's unfailing support provided performances for his growing list of compositions. Here he met Balakirev, who was the leader of a new school of Russian composers, and became acquainted with his future publisher, Jurgenson. He composed 3 piano pieces, *Souvenir de Hapsal,* including the favorite *Chant sans paroles,* which met with immediate popularity. His association with Balakirev led to the first performance of his symphonic fantasy, *Fatum,* which Balakirev conducted. In 1870, his first masterpiece *Romeo and Juliet,* an orchestral overture, had its premier with Nicholas Rubinstein conducting. In the same year, Tchaikovsky wrote the 6 *Songs Op. 6* of which *None but the lonely heart* is still a favorite. The first *String Quartet* with its graceful *Andante cantabile* established a Tchaikovsky idiom of lyrical sound which contrasted forcibly with frequent emotionalism and later driving restlessness.

In 1874, Tchaikovsky made preliminary sketches for the *First Piano Concerto*. The following year, he not only completed the *Concerto* but worked on the *3rd Symphony*, the ballet *Swan Lake,* and the *The Seasons*–12 piano pieces describing each month of the year. *The Seasons,* charming and descriptive salon pieces, are Tchaikovsky's best known compositions for solo piano. A year later, Tchaikovsky met Liszt in Bayreuth and heard the first performance of Wagner's complete Ring cycle. Although Tchaikovsky's own sounds were frequently massive, couched in strong emotion, he did not care for Wagner's music. He returned from Bayreuth to complete the famous *Marche Slave* for orchestra and the well known *Variations on a Rococo Theme for Cello and Orchestra.*

In 1877, Tchaikovsky married Antonia Milynkova, a woman of whom he knew very little. He undertook marriage to lessen suspicion of his homosexuality. The two month marriage was a disaster that brought Tchaikovsky close to nervous collapse. During the four years until Tchaikovsky secured a divorce, he maintained emotional stability through unique friendship with Nadezhda von Meck, a wealthy widow and discriminating admirer of music. The basis of their relation was a mutual distrust of physical involvement but an overwhelming attraction to the passion of music. Mme. von Meck freed him from financial obligation by presenting him with a annual income. After fourteen years of devoted yet remote friendship, Mme. von Meck suddenly broke with Tchaikovsky and discontinued his income. She died not long after, without having given her "beloved friend," or the world, an explanation of the strange end to an unusual friendship. Tchaikovsky was pathologically hurt by the affront and until his death suffered humiliation from it.

Before the break, while living with the consolation of Mme. von Meck's support, Tchaikovsky completed his *Fourth Symphony* in 1878 (dedicated to Mme. von Meck), the opera *Eugene Onegin,* and the *Violin Concerto.* The *Piano Sonata in G Op. 37* belongs to this period, followed two years later by the *Second Piano Concerto,* the *Serenade for Strings,* and the *1812 Overture.* In 1881, under the stimulus of the piano combined with other instruments, Tchaikovsky came again to lively piano writing far outstripping the previous *Piano Sonata Op. 37* in the virtuoso *Trio for Piano, Violin, and Cello Op. 50.* Its composition was influenced also by two other factors, the death of Nicholas Rubinstein and Mme. von Meck's desire to have a new work for her resident trio whose current pianist was Claude Debussy.

The last ten years of Tchaikovsky's life were marked with public recognition and esteem for his achievements as composer and conductor. He received the Order of St. Vladimir from the Tsar, membership in France's Academie Française, and an honorary Doctor of Music degree from Cambridge University.[1] Invitations to conduct came

---

[1]   Tchaikovsky received this degree along with Saint-Saëns, Bruch, and Boito; Grieg received his in absentia.

from many quarters, Leipzig, Hamburg, Berlin, Prague, Paris, London, and the United States. In composition, he completed the *Third Orchestral Suite* (the only one to stay in the repertoire), *Concert-Fantasy for Piano and Orchestra, Overture-Fantasy Hamlet,* the *5th* and *6th Symphonies,* the final set of *Piano Pieces Op. 72,* and the *Concerto No. 3 in E flat Op. 75* (1 movement).

Tchaikovsky drew little satisfaction from public acceptance. He grew increasingly unsettled, writing into his music the torment of his psyche. Shortly before his death, he conducted his recently finished *6th* or *Pathétique Symphony,*[2] a poignant chronicle of personal desperation. Soon afterwards, he committed suicide.

Style

The piano held little interest for Tchaikovsky. His musical ideas seemed to require the color of the orchestra, its variety of timbre and dynamics. His uninhibited emotionalism was more suited to the range and depth of the orchestra than to the relative inflexibility of the piano. His natural talent lay in long stretches of melody and heroic movements–the vast, rather than the subtle. These qualities found effective expression, not in the piano, but in the orchestral works, including six symphonies, operas, ballets, and overtures.

Because he wrote naturally for orchestra, Tchaikovsky spent little time learning piano idiom. He did not explore its resources or the possibilities of forms suited to it. What survived, with the exception of the *Concertos,* were light, charming works which captured a mood. Most of the piano pieces were given descriptive titles; when not specifically picturesque as *Barcarolle* or *By the Fireside,* they were lyrically expressive *Romances, Songs without Words,* or *Humoresques.*

Evaluation of Tchaikovsky's piano style is difficult because of his indifference toward pianistic idiom. The short works contain Slavic flavor, melodic spontaneity, and unusual rhythms, but are frequently weakened by murky texture, repetition of accompaniment figures, and literal restatement of theme. In contrast, the large works with orchestra carry the impetus of orchestral variety, invariably stimulating to Tchaikovsky. Conventional design and mechanical sameness are weaknesses which appear throughout Tchaikovsky's piano composition. A.E.F. Dickinson[3] concludes that Tchaikovsky was not really interested in the piano's artistic future. However over the rest of Tchaikovsky's production, like a giant, stands the *Concerto No. 1 in B flat minor,* possibly the most "popular" of all piano concertos.

[2]   A title suggested by Tchaikovsky's brother, Modeste, after the first performance.
[3]   Abraham, Gerald, ed., *The Music of Tchaikovsky,* W.W. Norton and Co., New York, 1974 Dickinson, A.E.F. (The Piano Music)

Compositions

Since Tchaikovsky wrote a large number of his piano compositions to order, they lacked the inspiration and ingenuity which might have made them come alive on their own. Yet exceptions appeared, among them *Theme and Variations Op. 19 No. 6*, certain of *The Seasons Op. 37b*, and *Sonata in C sharp minor Op. 80*, published posthumously and assigned a late opus number. The bulk of the solos shows Tchaikovsky's fondness for sets of pieces, nine in the complete listing, including *Opp. 2, 9, 19, 21, 37b, 39, 40, 51, and 72*. Among these:

Souvenir de Hapsal Op. 2 (3 pieces) (1867)

Dedicated to V.V. Davidova

The third *Souvenir* in the collection is the melodious *Chant sans paroles* recalling a holiday in Finland.

6 Pieces Op. 19 (1873)

Diverse dedications

Op. 19 includes *Humorous Scherzo No.2* and *Capriccioso No. 5* reminiscent of scherzos in Tchaikovsky's symphonies and ballets, vivacious and inventive. *Theme and Variations No. 6* is appealing in its well shaped theme and in the essentially melodic treatment of the *Variations*.

6 Pieces on a Single Theme Op. 21 (1873)

Dedicated to A.G. Rubinstein

The stately *Prélude No. 1* sings another *Song without Words;* the final *Scherzo No. 6* retains interest through unusual rhythm.

The Seasons, 12 characteristic pieces Op. 37b (1875-76)

Tchaikovsky published *The Seasons* month by month. Design is generally conventional, but certain months show expressiveness and personality: *March* evokes a rhapsodic tone picture of a lark's song; *November (In the Troika)* depicts a snow scene; and *December* celebrates Christmas with a waltz.

12 Pieces of Moderate Difficulty Op. 40 (1876-78)

Dedicated to M.I. Tchaikovsky

The *12 Pieces* hold an accepted place in the Tchaikovsky repertoire, particularly *Chanson triste No. 2* and the *Valses Nos. 8* and *9*.

Children's Album, 24 easy pieces Op. 39 (1878)

The *Album* contains brief sketches bringing to mind Schumann's *Album for the Young*. Not as sensitive to delicate changes of mood as Schumann, Tchaikovsky nevertheless provided engaging ideas. Best of the pleasant trifles are *March of the Wooden Soldiers No. 5, New Doll No. 9, Polka No. 14, Baba-Yaga No. 20*, and *Song of the Lark No. 22*.

---

6 Pieces Op. 51 (1882)

Diverse dedications

These salon pieces comprise light dance movements, *Polka, Minuet, Waltzes*, and a *Romance*.

---

18 Pieces Op. 72 (1893)

Diverse dedications

Although one sees in these late *Pieces* (written in the year of his death) Tchaikovsky's tendency to exact restatement of material, at least two of the *18 Pieces* are successful, *Concert Polonaise No. 7* and *Rustic Echo No. 13*. The virtuosity of *Concert Polonaise* is matched by *Rustic Echo's* sharp alternation of folk tune and music box effect, a perky device which brings to mind Debussy's *Minstrels*.

Individual works, apart from the sets, typical of Tchaikovsky's strongest traits are *Scherzo à la russe* and *Impromptu in E flat minor*, both of *Op. 1* (1867, dedicated to N.G. Rubinstein); *Dumka Op. 59* (1886, dedicated to A.F. Marmontel); and the *Sonatas in C sharp minor Op. 80* (1865) and *G major Op. 37* (1878). The *Scherzo* is based on a Ukranian folk song; the *Impromptu* contains furioso double octaves; and the *Dumka* brings fresh color to local folk themes. The *Sonatas*, both preceding the *Dumka*, hold a special place in Tchaikovsky's work, the *C sharp minor* a successful student composition and the *G major* a product of rare tranquility.

Sonata in C sharp minor Op. 80 (1865)

The year Tchaikovsky graduated from the St. Petersburg Conservatory, he composed the *C sharp minor Sonata*, a work of spontaneity and youthful directness. Of the four movements, the first is the strongest. The *Scherzo* also is effective, containing an *Adagio* epilogue which recalls Franck's chromaticism. The *Finale* has style and dash.

Sonata in G Op. 37 (1878)

Dedicated to Karl Klindworth

The *Sonata in G* contains no sign of emotional instability, an uncommon state of affairs in Tchaikovsky's internally stormy life. Although it was written just before the *Violin Concerto,* its emotions are cool, suggesting again that Tchaikovsky needed instrumental color to fire his imagination.

In combining the piano with orchestra, Tchaikovsky achieved musical results denied the piano solos. After a rocky start, *Concerto No. 1 in B flat minor* has established a seemingly immovable place in concerto repertoire. Two other *Concertos, No. 2 in G,* and *No. 3 in E flat* of a single movement, and a *Concert Fantasy* followed, but the *First Concerto* has never relinquished dominance.

Concerto No. 1 in B flat minor Op. 23 (1874-75)

Dedicated to Hans von Bülow (originally Nicholas Rubinstein)

The *B flat minor Concerto* reflects the violence and intensity of Tchaikovsky's nature. Tchaikovsky first played it for Nicholas Rubinstein who repudiated it by calling the *Concerto* trivial, clumsy, unplayable, and worthless. Stung by his words, Tchaikovsky withdrew the dedication to Nicholas Rubinstein and gave it instead to Hans von Bülow who played its first performance in Boston in 1875. Rubinstein later changed his opinion and played it widely in Europe, and Tchaikovsky in turn made certain revisions in the new edition of 1889. With Lisztian technique of runs, wide jumps, and double octaves, it thunders, rages, implores, and woos. Its appeal remains undiminished by the years.

The general plan of the *Concerto* is that of three movements, the first an *Allegro* in sonata form, the second an *Andante* with a *Prestissimo* middle section, and the last a modified *Allegro* with a rondo element. An unusual feature, a matter for surprise and speculation, is the introduction to the "proper" opening statement (theme and key) of the first movement. The strong theme of the introduction is not in the basic minor key of the *Concerto* but in its relative major. It does not return anywhere in the entire *Concerto.* Purists have called the first movement lop sided because of this; nevertheless, its musical message works and comes through sounding "all of a piece."[4]

Eric Blom describes the *Andantino semplice* second movement as a nocturne because it is more like Chopin's pieces of that genre than a Classical middle movement. The airy *Scherzo* is not a separate movement but instead is enclosed by the two sides of the *Andantino.* The *Finale's* first theme is based on a Ukrainian song. Its coda returns to B flat major, as does the first movement coda, an harmonic device which brings both movements to a virtuoso close.

---

[4]   Blom, Eric (Ed.), *The Music of Tchaikovsky: Works for Solo Instruments and Orchestra,* W.W. Norton and Co., New York, 1974, p. 47

Eric Blom[5] is quoted here on this controversial work: "...There are some fearful handfuls in this score for the pianist to tackle, some terrifying runs in four octaves and many breakneck jumps with notes widely stretched apart at one moment and closely bunched together the very next; and much of the figuration is so unusual as to demand a great deal of special study for which no other composer either of concertos or of technical exercises will prepare the player. But that is only another way of saying how original Tchaikovsky's keyboard writing is. What is more, it almost everywhere repays the effort made to master it..."

Concerto No. 2 in G Op. 44 (1879-80)

Dedicated to N.G. Rubinstein

The *G major Concerto* lacks the ardor and vitality of its predecessor, but nevertheless remains in the repertoire. It was revised and cut by the pianist Siloti in 1893.

Concert Fantasy Op. 56 (1884)

Dedicated to Sophie Menter (originally to A.N. Essipova)

Tchaikovsky wrote the *Concert Fantasy* not as a full scale *Concerto* but rather a short form, as Mendelssohn's *Rondo brilliant* and Schumann's *Introduction and Allegro appassionato*. It is well developed, with an agreeable Russian flavor.

Concerto No. 3 in E flat Op. 75 (1893)

Dedicated to L. Diémer

At his death, Tchaikovsky left the *Third Concerto* as a work of one movement. However, he had sketched an *Andante* and *Finale Op. 79* which his pupil, Taneyev, rightly or wrongly, completed and attached to *Op. 75*.

Between 1868-69, Tchaikovsky arranged 50 Russian folk songs for *Duet* taken from collections by Villebois and Balakirev. Many are charming miniatures, easy and pleasant to play. Most of them appear in Tchaikovsky's other works: Nos. 10, 17, 29, 32, and 34 were used in the *Oprichnik* dances; No. 6 was used in the 2nd mov't of the *2nd Symphony;* Nos. 28 and 43 were used in the *Finale of Serenade for Strings;* No. 47 was used in the *Andante cantabile* of *1st String Quartet;* No. 48 was used in the *1812 Overture;* and No. 49 was used in the arrangement of *Volga Boat Song.*

[5] Ibid., p. 57

Edition:

P.I. Tchaikovsky: Polnoye sobraniye sochineniy (Complete edition of compositions) (Moscow and Leningrad 1940-71)   T

Selected Works for Piano

Scherzo à la russe in B flat and Impromptu in E flat minor, Op. 1 (1867)

Souvenir de Hapsal, 3 pieces, Op. 2 (1867): *Ruines d'un Château; Scherzo; Chant sans paroles.*

Valse-Caprice in D, Op. 4 (1868)

Romance in F minor, Op. 5 (1868)

Valse-Scherzo in A, Op. 7 (1870)

Capriccio in G flat, Op. 8 (1870)

3 Pieces: Rêverie; Polka de salon; Mazurka de salon, Op. 9 (1870)

Nocturne in F, Op. 10 (1874)

Humoresque in E minor, Op. 10 (1876)

6 *Pieces*, Op. 19 (1873)

6 *Pieces on a Single Theme*, Op. 21 (1873)

The Seasons, 12 characteristic pieces, Op. 37b (1875-76)

Sonata in G, Op. 37 (1878)

Children's Album, 24 easy pieces, Op. 39 (1878)

12 *Pieces of Moderate Difficulty*, Op. 40 (1878)

6 *Pieces*, Op. 51 (1882)

Dumka, Op. 59 (1886)

18 *Pieces*, Op. 72 (1893)

Sonata in C sharp minor, Op. 80 (1865)

For Piano and Orchestra

Concerto No. 1 in B flat minor, Op. 23 (1874-75) (arr. for two pianos)

Concerto No. 2 in G, Op. 44 (1880) (arr. for 2 pianos)

Concert Fantasy in G, Op. 56 (1884) (arr. for 2 pianos)

Concerto No. 3 in E flat, Op. 75 (1893) (orchestrated by Taneyev after 1893)

Andante in B flat and Finale in E flat, Op. 79 (orchestrated by Taneyev after 1893)

For Piano Duet

50 *Russian Folk Songs*, after Villebois and Balakirev

June (Barcarolle)
from *The Seasons* Op.37a No.6

Born in Bergen, Norway,
June 15, 1843

Died in Bergen, Norway,
September 4, 1907,
Age 64 years

Edvard Hagerup Grieg

Historical Sketch

Edvard Grieg's father was a merchant of Scottish extraction connected with the British Consulate in Bergen. His Norwegian mother, a woman of unusual musical cultivation, studied the piano in Germany and England and played often in public before her marriage. Early in life Grieg showed a fondness for music, but it was the Norwegian violinist, Ole Bull, who helped him decide a career. Ole Bull recognized Grieg's unmistakable talent as a young pianist of 15 and persuaded Grieg's parents to enroll him in the Leipzig Conservatory for studies with E.F. Wenzel and later with Moscheles. As a close friend of Schumann, Wenzel imparted to Grieg an enthusiasm for Schumann's works that never left him. He attended the celebrated Gewandhaus concerts where he was exposed to many artists. It was here that he heard Clara Schumann play Robert's *A minor Concerto* which had a direct influence on his own *Piano Concerto* in the same key. In 1862 Grieg suffered an attack of pleuisy which was the forerunner of years of respiratory troubles. He left the Conservatory and returned to Bergen where he gave a successful public concert.

The following year he went to Copenhagen to study with Niels Gade, a friend of Mendelssohn and Schumann and leader of Scandinavia's Romantic school. In Copenhagen, he met Nina Hagerup, his cousin, who was born in Bergen but brought up in Denmark. She was a talented singer and later as Grieg's wife[1] performed his songs in her recitals. Among these were the songs, *Op. 5,* set to words of Hans Christian Andersen who was a celebrated figure in Copenhagen's cultural life.

The year 1864 was decisive for Grieg through his meeting with Rikard Nordraak, one of his most dymanic contemporaries. Nordraak interested him in Norwegian folksong as a source of musical material. Grieg recognized the power and beauty inherent in his country's folk style and began to employ it consistently. The *3 Humoresker Op. 6* are his first compositions to show the direct influence of Norwegian folk idioms. Nordraak's early death was a blow to Norwegian music and to Grieg who honored his memory with the *Funeral March* dated April 6, 1866. This was also the year that Grieg performed in Christiania, Sweden, a successful concert made up entirely of Norwegian music by himself, Nordraak, and Kjerulf. The occasion led to his acceptance as one of Norway's outstanding musicians. In Christiania he composed the first set of *Lyric Pieces Op. 12,* and on a sojourn in Denmark wrote the *A minor Concerto* which was later performed in Copenhagen.

Again in Christiania in 1868, Grieg received a financial subsidy from the state to study and travel in Italy. In Rome he played the *Humoresker* and parts of the *Piano Sonata Op. 7* for Liszt. Liszt in turn played through Grieg's *Piano Concerto* and praised it warmly. The next few years involved Grieg in conducting, composing, and performing. In 1874, he received an invitation from Henrick Ibsen, the celebrated Norwegian dramatist, to write the incidental music for Ibsen's stage version of his dramatic poem, *Peer Gynt.* Grieg received a government grant to compose and left Christiania for Denmark where he completed *Peer Gynt* the next year. After a year when he did no composing, he became the conductor of the Bergen Harmonic Society, a post he held for two years. A long European concert tour followed which reinforced his growing reputation throughout Europe.

In 1885, Grieg completed his permanent home at Troldhaugen and for the next twenty years devoted his time to composing, revising, and touring. The 1890's provided a fertile nationalist period during which he composed the 5th Book of *Lyric Pieces Op. 54,* the duo piano *Romance with Variations Op. 51,* and the *Haugtussa Song Cycle Op. 67.* He received outstanding honors which included an honorary doctorate from Cambridge and Oxford and membership in the Institut de France. He submitted critical writing for foreign journals and worked to improve standards of criticism and performance throughout Norway. Six years before his death, his health began to fail, but he continued to make concert tours. In 1907, he was preparing another tour to England but was ordered to the hospital where he died.

Grieg was buried near his villa in a grotto overlooking the water. Greatness and simplicity were uniquely combined in this man who said of his work:

> "It is not for me to build lofty palaces and mighty cathedrals of music, but rather cottages, in which men may dwell and rest their hearts."

---

[1]   Grieg wrote "Ich liebe Dich" for her.

Style

Grieg's inspiration was sharp, clear, and fresh, but his sense of formal development was restricted. Grieg himself spoke of his inability to handle "the larger forms" and he produced only three large works for piano solo, the *Sonata Op. 7*, the *Ballade Op. 24*, and the single *Concerto in A Minor for Piano and Orchestra Op. 16*. The short forms which comprise the majority of his works were obviously congenial to his style and suggest those of Schumann with their romantic flair for complete musical expression of an image or mood in a small framework. It is not surprising that Grieg's songs[2] form the most valuable part of his production, involving abundant melody, unfailing harmonic interest, and appropriate length. John Horton[3] characterizes Grieg's short forms, including the songs, as a mixture of poetry, idealism, philosophy, and common sense, with flights of vivid description.

Grieg's profound interest in harmony governed his musical language. Chromatic progressions appeared in bass lines and inner voices, and furnished enharmonic turning points to remote keys. Dissonant chords hinted at Impressionism as early as 1877 with the *String Quartet Op. 27* and spoke very clearly in the *Haugtussa Song Cycle Op. 67* twenty years later.

Maintaining his commitment to harmonic variety, Grieg created a pure folk song style and supported it with Norwegian dance rhythms. His characteristic stamp thus combined chromatic harmonies (and as with Schubert, quick alternations between major and minor), short lyrical melodies, and dotted rhythms with energetic syncopations.

Rikard Nordraak's early influence left a permanent stamp of nationalism on Grieg since he introduced Grieg to the variety and strength of Norwegian folk music and its adaptability to serious music. Nordaak's untimely death prevented his fuller exploration of folk idiom, but Grieg developed and furthered Nordraak's ideas to become one of Western music's most adept nationalists.

Compositions

Grieg's piano works divide into two general sections, the sixty-odd *Lyric Pieces* in ten volumes and the remaining compositions which surround them from *Op. 1* through *Op. 73*.

Lyric Pieces Opp. 12, 38, 43, 47, 54, 57, 62, 65, 68, 71

As the opus numbers suggest, the *Lyric Pieces* were Grieg's most numerous works in small form. With them he made complete, clear, and original statements in one or

---

[2]   Outstanding among them, the *Ibsen Songs Op. 25; Vinje Songs Op. 33*, 2 Volumes; *Haugtussa Cycle Op. 67*.

[3] Horton, John, *Grieg*, J.M. Dent and Sons, London, 1974

two pages. Like Mendelssohn in the *Songs Without Words,* Grieg wrote them during the course of his creative lifetime. The majority have suggestive titles. Among the many excellent *Pieces* are the following:

Book I Op. 12 (1867); *Arietta, No. 1* is the theme with which the final *Remembrances* of *Book X* closes, this time reharmonized and set in waltz style.

Book III Op. 43 (1884); *To Spring, No. 6,* needs no description. Just listen.

Book IV Op. 47 (1888); *Valse Impromptu, No. 1,* plays with a mixture of major and minor modes.

Book V Op. 54 (1891); *Notturno, No. 4,* compares with Debussy's *Claire de lune.* *Bell-Ringing, No. 6,* explores Norwegian folk idioms and uses superimposed perfect 5ths in a more revolutionary way than Debussy's *La Cathédrale engloutie* which it preceded by 20 years.

Book VIII Op. 65 (1896); *Wedding Day at Troldhaugen, No. 6,* is a bravura description of Norwegian style revelry.

Book IX Op. 68 (1898); *Valse mélancholique, No. 6,* hints at Ravel's bittersweet impressionist waltzes through use of 9th and 13th chords.

Book X Op. 71 (1901); *Peace of the Woods, No. 4,* again forecasts impressionism in its chord placing.

The compositions from *Op. 1* to *Op. 73* also include original, outstanding works: *4 Pieces Op. 1; Poetic Tone-Pictures Op. 3; Humoresker Op. 6; Sonata in E minor Op. 7; Funeral March in Memory of Rikard Nordraak* (without Opus); *Scenes from Peasant Life Op. 19* (including the popular *Norwegian Bridal Procession Passing By); Ballade Op. 24; Holberg Suite Op. 40; Norwegian Folk Melodies Op. 66;* and *Moods Op. 73.*

4 Pieces Op. 1 (1862)

The *4 Pieces,* student works influenced by Schumann, show positive talent and firm technique.

Poetic Tone-Pictures Op. 3 (1863)

Elegance and melancholy, reminiscent of Chopin's *Nocturnes* characterize the *Tone-Pictures;* at the same time, the *Tone Pictures* project strongly Nordraak's nationalist influence.

Humoresker Op. 6 (1865)

In contrast to the *Poetic Tone-Pictures,* the *Humoresker,* dedicated to Nordraak, show vitality through lilting rhythms and energetic fiddle drones.

Sonata in E minor Op. 7 (1865)

Grieg's only piano *Sonata,* his first work in classical form, is colored by nationalistic touches. A thoroughly musical and pianistic work, it shows Grieg's ability to compose successfully in extended form when he chose. It shares the vigor and open-air freshness of the *Humoresker* with harmonic sharpness and rhythmic drive.

Funeral March in Memory of Rikard Nordraak (1866)

The *Funeral March* strode ahead of its time, a remarkable piece with advanced harmony drawing from Grieg a profound tribute to young Nordraak.

Scenes from Peasant Life Op. 19 (1872): 1. Fields; 2. Norwegian Bridal Procession Passing By; 3. Carnival Scene

The *Scenes* are colorful and descriptive mood pieces.

Ballade Op. 24 (Ballade in the form of Variations on a Norwegian Folksong) (1875)

Grieg wrote the *Ballade* during the year when both of his parents died. It is a poignant work, considered one of his finest piano compositions. The folk song theme, titled "The Northern Peasantry," is taken from a collection by Lindeman. The nine variations are rhapsodical and unconventional, consistently masterful. Grieg felt the work was of such a personal nature that he never played it in public.

Holberg Suite Op. 40 (1884)

Piano and orchestral versions of the *Holberg Suite* appeared in the same year, the piano version being the original. A quaint, old fashioned aura surrounds the 5 baroque dance movements, among them, *Sarabande, Gavotte,* and *Rigaudon.*

Norwegian Folk Melodies Op. 66 (1896)

The 19 *Folk Melodies* were mainly the outcome of Grieg's own folk song collecting marking a fresh investigation of Norwegian folk idioms.

Moods Op. 73 (1906)

The *Moods,* important keyboard works, appeared the year before Grieg's death and mark the end of his piano composition.

The popularity of certain of Grieg's compositions for piano, duet, voice, and orchestra prompted him to arrange them for piano solo. Among these are *Norwegian Dances Op. 35, 6 Songs Op. 41* (including "Ich Liebe Dich"), *Peer Gynt Suites I* and *II Opp. 46* and *55,* and *Sigurd Jorsalfar Suite Op. 56.* Grieg's other transcriptions from his own works include *Opp. 34, 37, 50, 52,* and *63.*

Peer Gynt Suite I Op. 46 (1888) and *Peer Gynt Suite II Op. 55* (1891)

Peer Gynt Suite I Op. 46 (1888): *1. Morning; 2. Asa's Death; 3. Anitra's Dance; 4. In the Hall of the Mountain King.* Peer Gynt Suite II, Op. 55 (1891): *1. The Abduction and Ingrid's Lament; 2. Arab Dance; 3. Peer Gynt's Homecoming; 4. Solveig's Song*

The Peer Gynt music honors one of literature's finest dramatists, Henrik Ibsen, who was born in Norway in 1838 (died in Christiania, Sweden, 1906). Ibsen wrote satirical social dramas with realism and natural dialogue that marked a new development in dramatic art. His plays include *A Doll's House, The Wild Duck, Ghosts,* and *The Master Builder.* Ibsen requested Grieg to supply his dramatic poem, ''Peer Gynt'', with incidental music, 22 pieces which received their first performance in 1876 followed by Grieg's arrangement of the music into 2 *Suites* for piano solo in 1888 and 1891 respectively. Pianistically, they are of moderate difficulty.

Grieg's only work for piano and orchestra is the *Concerto in A minor Op. 16* written with youthful ardor at twenty-five. It is inventive, colorful, and melodious, undeniably his most successful and artistic work. Grieg probably composed it under the influence of Schumann's celebrated *Concerto for Piano and Orchestra* (in the same key of A minor) since the training he received at the Leipzig Conservatory stressed Schumann's technique and musical principles. Thus it is not surprising that Grieg's *Concerto* has an excellent orchestral score and contrasts mood and design in an original way. The dedication of the first edition bears Nordraak's name; however between the first and second editions, Nordraak died, and the second edition was then dedicated to the pianist Neupert. However, Grieg first performed it himself at a Gewandhaus concert in Leipzig.

Concerto for Piano and Orchestra in A minor Op. 16 (1868)

The *Concerto* opens with a brief kettle drum roll followed by the piano's fortissimo descending chords. The similarity to the opening of Schumann's *Concerto* is unmistakable. In the second movement, the *Adagio* speaks with Grieg's moving lyricism. The last movement is bright, rhythmic, thundering in its climax.

Grieg's single composition for *Piano Duo, Romance Op. 51* (1891), also called *Old Norwegian Melody with Variations,* uses the virtuoso technique of Liszt and Saint-Saëns and grafts it to folk music stock. The theme, like that of the *Ballade Op. 24,* is from Lindeman's folk song collection.

Two works for *Piano Duet* are original, *Norwegian Dances Op. 35,* (1881) and *Valses Caprices Op. 37* (1883). Seven other Opus numbers are arrangements: *Overture, In Autumn Op. 11; 2 Symphonic Movements Op. 14; Norwegian Bridal Procession Passing By Op. 19; Sigurd Jorsalfar, Suite Op. 22; Elegiac Melodies Op. 34; Two Norwegian Melodies Op. 63; Symphonic Dances Op. 64.*

Editions:

E. Grieg: Gesamtausgabe/Complete Works (Franfurt-am-Main 1977-   ).

Almost all publication was issued by Peters in Leipzig.

Selected Works for Piano

Four Pieces, Op. 1 (1862)

Three Poetic Tone-Pictures, Op. 3 (1863)

3 Humoresker, Op. 6 (1865)

Sonata in E minor, Op. 7 (1865)

Lyric Pieces Book I, Op. 12 (1867)

Norwegian Dances and Songs, Op. 17 (1869)

Pictures from Life in the Country, Op. 19 (1870-71) (also called *Scenes from Peasant Life)*

Ballade in G minor, Op. 24 (1875-76)

Album Leaves, Op. 28 (1878)

Improvisations on Norwegian Folksongs, Op. 29 (1878)

Elegiac Melodies, Op. 34 (Grieg's transcription of his Songs) (1881)

Norwegian Dances, Op 35 (Grieg's transcription from piano duets) (1887)

Valses Caprices, Op. 37 (Grieg's transcription from piano duets) (1887)

Lyric Pieces Book II, Op. 38 (1884)

Holberg Suite, Op. 40 (1884)

6 Songs, Op. 41 (Grieg's transcription) (1885): Cradle Song; Little Haakon; I love thee; She is so white; The Princess; I give my song to the spring.

Lyric Pieces Book III, Op. 43 (1884)

Peer Gynt Suite I, Op. 46 (Grieg's transcription from orchestra) (1888)

Lyric Pieces Book IV, Op. 47 (1885-88)

Prayer and Temple Dance from "Olav Trygvason", Op. 50 (unfinished opera) (1873)

6 Songs, Op.52 (Grieg's transcription) (1870-1890): A Mother's Grief; The First Meeting; You know not; Solveig's Song; Love; Old Mother

Lyric Pieces Book V, Op. 54 (1891)

Peer Gynt Suite II, Op. 55 (Grieg's transcription from orchestra) (1891)

Sigurd Jorsalfar Suite, Op. 56 (Grieg's transcription from orchestra) (1872)

Lyric Pieces Book VI, Op. 57 (1893)

Lyric Pieces Book VII, Op. 62 (1895)

Lyric Pieces Book VIII, Op. 65 (1896)

Norwegian Folk Melodies, Op. 66 (1896)

Lyric Pieces Book IX, Op. 68 (1898)

Lyric Pieces Book X, Op. 71 (1901)

Norwegian Peasant Dances, Op. 72 (1902-03)
Moods, Op. 73 (1906)

Without Opus Number

Funeral March in Memory of Rikard Nordraak (1866)
6 *Norwegian Mountain Tunes*
3 Piano *Pieces:* The Dance; Gnomes' Tune; White Clouds; Arrangement of a second
     pf. part to four Sonatas by Mozart.

For Piano and Orchestra

Concerto in A minor, Op. 16 (1868)

For Piano Duo

Romance, Old Norwegian Melody with Variations, Op. 51 (1891)

For Piano Duet

Overture in Autumn, Op. 11 (1866) (Grieg's arrangement)
2 *Symphonic Movements*, Op. 14 (1863-64) (Grieg's arr.)
Norwegian Bridal Procession Passing By, Op. 19 (1870-71) (Grieg's arrangement)
Sigurd Jorsalfar Suite, Op. 22 (1872) (Grieg's arr.)
Elegiac Melodies, Op. 34 (1881) (Grieg's arr.)
Norwegian Dances, Op. 35 (1881)
Valses Caprices, Op. 37 (1883)
2 *Norwegian Melodies*, Op. 63 (1869) (Grieg's arr.)
Symphonic Dances, Op. 64 (1896-97) (Grieg's arr.)

March of the Dwarfs
from *Lyric Pieces Book V* Op.54 No.3

*Born in New York City,
December 18, 1861*

*Died in New York City,
January 23, 1908,
Age 47 years*

Edward Alexander MacDowell

Historical Sketch

A sophisticated music that was indigenous to the United States developed a hundred years after the American Revolution. By the end of the 19th Century, there was a true American style–somewhat bland but certainly distinctive. However it was not until Edward MacDowell appeared that American music found its first internationally recognized native-born composer.[1] He was thought of in his day as an "American composer", but he actually did not aspire to organized nationalism. He allowed influences as diverse as Norse legends and American folk tales to run through his music, which had its real basis in the Classical and Romantic traditions of Germanic teaching.

When he was 8, Edward MacDowell began to study music with Juan Buitrago, a Colombian violinist living with the MacDowells. Buitrago introduced him to the Venezuelan pianist, Teresa Carreño, who became his next teacher and warm friend. Later, she played his compositions at her concerts when his budding career as a composer needed help from fellow artists. In 1876, MacDowell moved to Paris with his mother and Buitrago and entered the Conservatoire Nationale. Here he studied theory and composition. His piano teacher was Marmontel who later taught Debussy; a year

---

[1] See section on American School in this book.

after his entrance in the Conservatoire, he won a scholarship for outstanding piano performance.

At 17, MacDowell left Paris for further study in Germany. His teacher in Frankfurt was the composer Joachim Raff who arranged a meeting between the young composer and Liszt. Three years later, in 1881, MacDowell became a piano instructor at the Darmstadt Conservatory. He completed composition of the *1st Modern Suite* (begun under Raff) and a year later the *2nd Modern Suite* and *First Piano Concerto*. Liszt praised his work and arranged for the publication of the *1st Modern Suite*. In 1882, MacDowell appeared in a successful concert in Zürich. His reputation as a performer brought other teaching appointments in Frankfurt and Wiesbaden. At the same time, Teresa Carreño performed parts of the two *Modern Suites* in her concerts in New York and Chicago. The publishing firm of Breitkopf and Härtel now published both *Suites,* and by the end of 1884 when MacDowell was 23, German firms published ten of his works. In the same year, he married his former pupil, Marian Nevins, and settled briefly in Frankfurt. Two years later, he moved to Wiesbaden where he completed a variety of works–8 piano solos, 11 songs, a *Romanze* for cello and orchestra, the *2nd Piano Concerto,* and 3 orchestral tone poems. He also met fellow American composers, George Templeton Strong, Jr., George Whitefield Chadwick, and Arthur William Foote.

In 1888, MacDowell and his wife returned to the United States to settle in Boston where he was active as pianist and composer. The next eight years were among the most satisfying of his life, productive and financially rewarding. He was accepted as a leading figure in American musical life, composing, giving concerts, and teaching. There were performances of his new *2nd Piano Concerto* in New York and Boston, of the Symphonic Poem *Lancelot und Elaine,* and the *1st Orchestral Suite.* The compositions of this period included *The Woodland Sketches Op. 51,* the *Tragica* and *Eroica Sonatas Opp. 45* and *50, Songs Opp. 40* and *47,* and the *2nd Orchestral Suite.*

At 35, MacDowell was appointed professor of music at Columbia University with the duties of forming a new department. He held this position for 8 years, until he resigned because of administrative difficulties. Despite these problems, he produced many characteristic works, the *Sea Pieces Op. 55, Norse* and *Keltic Sonatas Opp. 57* and *59, Fireside Tales Op. 61,* and *New England Idyls Op. 62.* MacDowell wrote many of these works at his country house in Peterborough, New Hampshire, where a work cabin in the surrounding woods gave him seclusion.

After his resignation from Columbia, MacDowell stayed in New York teaching and working on behalf of cultural organizations, including the National Academy of Arts and Letters, American Academy of Arts and Letters, and the American Academy in Rome. In 1904, he was injured in a taxi accident which led to a mental collapse the following year. He had a few rational periods in his last years when he planned with his wife to transform the Peterborough property into an artists' colony.[2] At his death,

---

[2]   His widow founded the MacDowell Colony on the Peterborough estate in 1907 and managed it until 1946. It has 29 studios for writers and artists patterned after the original cabin. Composers who have worked there include Bernstein, Copland, Dello Joio, Virgil Thomson. The MacDowell Medal has been awarded yearly since 1960; among the composers receiving it have been Copland, Varese, Sessions, Schuman, and Piston.

his body was taken to Peterborough and buried close to the work cabin. Nearby stood a boulder bearing a plaque inscribed with MacDowell's own words:

"A house of dreams untold
It looks out over the whispering tree tops
And faces the setting sun."

Style

Musical characteristics and a generation in common made comparison inevitable between MacDowell and the man he much admired, Edvard Grieg. MacDowell was a complex musical figure–as was Grieg–with contradictory elements of greatness: both men tried extended forms and returned to sketches; both used idioms of their native lands with success; both shared Scottish ancestry and interest in Celtic and Nordic legends. But Grieg had stronger unity of feeling and idea. MacDowell's relative lack of unity stood in the way of his achieving greater ends.

While MacDowell's large works, the *Sonatas* and *Concertos,* are stylized rather than unified, this is not the case with the short works. Their language has meaning and direction; they are undiluted, fresh, youthful. Titles suggest musical content as do lines of poetry, often MacDowell's own, placed at the top of title pages. The most inspired are those which summon nature's moods, the sea in particular. Successful also are the ones that explore Native American folklore and legend, providing a subtle expression of Americana. Among these are the *Woodland Sketches* (with the famous *To a Wild Rose), Sea Pieces, Fireside Tales,* and *New England Idyls.*

A late Romantic under the influence of Schumann, Liszt, Wagner, and especially Grieg, MacDowell had strong poetic feeling which colored his melodies and made them consistently singable. He enhanced rhythmic vitality by frequent use of the "Scotch snap"[3] and worked basically diatonic harmonies into blocks of chords to furnish harmonic motion. MacDowell's own excellent pianism was reflected in his compositions which showed a thorough grasp of effective and idiomatic writing. All but the simplest of the short works required a well developed technique for performance. MacDowell never spared the performer as did Grieg.

Because of MacDowell's chronological place in music history, one might expect him to have introduced some of the aesthetic and structural innovations which blossomed around the start of the 20th Century. His position, however, was not that of innovator or modernist, but of tone colorist under the spell of past Romanticism. Brahms, closer by far than MacDowell to the traditions of Schumann and Chopin, turned to magnificent contrapuntal writing and new harmonic textures. MacDowell retreated instead to a Romanticism already established, but he lacked the ardor of the first Romanticists and the profundity of Brahms. He founded no school and failed to herald the musically exploratory nature of the early 1900's. His music is temporarily

---

[3]   A melodic figure with the rhythm of a stressed sixteenth note followed by an unstressed dotted eighth note, as ♪♩. . It was used in European art music between 1680-1800.

out of fashion, but there are signs on students' programs of awakening interest beyond the usual performances of the *2nd Piano Concerto* and a few small pieces.

Compositions

MacDowell's short forms began and closed his writing career, from *Op. 10* to *Op. 62*. The youthful works (from *Op. 10 - Op. 36)* include the *First* and *Second Modern Suites Opp. 10* and *14*, *Two Fantastic Pieces Op. 17*, *Six Poems after Heine Op. 31*, *Four Little Poems Op. 32*, and *Étude de concert in F sharp Op. 36.* [4]

First Modern Suite Op. 10 (1883):   1. Praeludium; 2. Presto; 3. Andantino and Allegretto; 4. Intermezzo; 5. Rhapsody; 6. Fugue

This was MacDowell's first published composition, printed in Germany. Revised a number of times, it remains one of his best known works. The *Praeludium* is a general favorite.

Second Modern Suite Op. 14 (1883); 1. Praeludium; 2. Fugato; 3. Rhapsody; 4. Scherzino; 5. March; 6. Fantastic Dance

Like the *First Modern Suite,* the *Second* also comprises 6 pieces in varying moods.

Two Fantastic Pieces Op. 17 (1884): 1. Legend; 2. Witches' Dance

Of these, *Witches' Dance* is occasionally heard.

Six Poems after Heine Op. 31 (1887): 1. From a Fisherman's Hut; 2. Scotch Poem; 3. From Long Ago; 4. The Post Wagon; 5. The Shepherd Boy; 6. Monologue

The *Scotch Poem* is a forceful, descriptive work foreshadowing the later *Sea Pieces* of *Op. 55.*

Four Little Poems Op. 32 (1888): 1. The Eagle; 2. The Brook; 3. Moonshine; 4. Winter

The character and individuality of *The Eagle* are heightened by the unusual dramatic touch of the last bars which describe the swoop of the eagle on its prey.

Étude de concert in F sharp Op. 36 (1889)

---

[4]   Less important works which fall within the period of *Opp. 10-36* are *Prélude and Fugue Op. 13, Serenata Op. 16, Two Compositions Op. 18, Forest Idyls Op. 19, Four Compositions Op. 24,* and *Six Idyls after Goethe Op. 28.* In this category also are two later sets of pieces, *Les Orientales Op. 37* and *Marionettes Op. 38,* as well as two sets of *Études (Twelve Studies Op. 39* and *Twelve Virtuoso Studies Op. 46).*

The *Étude* is one of MacDowell's finest works.

Following these compositions but preceding and interspersed with the short forms of the last period (from *Op. 49* to *Op. 62)* are the four *Sonatas* which cover a period of eight years, the *Tragica Op. 45, Eroica Op. 50, Norse Op. 57,* and *Keltic Op. 59.* They contain writing in grand style, frequently orchestral and invariably dramatic.

Sonata tragica Op. 45 (1893)

MacDowell explained that the first three movements express tragedy in detail and the last movement the overall power of tragedy. There are numerous chordal effects.

Sonata eroica Op. 50 (1895)

The *Sonata eroica* is a commentary on the Arthur legend: the coming of Arthur; a knight in the forest; Guinevere; the death of Arthur.

Norse Sonata Op. 57 (1900)

The *Norse* and *Keltic Sonatas* are dedicated to Edvard Grieg. In these works, MacDowell freed himself increasingly from the restrictions of form. He lengthened phrases and widened chord formations.

Keltic Sonata Op. 59 (1901)

MacDowell said that he used all the possible suggestions of tone painting to color what he called his "bardic" rhapsody. The work has power and passion.

In contrast to the extended construction of the *Sonatas* are the mature works in short form of the last period, *Air and Rigaudon Op. 49, Woodland Sketches Op. 51, Sea Pieces Op. 55, Fireside Tales Op. 61,* and *New England Idyls Op. 62.* In all of these, MacDowell introduced a wide choice of subjects: old airs, love songs, humorous sketches, and nature studies. The dramatic works are broad in idea; the tender ones are deftly poetic. With these works, MacDowell came to the fullest realization of his talents.

Air and Rigaudon Op. 49 (1894)

The *Air and Rigaudon* use the entire keyboard ingeniously in delicate staccato.

Woodland Sketches Op. 51 (1896): 1. To a Wild Rose; 2. Will-o'-the-Wisp; 3. At an Old Trysting Place; 4. In Autumn; 5. From an Indian Lodge; 6. To a Water-Lily; 7. From Uncle Remus; 8. A Deserted Farm; 9. By a Meadow Brook; 10. Told at Sunset

To a Wild Rose and *To a Water Lily* are dreamland salon pieces combining innocence and sentiment with musical refinement.

Sea Pieces Op. 55 (1898): 1. To the Sea; 2. From a Wandering Iceberg; 3. A.D. 1620; 4. Starlight; 5. Song; 6. From the Depths; 7. Nautilus; 8. In Mid-Ocean

The *Sea Pieces* are probably MacDowell's finest achievement, written at the height of his lyric and dramatic inspiration. They speak eloquently of the ocean's fascination–it is vast, cruel, beautiful, mysterious.

Fireside Tales Op. 61 (1902): 1. An Old Love Story; 2. Of Br'er Rabbit; 3. From a German Forest; 4. Of Salamanders; 5. A Haunted House; 6. By Smouldering Embers

These are simple, fanciful "folk tales" of the woods where it is easy to imagine haunted forests and supernatural revels.

New England Idyls Op. 62 (1902): 1. An Old Garden; 2. Midsummer; 3. Midwinter; 4. With Sweet Lavender; 5. In Deep Woods; 6. Indian Idyl; 7. To an Old White Pine; 8. From Puritan Days; 9. From a Log Cabin; 10. The Joy of Autumn

The last of MacDowell's piano compositions, the *Idyls,* were written largely at Peterboro. The lines of poetry which introduce the next to last, *From a Log Cabin,* formed MacDowell's epitaph.

The two *Concertos for Piano and Orchestra, A minor Op. 15* (1885) and *D minor Op. 23* (1890), were comparatively early works. MacDowell performed both in Boston and New York shortly after writing them, and in 1903 performed the *D minor* at a Philharmonic concert in London. They are effective but little performed, although the *D minor* appears occasionally on concert programs.

Concerto for Piano and Orchestra in D minor Op. 23 (1890)

Moods range from tender to dramatic, all with a certain fresh naïveté. Expressive chromatics add freedom of sentiment to the bravura first movement; emotional abandon and quick joking underlie the *Scherzo,* Uncle Remus fashion; New World vitality surges in a dazzling *Finale.*

For *Piano Duet* there are *Three Poems Op. 20* (1886) and *Moon Pictures after Hans Andersen Op. 21* (1886).

Edition:

A catalogue, entitled "Original Works of Edward A. MacDowell," can be obtained from Roberta S. Lysaght, MacDowell Artists Association, 416 South Euclid Ave., Oak Park, Ill. The catalogue contains information about getting copies of works which are not available from any other source.

Selected Works for Piano

Early works *(Opp. 1-7)*, published under the name of Edgar Thorn, with royalties going to an old nurse of his wife's:

"Amourette", Op. 1 (1896)

"In Lilting Rhythm", Op. 2 (1897)

"Forgotten Fairy-Tales," 4 pieces for pf., Op. 4 (1897)

"Six Pieces or Fancies", Op. 7 (1898)

First Modern Suite, Op. 10 (1880-81): Praeludium, Presto, Andantino and Allegretto, Intermezzo, Rhapsody, Fugue

Prélude and Fugue, Op. 13 (1881)

Second Modern Suite, Op. 14 (1882): Praeludium, Fugato, Rhapsody Scherzino, March, Fantastic Dance

Serenata, Op. 16 (1882)

2 *Fantastic Pieces for concert use,* Op. 17 (1883): Legend, Witches' Dance (Hexentanz)

Barcarolle in F and Humoresque in A, Op. 18 (1884)

Wald-Idyllen, Op. 19 (1884): Forest Stillness, Play of the Nymphs, Reverie, Dance of the Dryads

Four Compositions, Op. 24 (1886): Humoresque, March, Cradle Song, Czardas (Friska)

6 *Idyls after Goethe,* Op. 28 (1887): In the Woods, Siesta, To the Moonlight, Silver Clouds, Flute Idyl, The Bluebell

6 *Poems after Heine,* Op. 31 (1887): 1. We Sat by the Fisherman's Cottage; 2. Far Away, on the Rock-coast of Scotland (Scotch poem); 3. My Child, We Were Once Children; 4. We Travelled Alone in the Gloomy Post-Chaise; 5. Shepherd Boy's a King; 6. Death Nothing is but Cooling Night

4 *Little Poems,* Op. 32 (1888): The Eagle, The Brook, Moonshine, Winter

Étude de Concert, Op. 36 (1889)

Les Orientales, 3 pieces for pf., Op. 37 (1887-88): Clair de Lune, Dans le Hamac, Danse Andalouse

Marionettes, 6 little pieces for pf., Op. 38 (1888): Prologue, Soubrette, Lover, Witch, Clown, Villain, Sweetheart, Epilogue

Twelve Studies, Op. 39 (1889-90).*Book I:* Hunting Song, Alla Tarantella, Romance, Arabeske, In the Forest, Dance of the Gnomes; *Book II:* Idyl, Shadow Dance, Intermezzo, Melody, Scherzino, Hungarian

Sonata Tragica (No. 1) in G minor, Op. 45 (1891-92)

12 *Virtuoso Studies,* Op. 46 (1893-94): Novellete, Moto Perpetuo, Wild Chase, Improvisation, Elfin Dance, Valse Triste, Burlesque, Bluette, Träumerei, March Wind, Impromptu, Polonaise

Air and Rigaudon, Op. 49 (1894)

Second Sonata ("Eroica") in G minor, Op. 50 (1894-95)

Woodland Sketches, Op. 51 (1896): To a Wild Rose, Will o' the Wisp, At An Old Trystingplace, In Autumn, From an Indian Lodge, To a Waterlily, From Uncle Remus, A Deserted Farm, By a Meadow Brook, Told at Sunset

Sea Pieces, Op. 55 (1898): To the Sea, From a Wandering Iceberg, A.D. 1620, Starlight, Song, From the Depths, Nautilus, In Mid-Ocean

Third Sonata ("Norse") in D minor, Op. 57 (1899)

Fourth Sonata ("Keltic") in E minor, Op. 59 (1900)

Fireside Tales, Op. 61 (1901-02): An Old Love Story, Of Br'er Rabbit, Of Salamanders, A Haunted House, By Smouldering Embers

New England Idyls, Op. 62 (1901-02): An Old Garden, Mid-Summer, Mid-Winter, With Sweet Lavender, In Deep Woods, Indian Idyl, To An Old White Pine, From Puritan Days, From a Log Cabin, The Joy of Autumn

Without Opus Number

6 Little Pieces after Sketches by J.S. Bach

Technical Exercises for the pianoforte (2 books)

Many transcriptions of old harpsichord music

For Piano and Orchestra

Concerto No. 1 in A minor, Op. 15 (publ. 1885)

Concerto No. 2 in D minor, Op. 23 (publ. 1890)

For Piano Duet

Three Poems, Op. 20 (1885): *Nights at Sea; Tale of the Knights; Ballade*

Moon Pictures after Hans Andersen, Op. 21 (1886): The Hindoo Maiden; Stork's Story; In Tyrol; The Swan; Visit of the Bear

In Mid-Ocean
from *Sea Pieces* Op.55 No.8

6 | IMPRESSIONISM

In 1887, the painters Monet, Degas, Pissaro, Sisley and Renoir established a technique which provided a particular way of observing the outside world. They combined their talents with the Symbolist poets Verlaine, Baudelaire, and Mallarmé[1] to create an art of shifting values where sensation took the place of emotion. The resulting school of *Impressionism* substituted blurred outlines for hard edges and portrayed the constantly shifting effects of light and color. In the beginning, the term ''Impressionist'' was one of disdain, but by 1894 the new concept was accepted unconditionally. At the same time in music, Debussy created a range of sounds which the public was quick to label ''Impressionistic.'' Debussy himself did not accept any category for his music and did not want to be called an impressionist, but it is difficult not to draw a parallel between the fluid play of pigment and the liquid fall of sound. Debussy's experiments carried sound to a realm he alone explored, involving *unresolved dissonance, chords in parallel motion,* the *whole-tone scale,*[2] *modes,*[3] the *tri-tone,*[4] irregular and *fragmentary phrases,* and extreme *chromaticism.* [5]

---

[1]   Romanticism had already broken down the barriers between the arts, specifically, painting and poetry.

[2]   The whole tone scale consists of six whole steps within the octave, as c, d, e, f#, g#, a#, c.

[3]   Any of the various forms in which the octave was arranged in classical Greek and medieval church music, according to certain fixed intervals between the tones. Each of eight scales had a particular arrangement of fixed intervals and a name from the musical theory of the ancient Greeks which identified it: Dorian, Hypodorian, Phrygian, Hypophrygian, Lydian, Hypolydian, Mixolydian, and (adapted from the Greek) Hypomixolydian.

[4]   An interval (augmented fourth) formed by three whole steps in succession.

[5]   The use of successive half-tones (ie. c, c#, d, d#, etc.)

The late Romantic composers—Wagner, Bruckner, Wolf, Reger, and R. Strauss—all shared some of the characteristics of *Impressionism* at one time or another,[6] but Debussy was consistent in his Impressionistic style in departing from the largely Germanic features of Classical and Romantic music. Although Ravel was part of this movement, his characteristic feeling for form, dance-like rhythm and biting sound did not conform essentially to the new "ism."

The significance of Debussy's *Impressionism* was the awareness and acceptance of new sounds which avoided making a detailed tone-picture but conveyed the moods and emotions aroused by the subject. The exploration of new sounds triggered by Debussy has occupied the composers who followed him from his near-successor, Bartók, to the avant garde composers Messiaen and Boulez. The results of Debussy's solitary and prophetic experiments continue to wash up on contemporary shores and establish *Impressionism* as one of music's most important influences.

[6] Wagner used Impressionism's shimmering technique in his *Forest Murmurs* and *Magic Fire Music,* although his monumental conception of music drama ran counter to Impressionism's smaller forms.

ı in Saint-Germain-en-Laye, France,
August 22, 1862
Died in Paris, France,
March 25, 1918,
Age 56 years

Achille-Claude Debussy

Historical Sketch

Born to non-musical parents, Debussy showed no particular musical talent as a young child. But by the age of 9, he was taking piano lessons with Mme. Mauté de Fleurville, mother-in-law of the Symbolist poet Verlaine. She recognized Debussy's latent gifts and encouraged him to enter the Conservatoire Nationale in 1872. Here he studied the piano with Marmontel and theory with Lavignac. For a time, he studied informally with César Franck. His progress in two years indicated the possibility of a virtuoso career, but the idea was abandoned when he failed to achieve the necessary standards in the following four years. As a pianist of 18, he visited Italy and Austria, and in Russia became a tutor in Mme. von Meck's family. He was already one of those rare artists, a composer who was not also a dedicated instrumentalist. Marmontel is supposed to have said: "He doesn't like the piano very much, but he does like music."

On his return to Paris from summers with Mme. von Meck, Debussy turned to composition and in 1884 won the Prix de Rome (1st Prize) with his cantata, *L'Enfant prodigue.*[1] Although he did not find Rome congenial, he stayed there another three

---

[1]   The Prix de Rome are prizes which have been awarded annually since 1803 by the Institut de France to candidates selected by competition from composition students at the Paris Conservatory. The 1st

years, sending back to Paris several works, among them a new cantata, *La Damoiselle élue.*

For two years after his return from Rome, Debussy travelled and composed. At the World Exhibition of 1889 in Paris, he was introduced to the Javanese gamelan which inspired an awareness of timbre that became an underlying element of his music. He composed *Fêtes galantes* on poems of Verlaine, and for orchestra began the *Prélude a l'après-midi d'un faune* as well as the first version of *Nocturnes.* A performance of *La Demoiselle élue* at the Société Nationale brought his music to public attention.

In 1892, Debussy attended *Pelléas et Melisande,* a mystical play by the Belgian author, Maurice Maeterlinck. He began immediately to sketch an opera from the play but waited nine years for its performance at the Opéra Comique. At that time, it was greeted as a milestone of musical originality and in the next ten years received over 100 performances. While working on *Pelléas,* Debussy finished his *String Quartet in G minor* and the 3 *Chansons de Bilitis.*

In 1895, Debussy's mistress tried to commit suicide, and he suffered a period of paralyzing depression during which he could not compose. The situation improved with his marriage four years later to Rosalie Texier. But this marriage failed, and it was not until he married Emma Bardac, and his daughter Chou-Chou was born in 1905, that he had any kind of domestic fulfillment.

Several years prior to his daughter's birth, Debussy became a critic for *La revue blanche.* During this time, he wrote the 2nd set of *Fêtes galantes* for voice, *La Mer* for orchestra, and the piano pieces, *L'Isle joyeuse* and *Masques.* In 1906, he accepted a series of conducting and performing engagements in England, Belgium, Holland, Austria, Hungary, Italy, and Russia. Three years later, he was appointed to the advisory board of the Conservatoire Nationale and the following year began work on the 1st book of *Préludes* for piano.

The publisher, Durand, commissioned Debussy in 1915 to edit the works of Chopin. The direct result of Debussy's close study of the Chopin *Études* was the composition of his own *12 Études for piano.* At the same time he finished *En blanc et noir* for two pianos and the *Sonata for cello and piano,* the first of a projected series of 6 *Sonatas* for various instruments. He was suffering from cancer but lived three years longer, completing only the *2nd* and *3rd Sonatas (Sonata for flute, viola & harp* and the *Sonata for violin).* He played his final concert in 1917, which included the *Sonata for violin and piano,* and died in the spring of 1918 towards the end of World War I.

Prize entitles the winner to live in Rome for 4 years at the Villa Medici for study and creative work. Candidates must set to music a cantata on a given subject. Winners have been Berlioz, Gounod, Massenet, Debussy, and Charpentier. In 1968, the former channels of French competition were suppressed and promising young composers now go to Rome on teachers' recommendations. (See *Concise Oxford Dictionary of Music,* 3rd ed., 1980.)

Style

Debussy worked constantly to give the clearest expression of his thoughts in the briefest space; consequently, there are no extended works in the classical forms among his piano compositions. His most characteristic works, the 24 *Préludes,* are highly condensed, based on single impressions from painting, sculpture, literature, or his own fluid imagination. The great sentimental themes of the Romanticists are abandoned, replaced by vague sensations and recollections which are veiled in a mist of unreality. Applied to the piano these include delicacy of touch, interplay of the three pedals, and the combination of different registers to bring out unusual timbres.

Lack of traditional harmony, traceable melody, and explicit rhythm all aid in giving delicate and nebulous effects which suggest rather than describe the subject matter. Because of extreme chromaticism, the music lacks conventional key relationships and moves easily and without preparation from one key to another. It frequently sketches the harmony with only a few scattered notes in the bass; the melody may belong to any of several chords and is often indistinct from the accompaniment. Extending freedom beyond traditional harmony, clusters of tones are kept in vibration with the damper pedals while unrelated notes float high enough to mix without sharp dissonance.

For Debussy, virtuosity was not synonymous with bravura; rather it was the ability to vary sound quality to create the right tonal atmosphere. The technique involved was that of controlled dynamic gradation. Debussy's demands were subtle and sophisticated, and because they were widely different from classical tradition, they required a new outlook on the entire subject of expressiveness.

Debussy adapted the whole-tone scale[2] to his own style and created a type of music perfectly suited to the evocative qualities inherent in the scale. He became the greatest innovator of pianistic resources since Liszt, using (in addition to the whole-tone scale) church modes, plainsong, the "oriental" quality of open 4ths and 5ths, the major scale with sharpened 4th and flatted 7th, and his favorite chord of the major 9th.

While he closed his own field of Impressionism with these specific innovations, he opened the 20th Century to succeeding composers with his basic acoustical principles. These included awareness of sound for its own sake and the opposite of sound—powerful silence. His commitment to musical experimentation has influenced generations of 20th Century composers up to the present time. The composers referred to are his contemporary, Ravel, as well as Bartók, Webern, Varèse, Les Six,[3] Cage, Messiaen, Boulez, Stockhausen, and the composers of electronic music who are extending boundaries into the unknown.

---

[2]   See description of whole-tone scale in preceding chapter on Impressionism. It was presumably brought to Debussy's attention by Javanese and Cambodian musicians at the Paris Exposition of 1889.
[3]   Auric, Milhaud, Durey, Tailleferre, Honegger, and Poulenc.

Compositions

Debussy's piano music falls into two general sections: early works written from the time Debussy held the Prix de Rome in 1884 until he began the composition of *Pelléas* in 1892; later compositions dating a year before the completion of *Pelléas* in 1902 until his death. The early works include *Danse bohémienne*, two *Arabesques*, *Ballade*, *Danse*, *Nocturne*, *Rêverie*, *Valse romantique*, *Suite bergamasque*, *Mazurka*, and *Pour le piano*. While all these compositions have Debussy's unmistakable stamp, *Suite bergamasque* and *Pour le piano* are important as statements of his growing assurance in creating new qualities of sound.

Suite bergamasque (1890-1905): 1. *Prélude;* 2. *Menuet;* 3. *Clair de lune;* 4. *Passepied*

The third movement of this suite, the delicate *Clair de lune*, contains the germ of Debussy's ultimate Impressionism. It enjoys popularity beyond the rest of the *Suite* which is of an antique and archaic mood unlike *Claire de lune*.

Pour le piano, suite (1896-1901): 1. *Prélude;* 2. *Sarabande;* 3. *Toccata*

The virtuosity of the first movement *Prélude* is enhanced by rapid figures and octave passages. An unexpected harp-like cadenza closes the movement. The *Sarabande* and *Toccata* explore unusual sonorities and share the suite's general brilliance.

The later works begin with the important suites *Estampes*, *Images*[4] (2 sets of 3 each) and *Children's Corner*.

Estampes (1903): 1. *Pagodes;* 2. *Soirée dans Grenade*   3. *Jardins sous la pluie*

Dedicated to Jacques-Émile Blanche

Two years after completing *Pour le piano*, Debussy wrote three pieces to which he gave the group name *Estampes*. They are among the most descriptive, colorful, and highly organized of Debussy's piano works. *Pagodes* is built on the five-note scale.[5] In *Soirée*, the persistent Habanera rhythm carries overtones of gentle wind and glinting stars. *Jardins* describes a sudden shower in the Tuileries gardens. Two French songs, a round and a lullaby, add the charm of vanished childhood to this popular work. The rain clears in a burst of unexpected sunlight.

Images Set I (1905): 1. *Reflets dans l'eau;* 2. *Hommage à Rameau;* 3. *Mouvement*

---

[4]   In 1977, the manuscript of an additional piano suite, *Images (Oubliées)*, was discovered in a private New York library. Written in 1892, it follows the triptych form of the two later sets of *Images*.
[5]   c, d, e, g, a, c.

Debussy said to his publisher ''...I believe these three pieces will live and will take their places in piano literature...either to the left of Schumann...or to the right of Chopin...''

Reflets dans l'eau

This is a perfect example of Impressionism in music including chords and arpeggios which make up shifting, undulating harmonies based on the whole-tone and pentatonic scales.

Hommage a Rameau

Hommage is a grave, refined tribute to Rameau in which the grandeur of organ music is suggested.

Mouvement

The subtle humor of Mouvement is defined by a succession of triplets and enhanced by octaves and fifths tossed between the hands.

Images Set II (1907): 1. *Cloches à travers les feuilles;* 2. *Et la lune descend sur le temple qui fut;* 3. *Poissons d'or*

Cloches à travers les feuilles (Dedicated to Alexander Charpentier)

Distant chimes echo through the faint rustle of trees.

Et la lune descend sur le temple qui fut (Dedicated to Louis Laloy)

Blocks of hollow sounding chords veiled by the pedals bring to this *Image* ancient and mysterious overtones.

Poissons d'or (Dedicated to Ricardo Viñes)

This composition is a revelry of sound with flights of arpeggios, quick alternating chords, and shimmering tremolo. It was inspired by a descriptive oriental art object, lacquer or embroidery, in Debussy's possession.

Children's Corner (1906-08): 1. *Doctor Gradus ad Parnassum;* 2. *Jimbo's Lullaby;* 3. *Serenade for the Doll;* 4. *Snow is Dancing;* 5. *The Little Shepherd;* 6. *Golliwog's Cake-Walk*

Dedicated to Claude-Emma Debussy

Debussy composed this suite for his daughter, Chou-Chou, who prompted some of Debussy's most amusing and descriptive writing. The English titles suggest games played by a little French girl with an English governess. Chou-Chou died at 14 from diptheria a year following her father's death from cancer.

Doctor Gradus ad Parnassum

The opening five finger exercise, reminiscent of Clementi's great work, *Gradus ad Par-*

nassum,[6] brings a touch of humor suggestive of the diligent student at his morning practice.

Jimbo's Lullaby

Jimbo was Chou-Chou's enormous toy elephant; the ponderous musical allusion is inescapable.

Serenade for the Doll

In a child's caprice, the doll is serenaded with pianissimo staccato "plucking," the soft pedal depressed during the entire piece.

Snow is Dancing

Debussy's craftsmanship asks for a consistently feathery touch and sparing pedal.

The Little Shepherd

Debussy describes *The Little Shepherd* in a gentle melody supported by thin left hand chords much as he outlines *La Fille aux cheveux de lin* from the first book of *Préludes.*

Golliwog's Cake-walk

The *Cake-walk* adds another humorous touch to the collection. It is based on a popular dance step whose quasi-jazz rhythm provokes an impudent smile.

Appearing between the suites *(Estampes, Images, and Children's Corner)* and the following first book of *Préludes* are the single compositions, *L'Isle joyeuse, Masques,* and *La plus que lente.*

L'Isle joyeuse (1904)

This work represents a brief return to the form and spirit of Debussy's earlier works. More melodic than many compositions of this period, it is one of Debussy's few consistently bravura pieces. Watteau's "Embarquement pour Cythère" is the sensual, animated setting.

Masques (1904)

Masques takes place in a setting of Italian comedy with Scaramouche darting on and off stage.

La plus que lente (1910)

---

[6]   Muzio Clementi (1752-1832) wrote 100 technical studies which make up the *Gradus,* a collection respected to this day.

Debussy orchestrated *La plus que lente*, assuring it wider popularity than the original piano form. Its mood hovers between parody and seriousness.

Préludes (12) *Book I* (1910): 1. *Danseuses de Delphes;* 2. *Voiles;* 3. *Le Vent dans la plaine;* 4. *Les Sons et les parfums tournent dans l'air du soir;* 5. *Les Collines d'Anacapri;* 6. *Des Pas sur la neige;* 7. *Ce qu'a vu le vent d'ouest;* 8. *La Fille aux cheveux de lin;* 9. *La Sérénade interrompue;* 10. *La Cathédrale engloutie;* 11. *La Danse de Puck;* 12. *Minstrels*

Préludes (12) *Book II* (1910-13): 1. *Brouillards;* 2. *Feuilles mortes;* 3. *La puerta del Vino;* 4. *Les Fées sont d'exquises danseuses;* 5. *Bruyères;* 6. *General Lavine–eccentric;* 7. *La Terrasse des audiences du clair de lune;* 8. *Ondine;* 9. *Hommage à S. Pickwick, Esq., P.P.M.P.C.;* 10. *Canope;* 11. *Les Tierces alternées;* 12. *Feux d'artifice*

The 24 *Préludes* are the most polished, concise, and impressionistic of Debussy's piano works. The titles are highly suggestive, but Debussy chose to place them in small letters at the end, letting each work stand first by itself. There is some disagreement about the quality of the second book of *Préludes* in relation to the first; Debussy himself said they were not all good. However, the best of them project delicate sensations with remarkable success and show increasing perfection of means.

Twelve Études. Book I: *Pour les cinq doigts; Pour les tierces; Pour les quartes; Pour les sixtes; Pour les octaves; Pour les huits doigts*

Twelve Études . Book II: *Pour les degrés chromatiques; Pour les agréments; Pour les notes répétées; Pour les sonorités opposées; Pour les arpèges; Pour les accords*

The twelve *Études*, 2 books of 6 studies each (1915), bear the dedication, "To the memory of Frederic Chopin." Debussy began their composition three years before his death. They deal with the technical aspects of his music and present all the difficulties he felt were inherent in the execution and interpretation of his work.

Debussy's only composition for piano and orchestra is the *Fantaisie*, begun during his tenure of the Prix de Rome and completed in Paris in 1889. It was neither published nor performed publicly until after his death and is still little known as a concert work. Debussy withdrew it on the eve of its single possible performance for reasons still unknown. It is dedicated to René Chansarel.

Of the two compositions for *Piano Duo*, *Lindaraja* (finally published in 1926) and *En blanc et noir*, the latter is by far a finer work.

En blanc et noir (1915): 1. Dedicated to A. Kussevitsky; 2. Dedicated to Jacques Charlot; 3. Dedicated to Igor Stravinsky

---

Made up of 3 *Caprices*, as they were originally called, *En blanc et noir* contains overtones of World War I. The first is a rhythmic waltz, possibly a sardonic commentary on Debussy's physical handicap which kept him from military service. The second is a study in desperation. The third suggests a battlefield deserted in wind and rain.

For *Piano Duet*, Debussy composed *Symphonie en si mineur, Triomphe de Bacchus, Petite Suite, Marche Écossaise sur un theme populaire,* and *Six Épigraphes Antiques.* The *Petite Suite,* among the most popular of the early works, consists of *En bateau, Cortege, Menuet,* and *Ballet.* The *Petite Suite* (1888) became widely known in the orchestral transcription of Büsser.

Edition:

Durand and Cie, Editeurs, 4, Place de la Madeleine, Paris

Selected Works for Piano

---

2 *Arabesques,* 1888

Suite bergamasque (4), 1890: *Prélude; Menuet; Clair de lune; Passepied*

Ballade slave, Rêverie, Valse romantique, Nocturne, Danse (Tarantelle styrienne), 1890

Mazurka, 1891

Pour le piano (3), 1901: *Prélude; Sarabande; Toccata*

Estampes (3), 1903: *Pagodes; Soirée dans Grenade; Jardins sous la pluie*

D'un cahier d'esquisses, 1903

Masques, 1904

L'Ise joyeuse, 1904

Images (3), 1905: *Reflects dans l'eau; Hommage à Rameau; Mouvement*

Images (3) Second set, 1907: *Cloches à travers les feuilles; Et la lune descend sur le temple qui fut; Poissons d'or*

Children's Corner (6), 1908: *Doctor Gradus ad Parnassum; Jimbo's Lullaby; Serenade for the Doll; Snow is Dancing; The Little Shepherd; Golliwog's Cake-Walk*

Hommage à Haydn, 1909

La plus que lente, 1910

12 *Préludes,* 1910. *First set: Danseuses de Delphes; Voiles; Le Vent dans la plaine; Les Sons et les parfums tournent dans l'air du soir; Les Collines d'Anacapri; Des Pas sur la neige; Ce qu'a vu le vent d'ouest; La Fille aux cheveux de lin; La Sérénade interrompue; La Cathédrale engloutie; La Danse de Puck; Minstrels*

12 *Préludes,* 1910. *Second set: Brouillards; Feuilles mortes; La puerta del vino; Les fées sont d'exquises danseuses; Bruyères; General Lavine–eccentric; La Terrasse des audiences du clair de lune; Ondine; Hommage à S. Pickwick, Esq., P.P.M.P.C.; Canope; Les Tierces alternées; Feux d'artifice*

Berceuse héroïque, 1914 (also for orchestra)

6 *Études* Book I (dedicated to the memory of Chopin) (1915)

6 *Études* (Book II dedicated to the memory of Chopin) (1915)

Miscellaneous

For Messrs. Durand, an edition of the complete piano works of Chopin.

La Bôite à joujoux, a ballet for children in piano score only.

For Piano and Orchestra

Fantaisie (1889)

For Piano Duo

Lindaraja (publ. 1926)

En Blanc et noir, 3 pieces (1915)

For Piano Duet

Symphonie en si mineur, 1880 (dedicated to Mme. von Meck) (Exists only as a piano duet.)

Triomphe de Bacchus, 1880's (An interlude intended for orchestra: a student work.)

Petite Suite: En Bateau, Cortège, Menuet, Ballet, 1888

Marche écossaise sur un theme populaire, 1891 (A primitive Scotch fighting tune in the form of a march.)

Six Epigraphes antiques, 1915 (also for piano solo)

For Piano Duo (Transcriptions)

Schumann's *6 Studies on Canon,* (also called 6 Études in the form of a canon for pedal-piano) *Op. 56;* also *Am Springbrunnen* of Schumann

Saint-Saëns's *Second Symphony in A minor*

Saint-Saëns's *Introduction* and *Rondo capriccioso*

Wagner's overture to *The Flying Dutchman*

Claire de lune
from *Suite bergamasque*

Andante

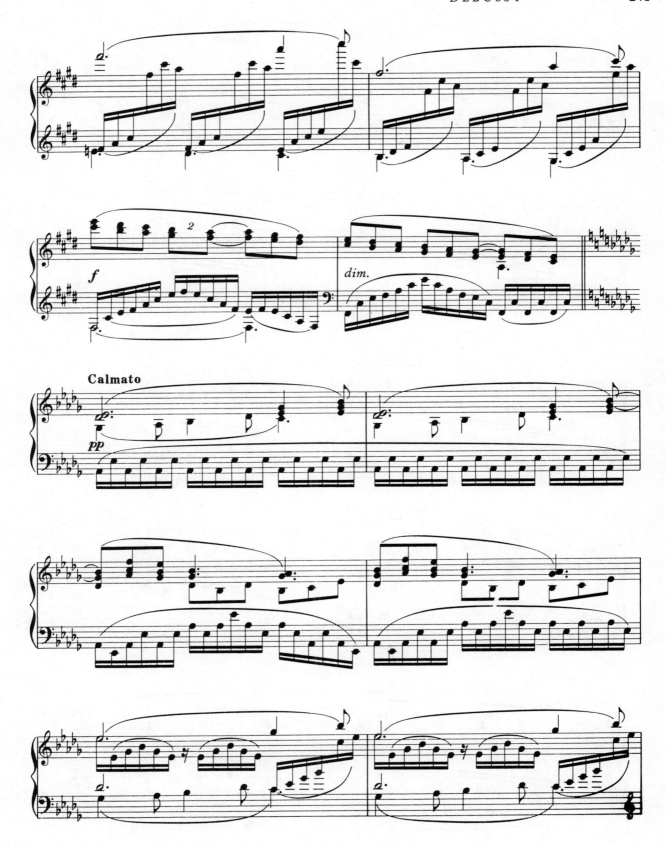

7 | MODERNISM AND CONTEMPORARY TRENDS

The piano repertoire of the 20th Century is larger than that of any other instrument. Its development has marked the direction of all musical exploration in this century from Debussy and Bartók through Schoenberg (1874-1951) to Boulez (1925-) and Stockhausen (1928-   ).

In general, three trends have marked musical progress from the first quarter of this century: incorporation of folk elements (not only from aboriginal music of various parts of the world as in *primitivism,* but also indigenous national themes and rhythms); a deep probing of psychological responses at the expense of form as in *expressionism;* and finally, a concern for *sound in itself,* divorced from meaning and from emotional response. This latter spirit of detachment (i.e. sound for its own sake) has been evident in *objectivism, machine music* (which sought to use the sounds of the workaday world), and the *new objectivity.* Hindemith carried it into music written for special purposes such as film, radio, or school--that is, music with a purpose outside the composer's personal feelings and goals. The Russian emphasis on music as an active propaganda force falls within this category.

Neo-classicism, though broader in concept and making use of the forms of past centuries, has continued the trend away from psychological overtones in music. *Musique concrète* has expanded the exploration of nature and quality of sound, even making use of everyday sounds such as traffic noises, running water, children's voices, street cries, etc., all recorded on tape. *Aleatory* and *indeterminate music* has added another new aspect–chance–since this music cannot be predicted before performance and is composed through chance procedures, either statistical or computerized.

Such radical changes in the conception of the nature of music obviously required equally drastic changes in methods of composition. In *atonality,* there is no tonal center, and the 12 notes of the octave function independently without relation to any key. *Serialism* is based on a structural series of notes which governs the total development of the composition, involving in turn all twelve notes of the chromatic scale in any order selected by the composer. This was extended to the *new serialism* which included all the components of the composition–time, pitch, dynamics, etc. The methods employed are of such complexity that they require a detailed study of their own. With *neo-lyricism,* there was a return to incorporating native lyricism into the fabric of structural music, a method used by the Italian composers Maderna and Nono. Piano usage in itself has undergone startling changes since the days of Liszt. The composers who followed Debussy and Bartók have gone beyond the mechanical limitations of the instrument. Henry Cowell (1897-1965) even treated string sound separately from keystruck sound by stroking and plucking the strings in combination with the sustaining pedal. He also altered keystruck sound in his prepared piano by inserting such objects as metal wedges, hat pins, rubber bands, and tacks between the strings.

The sustaining pedal has become as important to present-day piano writing as dynamics and phrasing. The descriptive terms of half-pedaling, after-pedaling, and flutter-pedaling are standard. The center pedal is commonly used for occasional groundbass effects. In most contemporary composition, pedal effects are not left up to the performer but are directed by the composer.

The invention of the electronic instruments which have come to dominate popular music have had a profound effect on the composers of serious music. Here was a new supply of unlimited acoustics. Not only the electronic piano and organ themselves were put to use, but tapes, loudspeakers, film sound tracks, oscillators, and recordings were combined in new ways. Even long silences came into conscious use.

The jazz from the southern part of the United States has had a deep and continuing influence on many of these developments. A popular style with rhythmic elements from West Africa and from Gospel singing, it was consciously used by a number of composers, particularly by George Gershwin who was unique in building a bridge between jazz and symphonic form. Its often spontaneous performance challenged the predictability of the written note. In the 1960s, with the general advent of electronic instruments, jazz was the decisive influence in the growth of hard rock, although young rock composers of the day often turned to the past–especially Bach and Vivaldi–for musical inspiration and ideas. The influence of jazz has gone far beyond the boundaries of its native United States and has had strong effects on both popular and serious music in all parts of the world.

A feature of contemporary music impossible to ignore is its creation of an audience gap. From Bach to Debussy, developments took place within the framework of a basic musical language. Mozart knew his audience and both wrote and performed for his listeners. So, in their own way, did Beethoven, Liszt, and Chopin. Today this is no longer so. The absolute novelty of some contemporary works is offensive to many people. That the musical language of composers seems so remote from their audiences may also be a commentary on the isolation of the artist in modern industrial society. An understanding of trends and a growing familiarity with composers' styles will certainly provide some remedy for present alienation.

With the enormous number of fine composers at work today, with the new resources of electronic instruments (not to mention today's magnificently built pianos), and with the technical equipment to bring the best of music into every home, the time is ripe for the greatest musical flowering yet known.

Born in Nagyszentmiklós, Hungary,
(now Sannicolaul, Romania),
March 25, 1881
Died in New York, New York,
September 26, 1945,
Age 64 years

Béla Bartók

Historical Sketch

Bartók's parents quickly recognized his precocious talent as a young pianist and composer. His mother, a respected piano teacher, gave Bartók his first piano lesson when he was 5; at 9, he wrote his first compositions. Since his father, an amateur pianist and cellist, died early in Bartók's life, his mother directed his musical education. In 1891, she accepted a teaching post in what is now Oradea, Romania. Bartók entered the Gymnasium there and studied with a professional teacher, Kersch. The next year, Bartók made his first public appearance in Nagyzöllös, as pianist and composer. At 13, he moved to Pozsony where for the next five years he studied piano and composition. His teachers, Erkel and Hyrtle, were first rate musicians. Bartók took part in the musical life of Pozsony, played chamber music and attended the symphony and opera. Through his organ playing at the Pozsony Gymnasium, he became familiar with the classical repertoire from Bach to Brahms and showed a quick and thorough grasp of classical style.

At 18, Bartók, entered the Budapest Academy of Music in preference to the Vienna Academy. He was influenced in this choice by a countryman, Dohnányi, who was interested in folk song and persuaded Bartók to learn more about his Hungarian cultural background. Bartók's excellent teachers at the Budapest Academy introduced him to celebrated artists and musicians who broadened his musical interests. The heritage of Wagner and Richard Strauss, along with Liszt and Debussy, exerted a strong influence on the young musician. In Hungary at this time, the very air was humming with ideas of national independence. Far from holding aloof, Bartók was intensely aware of this nationalism and interested in translating it into musical terms through folk music. When Bartók graduated from the Academy in 1903, he seemed destined for a virtuoso piano career. He was a fine sight reader and chamber player, a brilliant and dedicated Liszt performer, and a favorite of the musical patrons of the day. By 1904, he had written the *4 Piano Pieces DD 71, Rhapsody Op. 1, Violin Sonata,*[1] and *Piano Quintet.* A public performance of the *Violin Sonata, Posa Songs,* and *4 Piano Pieces* introduced him as a rising composer.

Bartók made his first notation of a Hungarian peasant song in 1904. Here, he discovered, was a wealth of indigenous material ready for serious use. He began a lifelong collaboration with another countryman, Kodály, who was also engaged in folk song research. Bartók began to make annual trips through Hungary to transcribe and record folk material. He became a piano professor at the Budapest Academy in 1907 but continued folk song research and expanded it to include Slovakia, Romania, and Transylvania. The *1st String Quartet, 10 Easy Pieces SZ 39,* and the last 2 of the *14 Bagatelles Op. 6 SZ 38* are works of this period. His marriage to Márta Ziegler in 1907 inspired *Portrait of a Girl* from the *Sketches Op. 9 SZ 44* and *The Quarrel* from *3 Burlesques Op. 8c SZ 47.* She became the mother of Bartók's first child, Béla.

Between 1910 and 1915, Bartók was engaged primarily in collecting folk songs. He extended his field to include North Africa, Ruthenia, Bulgaria, and Serbia and prepared 2721 Hungarian, 3500 Romanian, and 3000 Slovak folk songs for publication. During these five years, the public lost interest in Bartók's compositions, but, in 1915, his reputation returned with a surge of creativity. He completed several piano works, the *2nd String Quartet,* songs of the *Ady Cycle,* the ballet *The Wooden Prince,* the opera *Bluebeard's Castle,* and the ballet *The Miraculous Manderin. Universal,* in Vienna, took over his publication. He was now an international figure whose success included commissions and performances in many European countries.

In 1923, Bartók divorced his first wife and married Ditta Pásztory,[2] an excellent pianist who performed many two-piano concerts with him. She was the mother of his second son, Péter. For the next eight years until his 50th birthday, Bartók composed and performed with great success. His concert and lecture tours to the United States, Russia, Switzerland, Czechoslovakia, and Egypt featured the folk songs he and Kodály had researched and classified. On his 50th birthday, Bartók received the Légion d'Honneur.

[1]   1903, unpublished, not to be confused with the two later *Sonatas for Violin and Piano, No. 1* of 1921 and *No. 2* of 1922.

[2]   After Bartók's death, she moved from the United States to Budapest, Hungary and continued to play two-piano recitals which included his works.

The 1930's were years of extreme changes in world stability, and Bartók felt them keenly. After 1933, as a protest against the rise of fascism, he never played again in Germany; for the same reason, he quit Universal in Austria for the English firm of Boosey and Hawkes. He made plans to leave Hungary because of the repressive situation there.

Before Bartók decided to settle in America, he made a successful tour of the United States accepting commissions both here and in Europe. These represent some of his finest works—the *5th String Quartet* (commissioned by Elizabeth Sprague Coolidge in 1934); *Music for Strings, Percussion and Celesta* (for Paul Sacher in 1936); *Violin Concerto No. 2* (for Zoltán Székely in 1937-38) and *Contrasts* (for Joseph Szigeti and Benny Goodman in 1938). The last significant composition he wrote in Europe was the *6th String Quartet* of 1939. In the spring of 1940, he emigrated to the United States and settled in New York City. The Ditson Foundation of Columbia University gave him a limited grant to work on some unclassified recordings of Yugoslavian folk music, and Columbia University presented him with an honorary doctorate.

In 1942, Bartók's health declined, but he could still produce the *Concerto for Orchestra* in 1943 for the Koussevitzky Foundation, the *Solo Violin Sonata* in 1944 for Yehudi Menuhin, and the *Viola Concerto* (left unfinished but completed by Tibór Sérly) for William Primrose. Bartók's connection with Hungary ended when he came to live in the United States during World War II. After the war, he was told by Hungarian authorities that "official difficulties" made his return to Hungary impossible. By 1945, he was mortally ill and died from leukemia in a New York hospital, leaving behind unfinished works and, in his words, "a trunkful of fresh ideas."

Style

Bartók himself declared that the study of native folk music was the underlying artistic influence of his musical life. To him, this study suggested the fruitful use of melodies based on the chromatic scale (where every note had equal melodic value), rhythms which were combinations of folk patterns, and harmonies free from traditional use of major and minor keys. Combining these folk traits, he achieved new virtuosity of each musical element and transformed every style he touched, traditional, classic, romantic, expressionist, and neo-classic.

Bartók's melodies often appear as parts of single or double scale passages and reflect folk influence in avoidance of long lines. They are not suited to ordinary counterpoint, but, because of mathematical form and mechanical symmetry, they furnish an ever varied spring board for Bartók's characteristic, complex polyphony. With a debt to Liszt, Bartók uses melodies successfully in cyclic treatment, compressing rather than expanding them. Purely pianistic melodic devices, again reminiscent of Liszt, employ glissando passages and ornamented grace notes.

Rhythms favor decisive first beats over up-beats, and incorporate strong dotted patterns. Time signatures change frequently within the body of the composition, adding rhythmic vitality.

The strong physical feeling of Bartók's harmony is channeled in combinations that fall naturally under the hands. It is typically free of restraints and explores every kind of chord and interval, making satisfactory balance of consonance and dissonance. Foreign chords appear without reference to modulation, while major and minor intervals often sound simultaneously. Although intervals from seconds to sevenths provide unlimited combinations of note patterns by the addition of sharps or flats, it is the interval of the third, either major or minor, which is the most constant and individual element of Bartók's harmony. Frequently, dissonant harmonic climaxes are marked by shocks of consonance.

In the matter of formal structure, Bartók combines the forceful but fragmentary qualities of folk music with a strong feeling for extended form. Structural balance and use of sonata form mark his works and bear out his often expressed conviction that the true test of creative talent lies in form.

Drawing new sounds from every instrument he touched, Bartók demands from the piano an extraordinarily wide tonal response from pure beauty to raw percussiveness. Extremes appear on almost every page: keyboard compactness contrasts with extension; simplicity of line with bizarre dynamics; primitive percussiveness with shimmering delicacy. Shading and quality of sound range from bell-like accents, ostinatos, glissandos, and sliding chromatic progressions to trills producing percussive clangor. The gradations are subtle, foreshadowing contemporary use of percussiveness which creates expressiveness beyond special effects for their own sake. Only when he chose, was Bartók's personal use of percussiveness unrelenting. Awesome, it never banged; its quality was clear, incisive, accented, harsh–but always musical.

Bartók was a constant experimenter, bold innovator, borrower and master transmuter of ideas and methods. He explored fresh melodic, rhythmic, and harmonic means; he opened doors with a zest for discovery which was constantly growing. Presiding over all was his demand for unremitting concentration, a formidable challenge to performer and listener unsurpassed among his contemporaries.

Compositions

Five periods have been suggested[3] as a general guide to Bartók's compositions: they encompass the early works, 1889-1907; the mature style, 1908-1911; years of Extension, 1911-1924; classical middle period, 1926-1937; last works, 1938-1945.

Rhapsody Op. 1 (1904) SZ 26

The *Rhapsody*, originally written for piano solo, appears in two other versions, piano and orchestra and two pianos. Written as a virtuoso work for Bartók's own concert performances, it is in the grand style of Liszt's *Rhapsodies* but more compact. Themes are neo-Hungarian, the setting reflective of German Romantic traditions. However,

---

[3]   See New Grove 1980, Bartók.

Bartók added frequent chromaticism and abrupt harmonic changes, giving the *Rhapsody* an air of passionate improvisation. In contrast to later works, its pages are frequently black with notes.

Bagatelles Op. 6 (1908) 14 pieces *SZ 38*

The *Bagatelles,* almost all short, bear Bartók's distinctive stamp of experimentation in structure and tonality. For instance:

No. 1: In *Molto sostenuto,* Bartók deals with bitonality in opposing hands, a method appearing frequently in later compositions.

No. 2: *Allegro giocoso* is a study in major seconds.

No. 5: *Vivo,* in Dorian mode, is an arrangement of a Slovak folk song.

No. 9: The expressive melody of *Elle est morte* is supported by two chords only.

Ten Easy Pieces (1908) *SZ 39*

The *Ten Easy Pieces,* with the *Bagatelles,* forecast concentration of idiom that characterizes Bartók's later work and shows his adventurous, ever-renewing way of looking at musical materials. The two most popular of this collection are *No. 5, Evening with the Széklers,* and *No. 10, Bear Dance.*

Two Elegies Op. 8b (1908-09) *SZ 41*

In contrast to the *Ten Easy Pieces,* the first *Elegie* shows a return to early romantic virtuosity with arpeggios, tremolos, bravura chords and cadenzas. In the second *Elegie,* Bartók points to future simplicity of structure.

Two Romanian Dances Op. 8a (1909-10) *SZ 47*

These *Dances* are harmonically complex, percussive, vigorous, and rhythmic. Violence of contrast is marked from *ppp* to *fff.*

Three Burlesques Op. 8c (1908-11) *SZ 47*

Sharply dissonant and harshly accented, the *Burlesques* introduce polyrhythms of 2 against 3, and 3 against 4. They are sparse, with no harmonic enrichment. The middle *Burlesque, A Bit Drunk,* contains parallel triads played in descriptive, unstable rhythm.

Allegro barbaro (1911) *SZ 49*

Authentically Magyar, the *Allegro barbaro* shows Bartók's complete assimilation of folk elements. Martellato chords and driving rhythm give it unrelenting, savage energy.

With this work, Bartók embraced the piano as a percussion instrument capable of sounds which expanded keyboard coloring through gradations and quality of attack.[4]

Following *Allegro barbaro* came the *Sonatina* (1915) *SZ 55*, *Suite Op. 14* (1916) *SZ 62*, *Three Studies Op. 18* (1918) *SZ 72*, and 8 *Improvisations on Hungarian Peasant Songs Op. 20* (1920) *SZ 74*. Of these, the *Three Studies*, pushing beyond Bartók's previous writing, pursue experiments in contrapuntal atonality which parallel Schoenberg's development of 12 note technique. Pianistically the *Studies* are concerned with extension and contraction of the hand necessary for playing 12 note music.

Bartók, an acclaimed international virtuoso by 1926, composed for his own performance in this one year the *Sonata, First Concerto, Out of Doors* (5 pieces) and *Nine Little Piano Pieces*.

Sonata (1926) SZ 80

The *Sonata* bears resemblance to *Allegro barbaro* in percussive rhythmic figures. Counterpoint expands from single notes to intervals, chords, and tone clusters. The largest of Bartók's solo compositions, the *Sonata* underlines its primitive origins with machine-like energy.

Out of Doors (1926) SZ 81 (5 pieces)

Although repeated percussive figures suggest the *Sonata*, *Out of Doors* differs in a variety of suggestive sounds and emotional contrast of inner movements.

No. 4 The Night's Music

Dedicated to Bartók's wife Ditta, this movement is the most unusual of the suite. It shows Bartók's exceptional awareness of nature's voices in which *pp* cluster chords make a delicate, blurred web of sound.

Nine Little Piano Pieces (1926) SZ 82

The first four, *Dialogues*, are contrapuntal studies in two voices, while the last, *Preludio, all'ungherese* is a dance tune with percussive accompaniment.

---

[4]   Halsey Stevens asserts that with *Allegro barbaro* "...Bartók recognized the piano for what it is, an instrument of percussion, and turned his creative energies to the production of music in keeping with its nature, music which culminated in the *Sonata*, the *Concertos*, and the *Sonata for Two Pianos and Percussion.*" Stevens, Halsey, *The Life and Music of Bela Bartók* (Revised ed.), Oxford University Press, London, 1978, pp. 120-121.

The set of 153 short graded pieces, *Mikrokosmos SZ 107,* shows Bartók's range of creative styles and ideas from 1926 to 1939. Originally designed for Bartók's son Péter, the pieces progress from simple studies to the most difficult compositions suitable for concert performance. Stating essential characteristics of 20th Century music in brief form (the origin of the title), they bring together favorite harmonic, contrapuntal, and rhythmic features: whole-tone, pentatonic, and modal scales support bitonality and cluster chords to create harmonic bases; inversion and free canon expand contrapuntal treatment; syncopation and irregular accents in endless variety provide new rhythmic language. But *Mikrokosmos* is also a graded study of piano technique which includes exercises in legato and staccato, extension and contraction, finger and hand independence. These are definitive studies for 20th Century language as Chopin's, Liszt's, and Debussy's *Études* are for Romanticism and Impressionism.

Sonata for Two Pianos and Percussion (1937) SZ 110

In 1937, Bartók produced a work which stands by itself, unique in the entire field of music, the *Sonata for Two Pianos and Percussion.*[5] In the new vein of mellow sound, i.e. percussive sections contrasting with rich sonorities, Bartók introduced a variety of moods and colors with the ever-present goal of combining piano resonance and percussion timbre. The *Sonata* is a masterpiece, one of Bartók's most important works. Its three movements (including many tempo changes within each movement) are, I *Assai lento,* II *Lento,* and III *Allegro non troppo.*

Exemplifying meticulous attention to detail in everything he wrote, Bartók provided a diagram of instruments and performance notes as a preface to the published edition. Instruments called for are 3 timpani, xylophone, side drum with snares, side drum without snares, cymbal suspended, a pair of cymbals, bass drum, triangle, tam-tam, and two pianos.

Focusing on the pianist, Bartók wrote the first two *Concertos for Piano and Orchestra* as additions to his personal repertoire. The *Third Concerto,* which Bartók knew he would never play and left unfinished, concentrated on serenity, simplicity, and refinement.

Concerto No. 1 for Piano and Orchestra (1926) SZ 83

The year 1926 is the clue to Bartók's style in this *Concerto,* vital, sharp, brittle, and homogeneous in avoidance of personal expressiveness. Harmonically, tone clusters appear frequently, as does polytonality (in the *Adagio,* woodwinds play in four different keys simultaneously). It is apparently the last time Bartók used key signatures in a large work, preferring the freedom of ad lib accidentals and enharmonic writing.

[5]   Bartók transcribed it as a *Concerto for Two Pianos and Orchestra SZ 115* in 1940.

Concerto No. 2 for Piano and Orchestra (1930-31) *SZ 95*

The bravura *Second Concerto* represents a transition between scores of the 1920's and Bartók's final two decades. Development is polyphonic with an economy of themes. Extremely active outside movements are reminiscent of the incessant activity of Bach's *Concertos*.

Concerto No. 3 for Piano and Orchestra (1945) *SZ 119*

Showing serenity unusual among Bartók's large works, the *Third Concerto* possesses tenderness, delicacy, and fragility. Modest scoring and simple single line writing reflect Bartók's new direction toward simplification of structure and tonality. On Bartók's death, his countryman Tibór Sérly finished the last seventeen measures.

Editions:

D. Dille: Thematisches Verzeichnis der Judenwerke; Béla Bartók's 1890-1904 (Budapest 1974)   DD

A. Szöllösy: Bibliographie des oeuvres musicales et ecrits musicologiques de Béla Bartók, in B. Szabolcsi, ed.: Bartók: sa vie et son oeuvre (Budapest 1956)   SZ

Selected Works for Piano[6]

Rhapsody Op. 1, SZ 26 (1904) (2nd version for Piano and Orchestra SZ 27)
Three Hungarian Folksongs, SZ 35a (1907)
Fourteen Bagatelles Op. 6, SZ 38 (1908)
Ten Easy Pieces, SZ 39 (1908)
Two Elegies Op. 8b, SZ 41 (1908, 1909)
For Children, 85 pieces SZ 42 (1908-09)
Seven Sketches Op. 9, SZ 44 (1908-10)
Two Romanian Dances Op. 8a, SZ 43 (1909-10)
Four Dirges Op. 9a, (Nenies) SZ 45 (1910)
Three Burlesques Op. 8c, SZ 47 (1908-11)
Allegro barbaro, SZ 49 (1911)
The First Term at the Piano, 18 pieces SZ 53, (1913)
Sonatina, SZ 55 (1915)
Romanian Folk Dances from Hungary, 7 pieces SZ 56 (1915)

---

[6] For a complete listing of early works between 1889 and 1904, see New Grove 1980 article on Bartók, Vol. 2, p. 221.

Romanian Christmas Songs, 20 pieces, SZ 57 (1915)

Suite Op. 14, SZ 62 (1916)

Fifteen Hungarian Peasant Songs, SZ 71 (1914-17)

Three Hungarian Folk Tunes, SZ 66 (1914-17)

Three Studies Op. 18, SZ 72 (1918)

Eight Improvisations on Hungarian Peasant Songs Op. 20, SZ 74 (1920)

Sonata, SZ 80 (1926)

Out of Doors, SZ 81 (1926): 1. With drums and pipes; 2. Barcarolla; 3. Musettes; 4. The night's music; 5. The chase

Nine Little Piano Pieces, SZ 82 (1926)

Three Rondos on Folk Tunes, SZ 84 (I, 1916, II and III, 1927)

Petite Suite, SZ 105 (1926)

Mikrokosmos, 153 progressive pieces for piano, 6 vol. SZ 107 (1926-39)

For Piano and Orchestra

Scherzo, Op. 2, SZ 28 (1904)

Concerto No. 1, SZ 83 (1926)

Concerto No. 2, SZ 95 (1930-31)

Concerto No. 3, SZ 119 (1945) (completed by Tibór Sérly)

For Piano Duo

Sonata for Two Pianos and Percussion, SZ 110 (1937) Transcribed as Concerto for Two Pianos and Orchestra SZ 115, 1940)

A Little Tipsy, No. 2
from *Three Burlesques*, Op. 8c

8 | SCHOOLS

The following sections give the historical background and contemporary development of the major schools of keyboard composition throughout the world.

Austro-German School

Bach and Handel represent the culmination of composition for the harpsichord and clavichord. Among their lesser predecessors were *Hassler* (1564-1612), *Froberger* (1616-1667), *Georg Muffat* (1653-1704), and *Buxtehude* (1736-1707).[1] All of these composer-performers, like Bach and Handel, wrote for the harpsichord, clavichord, and organ. Following Bach and Handel, the Austro-German genius produced a succession of additional composers who hold their position without challenge: Haydn, Mozart, Beethoven, Schubert, Mendelssohn, Schumann, and Brahms.

After furnishing this tremendous impetus to the course of music from late Baroque through Classicism and Romanticism, the Austro-German school continues its innovative spirit today. Following the late Romantic composers[2] and the cataclysm of World War I, *Arnold Schoenberg* (1874-1951) originated the concept of *atonality* in which the consonances and dissonances of traditional harmony are disregarded. Soon Schoenberg's atonality gave rise to his *12 note row,* or *serial technique,* and he was joined

---

[1]   Buxtehude was Danish but lived in Germany.
[2]   See chapter on Romanticism and late Romantic Austro-German composers whose skill was largely orchestral, i.e., Wagner, Strauss, Mahler, and Bruckner.

by his contemporaries *Anton Webern* (1883-1945) and *Alban Berg* (1885-1935) as exponents of *expressionism* through *serialism* as well as atonality.[3]

Schoenberg pioneered the concept of atonality in his *3 pieces for piano Op. 11* and in *Pierrot Lunaire* for voice and chamber orchestra. Although he was not a pianist, his two important concepts of atonality and serialism were born through the medium of the piano. In 1923, the *5 piano pieces Op. 23* introduced his mature 12 note method of composition. He remains a controversial figure; he is respected if not yet loved. He was steadfast in his arresting ideas and became a powerful influence on 20th Century music. Webern wrote at first in a free atonal style but later made increasingly complex use of the 12 note row. His homage to contrapuntal forms such as the passacaglia and canon, and his new approach to extended contrapuntal lines brought about the compelling sight and sound of frequent hand crossing. Among his piano works are *Variations for piano Op. 27,* and chamber music with piano.

Berg's compositions for piano came early in his career and were not representative of his mature style of emotional magnetism which came with the operas *Wozzeck* (1914-20) and *Lulu* (1928-35), and the *Lyric Suite for string quartet* (1925-26).

Unlike the serialists, *Hindemith* (1895-1963) wrote music firmly based on tonality. His buoyancy, rhythmic drive, and effective counterpoint have overcome the public's initial hostility. His best known work is *Mathis der Maler* (1934) for orchestra. Among his piano works are *Kammermusik No. 2 (Op. 36 No. 1)* which is a concerto for piano and 12 solo instruments, *Suite 1922* with suggestions of jazz, and *Ludus Tonalis* (studies in counterpoint for the piano).

Unrivalled among his contemporaries, *Stockhausen* (1928-   ) along with the Frenchman, Boulez, has written more piano compositions than any other post World War II composer. Like Liszt, he has enlarged the standards and range of virtuoso performance with demands for extreme speed and agility. His variety of touch and attack creates dynamics ranging from ppp to fff–and beyond. With cluster chords, he defines their boundaries and irregular shape as accurately as traditional scales and arpeggios. The *Klavierstücke I-XI* form the body of his compositions for piano solo. Stockhausen has also composed a large number of electronic works which incorporate tape, tam-tam, Hammond organ, feed-back, and short-wave receiver.

French School

Founder of the French harpsichord school, *Jacques Champion de Chambonnières* (1602-1672) published two books of *Piéces de Clavecin* in which he set forth the elegant harpsichord style of decorative trills, turns, and mordants. He was followed half a century later by *François Couperin* (called *Le Grand,* 1668-1733), a composer, organist, and the most distinguished musician of his family. He was a virtuoso harpsichordist and published over 230 compositions grouped in *ordres* (suites) in 4 volumes called *Piéces de Clavecin.* His famous instruction book, *L'Art de toucher le clavecin,* was a strong influ-

---

[3]   These terms are explained in Chapter on *Modernism and Contemporary Trends.*

ence on Bach's harpsichord style.   Other contemporaries of Couperin were *Marchand* (1669-1732), also a harpsichord composer and virtuoso; *Rameau* (1683-1764), the author of an important treatise on harmony, *Traité de l'harmonie* (1722); and *Daquin* (1694-1772), a prodigy organist and harpsichord composer. Rameau composed in many fields and through his operas and ballets established himself as *Lully's* (1632-1687) successor in French opera. He was also a harpsichordist and composed many works for the harpsichord which were published in 3 volumes in his lifetime and bear such imaginative titles as *Les Tendres Plaintes, Le Rappel des oiseaux, L'Indifférence, La Timide,* and *L'Indiscrète.*

These composers were the last of the major French harpsichord writers. It was not until the era of Romanticism that French music returned to a comparable flowering. With Romanticism, French music blossomed under the influences of Chopin, Berlioz, and Franck. Chopin, although not French, lived in Paris and wrote with an elegance and poetry compatible with the French spirit. *Hector Berlioz* (1803-1869), though not a pianist or composer for the piano, influenced his contemporaries through vivid operatic, orchestral, and vocal writing. The Belgian, Franck, lived in Paris from his 22nd year and inspired his pupils, particularly d'Indy, as a teacher of "pure" music.

The native French Romantic composers who followed Chopin, Berlioz, and Franck at the end of the 19th Century formed what might be called a "school" because of their mutual feeling for restraint, lyricism, and Franch *clarté. Camille Saint-Saëns* (1835-1921) in the *Variations on a Theme by Beethoven for 2 Pianos* and *5 Concertos* for solo piano, and *Paul Dukas* (1865-1935) in the orchestra scherzo *L'Apprenti sorcier* and in the *Variations, Interlude et Finale* for piano showed continuing traits of Romanticism. *Gabriel Fauré* (1845-1924) was slow to win recognition but is now regarded as one of France's major composers. His song cycles, chamber music, and piano pieces are poetic and profound. Among the piano works are the *Ballade* for piano and orchestra, *Theme and Variations Op. 73,* and many distinguished *Impromptus, Nocturnes, Barcarolles,* and *Préludes.* Fauré taught two prolific piano composers, *Charles Koechlin* (1867-1951) and *Florent Schmitt* (1870-1958) both of whom wrote with facile charm for piano solo and duet.

With varied interests in education and schools of composition, *Vincent d'Indy* (1851-1931), a Franckist, was able to combine Romanticism with the emerging neo-classicism in his *Symphony on a French Mountain Air* for piano and orchestra (1886). Standing between Romanticism and neo-classicism, d'Indy created music bonded to the concept of timbre. The concept of timbre became an absorbing concern for Debussy[4] and opened doors to the new sounds of Impressionism. D'Indy's and Debussy's contemporary, *Ravel* (1875-1937) combined the sonorities of Impressionism with keyboard virtuosity, incorporating savagery *(La valse* for orchestra), jazz (the 2 *Concertos* for Piano, one of which is for the left hand), and neo-classicism *(Valses nobles et sentimentales,* and *Tombeau de Couperin).* Additional works for piano include *Jeaux d'eau, Sonatine, Miroirs,* and *Gaspard de la Nuit.*

A contemporary of Debussy and Ravel, *Eric Satie* (1866-1925) added variety to the

---

[4]   See chapter on Debussy.

concept of neo-classicism and created simple, impersonal, and thinly scored music in a large number of piano solos with such witty titles as *3 Pieces in the Shape of a Pear* (1903). At this time, a group of composers came together who called themselves *Les Six*. Although *Durey* and *Tailleferre* soon dropped from sight and *Auric* devoted himself to music for films, *Milhaud, Honegger,* and *Poulenc* became the leaders of the modern French school. Always a champion of Les Six, Satie continued his influence by writing unaffected music, free from sentimentality. His move away from Romanticism and concern with timbre led to music of satire, with a touch of jazz, irony, and humor. *Milhaud* (1892-1974), in *Trois Rag Caprices for Piano* and *Création du Monde* for ballet, explored the powerful energizing idiom of jazz, syncopation and polyrhythms, while *Honegger* (1892-1955) expressed the mechanical power of turbines and dynamos in *Pacific 231* for orchestra. *Poulenc* (1899-1963) wrote with wit and incisiveness. His bitter-sweet, quasi cabaret melodies were a reflection of his own melancholy. The music of these composers conveyed (as music had not before) the hunger and nervous excitement of a world overstimulated and disillusioned by war.

With the second World War, ideas were shared and styles observed in France and elsewhere through the instant communication made possible by electronic developments. Electronic music, new sounds made by electrical impulse, caught the fancy of experimentally minded composers. It came to fruition in *Poème électronique* of *Edgar Varèse* (1883-1965), a work composed for the most part directly on tape. Another Frenchman, *Pierre Schaeffer* (1910-   ) coined the term *concrète* in 1948 for compositions which replaced traditional instruments and the human voice with assemblages of recorded sounds either natural or man-made. His first work in this genre was *Étude aux chemins de fer* made from the sounds of a railway train.

Olivier Messiaen (1908-   ) has returned to unmistakeable pianism without distortion or additives in his enormous *Catalogue d'oiseaux* (1956-58). A deep religious mysticism distinguishes all his work. He has created a range of new keyboard color and new rhythmic combinations and extensions which have influenced another innovative serialist, *Pierre Boulez. Boulez* (1925-   ), the most important French composer of the avant-garde, studied with Messiaen and says of his own creed, "I think that music should be collective magic and hysteria." To this end he has experimented with musique concrète and combined it with electronic sounds. His use of serial technique (applied to dynamics, pitch, rhythms, and sonority) is seen in his first 2 *Sonatas for Piano* (1946 and 1947) and *Structures for 2 Pianos* (1951-52); he used indeterminacy in the *3rd Sonata* of 1957. His most ambitious work to date is *Pli selon pli* for soprano and orchestra. It is a 5 part portrait of Mallarmé developed from earlier improvisations. The 5 parts are sung or declaimed in a variety of ways. With the Greek Xenakis (1922-   ), German Stockhausen, and Messaien, Boulez stands with the giants of the late 20th Century avant garde.

Italian School

The writing of opera has been an Italian specialty since *Monteverdi* (1567-1643) wrote his *Il combattimento di Tancredi e Clorinda* in 1624. His contemporary, *Frescobaldi* (1583-1643), used the vocal forms of the *motet* and *madrigal* but achieved his greatest celebrity as an organist and composer for the organ. *Alessandro Scarlatti* (1660-1725), father of the harpsichord composer Domenico, continued Monteverdi's development of Italian opera and was considered the founder of the Neapolitan school. His contemporary, the great Venetian *Vivaldi* (1678-1741), wrote not only many operas (around 50 are extant) but also an enormous body of church and instrumental music still used today. With interest in opera and instrumental music, *Domenico Scarlatti* (1685-1757) wrote operas for the Queen of Poland's private theatre in Rome as well as 550 single movement harpsichord sonatas which included technical innovations[5] and foreshadowed the development of sonata form. *Salieri* (1750-1825), the teacher of Beethoven, Schubert, and Liszt, wrote over 40 operas, although his distinguished pupils were all primarily instrumental composers (except for Beethoven with his single opera, *Fidelio*). *Muzio Clementi* (1752-1832), a contemporary of Salieri, conducted opera even as he wrote over 100 piano sonatas and his *Gradus ad Parnassum* studies. The line of operatic succession from Monteverdi was strong, and the 19th and first half of the 20th Centuries produced composers whose works continue to fill the Western world's opera houses–Rossini, Donizetti, Bellini, Verdi, Leoncavallo, Mascagni, Puccini, and Montemezzi.

One of the first 19th Century Italian composers to awaken his country to instrumental developments in other countries was *Sgambati* (1841-1914). As a pianist and conductor, he introduced German classics to Italian audiences. He wrote chamber music, two symphonies, a piano concerto, and piano pieces, but they have not held a place in the continuing piano repertoire. Twenty years later, *Busoni* (1866-1924) established a compelling style of grandeur and poetry in his own playing and in transcriptions of Bach's works in particular. His late style, seen in the *Elegies* for piano (1907), was prophetic of the 20th Century composers Webern, Bartók, and Messiaen.

With *Respighi* (1879-1936), *Malipiero* (1882-1973), and *Casella* (1883-1947) it was time to challenge the "tyranny" of the formidable operatic composers and bring the Italian gift for instrumental music also into the open. Respighi studied at the beginning of his career with Rimsky-Korsakov in Russia and later with Bruch in Germany. His music is based on classical forms but shows the influence of Rimsky's brilliant and colorful scoring. He wrote operas, ballets, orchestral works *(Pines of Rome,* 1924) and a *Fantasy* for piano (1907). Malipiero and Casella took part in the revival of interest in Renaissance and Baroque music through their editions of Monteverdi's and Vivaldi's music. A prolific composer in all fields, Malipiero composed concertos for piano and individual pieces for piano in which he did away with both key and time signatures. After 1920, Casella identified himself with neo-classicism. His piano pieces include

[5]   Rapid repetitions, crossed hands, double-note passages, etc.

Scarlattiana for piano and orchestra (1926) and two series entitled *In the style of...* (1911-13, 2nd series collab. Ravel). A pupil of Malipiero and Casella, *Rieti* (1898-   ) wrote ballet and film music somewhat under the influence of Stravinsky and Les Six. His piano works include two piano concertos, a concerto for 2 pianos, and piano pieces.

The three avant-garde composers *Maderna* (1920-1973), *Nono* (1924-   ), and *Berio* (1925-   ) have used serialism, electronic sounds, and prerecorded tape as basic writing techniques for their extraordinarily complex music. Maderna, a pupil of Malipiero, and Nono, a pupil of Maderna, have preserved a measure of Italian lyricism in works which include theatre pieces, instrumental and vocal works, operas, concertos, and pieces for tape. Among them are Maderna's composite pieces *Dimensioni* and *Hyperion,* and Nono's *Epitaffio per Garcia Lorca* for chorus and orchestra. Berio, who founded the electronic studio at the Italian Radio, explored the additional technique of *collage,* incorporating fragments from other composers and superimposing them on his own music. He has written a two-piano concerto and shorter works for piano. His large list of compositions includes works for the theatre, orchestra, voice, and tape. The current avant-garde has brilliant champions in these composers who are committed to experimentation in a scientific age. By the 21st Century, we should know the extent and durability of their probing.

English School

As early as the 15th Century, organs were built and choirs were founded in English cathedrals and monasteries, while Oxford and Cambridge first conferred musical degrees in 1463. A century later, under King Henry VIII (d. 1547), a musician himself, the *Chapel Royal* (a group of clergy and musicians whose records go back to 1135) increased its ranks to 70. Under Elizabeth (as Queen from 1558-1603) and James I (as King from 1603-1625), the Chapel's musicians included Tye, Tallis, Byrd, Gibbons, Morley, Tomkins, and Bull, all either organists or virginal players. They developed the English *Madrigal* and laid the foundations of English keyboard music. Their numerous keyboard works are collected in the 17th Century *Fitzwilliam Virginal Book* (297 pieces) and in the *Parthenia,* printed in 1611, which contains 21 keyboard pieces by Byrd, Gibbons, and Bull. Somewhat later, *Henry Purcell* (1659-1695) became ''Composer in Ordinary'' to the Chapel Royal and was recognized as one of England's greatest composers. His works include the opera, *Dido and Aeneas,* stage spectacles, incidental music, many choral works and songs, instrumental works, and numerous harpsichord suites. After Purcell, English clavier music of the 17th-18th Centuries was overshadowed by developments in France, Italy, and Germany.

With the extension of the oratorio and opera from the early motet and madrigal, English composers in the 18th Century began to develop their particular feeling for choral music. This gift continued through the 19th Century, surpassing more modest accomplishments in keyboard music.

One of the first English composers of piano solos as well as sacred works was

William Sterndale Bennett (1816-1875). He won recognition from Mendelssohn and from Schumann who dedicated the *Symphonic Études* to him. *Sir Charles Hubert H. Parry* (1848-1918) was in the forefront of British composers in his lifetime and was the scholarly writer of *Evolution of the Art of Music*. For piano he wrote a single *Concerto* (1879-80) and individual piano pieces. Parry's Irish contemporary, *Sir Charles Villiers Stanford* (1852-1924) was at his strongest in works for voices. He was a gifted teacher whose pupils included Vaughan Williams, Bliss, Ireland, and Holst. *Sir Edward Elgar* (1857-1934), one of the most prolific and distinguished English composers of choral and orchestral music, is best known for his choral setting of *The Dream of Gerontius,* the *Enigma Variations* for orchestra, and the *Pomp and Circumstance* marches. His piano compositions are the least important of his works.

In contrast to the 19th and early 20th Century choral and instrumental composers, *Tobias Matthay* (1858-1945) concerned himself primarily with the piano. He gave up his career as a concert pianist to teach and write books on the piano. His method was based on the psychological as well as physical aspects of piano playing. One of his eminent pupils was Dame Myra Hess, a distinguished international pianist who played valiantly in public concerts in London's National Gallery during World War II.

With *Sir Arnold Bax* (1883-1953), English music found a superior pianist who wrote fluently and expressively for the piano–both solo and chamber music. His piano works include 4 *Sonatas* (1910, 1919, 1926, and 1932). *Gustav Holst* (1874-1934) and *Ralph Vaughan Williams* (1872-1958) added impetus to English music of the 20th Century through original and visionary choral and orchestral writing. Holst is best known for *The Planets* for orchestra, but he also wrote 4 operas, many choral compositions, and a few piano pieces, such as *Chrissemas Day in the Morning Op. 46 No. 1* (1926). Vaughan Williams wrote many works in almost every genre combining modal harmonies characteristic of folk song (he was a folk song collector) with the French influences of Debussy, and of Ravel, with whom he studied. His many works include the opera, *Riders to the Sea* (1925-32), 9 symphonies, *The Lark Ascending* (Romance for violin and orchestra), *Serenade to Music* for chorus and orchestra, and a small number of piano pieces including the *Introduction and Fugue* for 2 pianos.

On his return to England from the first World War, *Sir Arthur Bliss* (1891-1975) brought to English music the influence of Stravinsky and of Poulenc and Auric of the French avant garde. His works are lively and often humorous, like the film music, *Things to Come,* and the ballet, *Checkmate*. His *Piano Concerto* for the N.Y. World's Fair of 1939 is cleverly cast in the grand manner of the late 19th Century. *Sir Michael Tippett* (1905-   ), one of England's most distinguished composers, now in his 70s, has developed his music in three periods, the early lyrical style, a dramatic middle style, and a fusion of the first two plus a tighter control of form. The oratorio *A Child of Our Time* represents the first period; the opera *King Priam, Concerto for Orchestra,* and the *2nd Piano Sonata,* the second period; and finally the *Piano Concerto* of 1953-5 and *3rd Piano Sonata* of 1972-3. His works are not only lyrical but technically sophisticated.

Benjamin Britten (Lord Britten) of Aldeburgh (1913-1976) ranks as one of Britain's greatest composers. He was essentially a vocal composer with 13 operas and distinguished song cycles to his credit. He never abandoned tonality and was a conservative of striking imagination. His originality won the respect of radicals and the public alike. His piano works composed early in his career do not reflect his extraordinary gifts shown later in the *War Requiem* and the opera, *Peter Grimes.*

Thea Musgrave (1928-   ), the Scottish composer, achieves expressiveness through use of serialism, jazz *(Clarinet Concerto,* 1968), and prerecorded tape. She is best known for her opera, *Mary, Queen of Scots* (1976).

One of the most important of England's avant garde composers, *Peter Maxwell Davies* (1934-   ), has specialized in unusual sounds which include combining medieval music with his own sometimes angular idiom and using the 1920's fox-trot rhythm for special effects. He has written 4 operas including *Taverner* (1970), 2 symphonies, a large amount of vocal music with orchestra, chamber music with piano, and a small number of piano pieces which include *5 Little Pieces* and *Stevie's Ferry to Hoy.* Among his theatre pieces is *Miss Donnithorne's Maggot* for one singer and an ensemble of 4 metronomes, football rattle, bosun's whistle, and leather rubbed on glass. If title and subject matter seem odd, they can only be compared to others of this free wheeling generation.

American School

Long after Germany, Austria, France, Italy, and England had established musical traditions, America began her fledgling career. Her first native pianist-composer, *Louis Moreau Gottschalk* (1829-1869), had ties with Europe; he studied in Paris and was praised by Chopin at his piano debut of 1844. He composed 2 symphonies, 2 operas, and piano pieces such as *The Dying Poet* which emphasized virtuosity over deeper musical feeling. He was followed by four pioneer American composers, three of whom studied in Germany but left their stamp on American training and style–*John Knowles Paine (1839-1906), Arthur William Foote* (1853-1937), *George Whitefield Chadwick* (1854-1931), and *Horatio William Parker* (1863-1919). Paine was the teacher of *John Alden Carpenter (Adventures in a Perambulator* for orchestra, 1915), an organist, and composer of 2 operas, 2 symphonies, choral and chamber works. Foote founded the American Guild of Organists and composed orchestral suites and piano and organ pieces as well as vocal works. Chadwick, also an organist and director of the New England Conservatory, wrote an opera, 3 symphonies, and 5 string quartets. Parker was an early teacher of Charles Ives at Yale. He composed oratorios, 2 operas, a symphony, chamber music, organ pieces, and songs. These well-trained composers were beginning to establish a valid American voice, but it was their somewhat younger contemporary, *Edward MacDowell* (1861-1908), who became America's first widely recognized American composer. Like his predecessors, he was trained in the German Romantic tradition, but combined it with his own strongly individual pianistic expression to catch the fancy of 19th Century European and American audiences. The only woman composer of this period was *Mrs. H.H.A. Beach* (1867-1944). She wrote the *Mass in E flat* and *Gaelic Symphony,* and as a piano soloist gave distinction to her own *Concerto for Piano.*

MacDowell's near contemporary *Charles Ives* (1874-1954) quickly shed the cloak of Romanticism and Horatio Parker's teaching at Yale to start on his way toward being "one of the most extraordinary and individual figures in the history of Western music."[6] Several years after graduation from college, he and a friend formed a successful insurance agency. He divided his time between music and business, an incongruity which seemed to apply to his music in its continually surprising combinations: the straightforward with the sophisticated; hymns with jazz; tonality with atonality; double tonality; and whole tone scales, 12 note row, and tone clusters all at the same time. With a typically original approach to the keyboard, Ives disregarded the limitations of the pianist's two hands and ten fingers. For chordal effects he simply used his arms or borrowed another pianist's hand. His piano pieces include the celebrated *Concord Sonata* (1909-15) with solos for viola and flute, *20 Studies* for piano including *Some South-Paw Pitching,* and *3 Quarter-Tone Piano Pieces* for 2 pianos. He also composed 4 symphonies, many choral works, and a variety of chamber music.

Henry Cowell (1897-1965) and *John Cage* (1912-   ) breathed the same heady avant garde air as Ives and followed him as musical radicals who placed experimentation first in the order of their composition. Cowell in the 1920's used tone clusters played with arms, hands, and elbows and created harmonic *areas* in place of actual chords. He drew sounds from the piano strings themselves by stroking and plucking and muting them with cardboard, metal wedges, rubber bands, hatpins, and tacks. He was a co-inventor with Theremin of an early electronic instrument which reproduced complicated rhythmic combinations. He was also one of the first composers to introduce indeterminacy into music by letting the performers assemble and perform the individual parts as they chose. In *Hymn-and-Fuguing Tunes* for orchestra he expressed early American musical culture. Cowell's many piano pieces, especially the *Banshee* and *Aeolian Harp,* explored controversial pianistic approaches. Cage furthered Cowell's use of the piano frame and pedals to create resonance. He also established aleatory methods where the musical results were not planned but were left to the discretion of the performers. They might choose as they liked from the composer's instructions. Sounds of "chance" like ringing a bell, maintaining stretches of silence, and even crossing the stage were taken seriously. Cage's many compositions included the devices of tape, prepared piano (materials wedged between the strings), variable speed phonograph turntables, and radios.

A number of other important composers also shared roughly the first half of America's innovative 20th Century. *Carl Ruggles* (1876-1971), a craggy individualist, studied with Paine from 1903-1907 and used atonality long before it was generally accepted as a method. Among other compositions, he wrote *Men and Mountains* (1924) and *Sun Treader* (1931-32) for orchestra; *Polyphonic Composition for 3 Pianos* (1940); and *Evocations* (1937-44) for solo piano. *Charles Griffes* (1884-1920) was influenced by

---

[6] The *Concise Oxford Dictionary of Music,* Third Edition, 1980, p. 323.

French Impressionism, but he also used Japanese and Native American themes and combined them with polyrhythms and polytonality. *Wallingford Riegger* (1885-1961) used atonality and contrapuntal forms combined with strong rhythmic drive in a variety of compositions, symphonies, songs, chamber music, concertos, and piano pieces. *Douglas Moore* (1893-1969) studied with Parker and was steeped in American legend which inspired his operas, *The Devil and Daniel Webster* (1939) and the *Ballade of Baby Doe* (1956). *Walter Piston* (1894-1976) was the author of 3 important text books: *Harmony; Counterpoint;* and *Orchestration.* He studied in Paris with Boulanger and later became a professor of music at Harvard. He wrote 8 symphonies, concertos including a piano *Concertino* (1937), and chamber music using the piano. He is perhaps best known for his ballet, *The Incredible Flutist.*

Two composers who became tireless champions of 20th Century music, and music by American composers, are *Virgil Thomson* (1896-　　) and *Howard Hanson* (1896-1981). Thomson studied in Paris with Boulanger, associated with Les Six, and was influenced by Debussy and Satie. He was music critic of the N.Y. *Herald Tribune* from 1940-1954. He has written film scores, operas *(Four Saints in 3 Acts* to a libretto by Gertrude Stein, 1928), chamber music, songs, and 4 piano sonatas. Hanson won the American Prix de Rome in 1921 and returned to become director of the Eastman School of Music in Rochester, N.Y., for 40 years. He was responsible for festivals in Rochester which saw the performance of hundreds of works by American composers. His compositions are Romantic and tonal. They include 6 symphonies and an opera, *Merry Mount* (1934).

To Hanson in particular, as a sponsor of American music, must be added the names of *Ruth Crawford* (1901-1953) and *Elie Siegmeister* (1909-　　). Crawford transcribed several thousand American folk songs, wrote piano accompaniments for 300 of them, and composed among other works 9 piano *Préludes* (1926). Siegmeister studied in Paris with Boulanger and returned to study at the Juilliard School in New York. He founded the American Ballad Singers in 1930 and through them was active in the promotion of American folk music and the use of folk themes in serious musical composition. He has written an opera, the *Plough and the Stars* (1963), 5 symphonies, concertos, choral works, chamber music, and 2 piano sonatas.

George Gershwin (1898-1937) occupies an unusual and solitary place in American music. His early formal training was sketchy. He worked as a pianist for a publisher of popular music and for 14 years wrote successful musicals for Broadway. With this background, he created a new genre, concert works made up of jazz idioms.[7] The first example of this was *Rhapsody in Blue* for piano and orchestra written in 1924. His gift for melody has made many of his songs (he wrote hundreds) classics in themselves, creating a kind of 20th Century folk song tradition. This element is strong in his well known opera, *Porgy and Bess* (1934-35). His four works for piano and orchestra include the *Rhapsody in Blue, Piano Concerto in F* (1925), *Second Rhapsody* (1931), and *I Got*

---

[7]　Scott Joplin (1868-1917), a black American composer, preceded Gershwin in the area of "popular" music through his composition of the first ragtime opera, *Treemonisha* (publ. 1911). The popularity of Joplin's music surged again in the mid-1970's.

Rhythm Variations (1934). For solo piano he composed 3 *Préludes* in 1926 which have been transcribed by Heifetz for violin and piano.

Four of America's major living composers–Sessions, Copland, Carter, and Crumb–have worked or are working within recognized musical forms, i.e., the sonata, quartet, concerto, symphony, etc. But they are finding new voices for these traditional forms in their extensions and transformations of music's basic materials of melody, harmony, and rhythm. They are re-evaluating and refining piano color, avoiding freakishness, and composing piano works whose structure is comprehensible. *Roger Sessions* (1896-   ), described as "constructively eclectic," has composed a range of knotty and serious music from opera through symphonies, chamber and choral works to piano. He is a dedicated teacher with influence spreading to his pupils, Babbitt, Imbrie, and Diamond. His piano works include 3 *Sonatas* (1930, 1946, 1965).

Aaron Copland (1900-   ) is the first important American nationalist composer to be recognized outside the U.S. He studied in Paris with Boulanger and returned to the U.S. to compose in a style which incorporated jazz and the regional flavor of the West, Appalachia, and Mexico. His major piano works are the Schoenbergian *Piano Variations* of 1930, the *Piano Sonata* of 1939, and the *Fantasy* of 1957. He is well known for the ballets *Billy the Kid* and *Rodeo,* the opera *The Tender Land,* and the orchestral suite *El Salon Mexico.*

Elliott Carter (1908-   ) studied at Harvard with Walter Piston on a recommendation from Ives. Like Copland, he also studied in Paris with Boulanger. He has developed metric modulation which establishes a new tempo from a cross-rhythm within the old tempo giving the feeling of 2 tempos existing simultaneously. His music is uncompromising and intellectual. The *Sonata* for piano (1945-46) is an important creation, and the 3 *String Quartets* are possibly the most significant in this medium since Bartók. Carter's recent *Night Fantasies* for piano makes a distinguished addition to contemporary repertoire.

George Crumb's ideas (he was born in 1929) remain comprehensible, and his unusual pianistic effects are not quirky but poetic. His 1972 fantasy-pieces titled *Makrokosmos* use an amplified piano and are representative of his exploratory but listenable style.

America has come of age.

Russian School

The rich background of native folk music in Russia has furnished material for its major composers beginning with *Mikhail Glinka* (1804-1857) who created enthusiasm for national music in his opera, *A Life for the Czar.* He wrote a sextet for piano and strings and miscellaneous pieces for the piano. *Anton Rubinstein* (1829-94), later influenced by Western European music as well as his native Russian, founded the St. Petersburg Conservatory in 1862. He was a virtuoso performer and prolific but uncritical composer. His *Melody in F* is familiar to pianists, but he also wrote 5 piano concertos and other piano pieces. *Tchaikovsky* stands alone in 19th Century Russian music; he never identified himself with nationalism *per se* nor the Germanic influences of

Brahms or Wagner. He admired the French music of Bizet and Saint-Saëns, and had a life-long love for Mozart. His style combines delicacy with unrelenting emotionalism–particularly successful in the songs, ballets, orchestral works, and operas.

A group of nationalist composers called *The Five* (sometimes *The Mighty Handful)* ran counter to Rubinstein and Tchaikovsky and under the leadership of *Mily Balakirev (1837-1910)* developed a nationalist school. Balakirev wrote the virtuoso showpiece, *Islamey,* and other piano works in the same vein as well as a number of orchestral overtures and 3 symphonies. Other members of *The Five* were *Cesar Cui (1835-1918)* who was a prolific composer with nationalist ideas, and a witty prose writer who also composed songs and piano pieces; *Modest Mussorgsky (1839-1881)* whose *Pictures at an Exhibition* continues to fascinate listeners with its sharp color and rhythm; *Alexander Borodin (1833-1887)* who wrote the *Petite Suite* for piano in 1885 but is remembered for his (unfinished) opera *Prince Igor* and the tone poem *In the Steppes of Central Asia; Nikolay Rimsky-Korsakov (1844-1908)* who was a master of clear, colorful orchestration and in this capacity an influence on Stravinsky's *The Firebird.* He wrote a few piano pieces but is best known for his editing of 100 Russian folk songs, the opera *The Snow Maiden,* and *Sheherazade* for orchestra.

Outside the circle of *The Five,* were two students of Rimsky-Korsakov, *Anton Arensky (1861-1906)* and *Alexander Glazunov (1865-1936).* Arensky is known for the exceptionally attractive *Piano Trio in D minor,* the *Piano Concerto,* and many piano pieces. Glazunov, early in his life, came under the influence of Liszt and Wagner. After his years as Director of the St. Petersburg Conservatory, he left Russia to live in Paris. His music is colorfully Romantic and more cosmopolitan than nationalist. Among his piano works are the *Concerto in F minor Op. 92, 2 Sonatas Opp. 74* and *75,* and *Theme and Variations Op. 72.*

Alexander Skryabin (1872-1915) was a pupil of Arensky and a brilliant pianist who introduced many of his own works on concert tours. He originated the "mystic" chord, which was a series of 4ths producing extreme chromaticism, and used it in the 5th Symphony *Prometheus, The Poem of Fire* (1909) and in the 7th piano *Sonata.* He regarded his works as preparation for a "supreme ecstatic mystery" and in this vein wrote a large number of piano compositions, 10 *Sonatas,* 24 *Études,* 85 *Préludes,* and additional short pieces.

With *Sergey Rachmaninov (1873-1943)* the legend of Lisztian piano technique reasserted itself. *Rachmaninov* was one of the greatest of pianists who also wrote idiomatic and colorful music for the piano. The 4 piano concertos are an important part of the Romantic repertoire as are the *Rhapsody* on a *Theme of Paganini* for piano and orchestra and numerous *Préludes* and *Études tableaux* for piano solo.

Although *Igor Stravinsky (1882-1971)* seemed to wear many coats, he remained fundamentally himself–and he chose that self to be a sophisticated eclectic. His early years were concerned with the flamboyant music for Diaghilev's *Ballets Russes–The Firebird, Petroushka,* and *Rite of Spring.* After combining Russian folk rhythms and American jazz in the theatre piece *The Soldier's Tale,* he entered a neo-classical phase. The results of this period were the *Piano Concerto, Capriccio for Piano and Orchestra,* and the Hogarthian opera, *The Rake's Progress*. Stravinsky was one of the first to establish the piano as an instrument of the orchestra which he did in the *Symphony in 3 Movements* and *Petroushka*. After a period of interest in Baroque style, Stravinsky worked with serialism and atonality in the *Movements for Piano and Orchestra*. His final expression was in short, bare works of occasional religious form and feeling. Rhythm was the underlying element in all his work, leading perhaps to the enormous success of his ballets. His pleasure in childlike fun and sardonic humor showed itself in *Circus Polka* for piano, *Piano Rag-Music,* and *The Owl and the Pussycat* for violin and piano.

Sergey Prokofiev (1891-1953) was considered a member of the avant garde in his youth; he is now seen in a direct line from the colorful 19th Century nationalists. He combined sharp wit and dramatic incisiveness with innate lyricism to produce successful ballets, operas, symphonies, film music, and piano works. His 9 piano *Sonatas* and 5 *Concertos* for piano and orchestra are crucial to the 20th Century repertoire. *Peter and the Wolf,* a young people's guide to the orchestra, is in a bewitching class by itself. Prokofiev's piano style adds Lisztian virtuosity to the particular percussiveness pioneered by Bartók and Stravinsky.

Dimitry Shostakovich (1906-1975) was world famous at 20 through performances of his *1st Symphony*. Reflecting the temporary liberalism in post-Revolutionary Russia, Shostakovich studied the Western avant garde of Berg, Hindemith, and Krenek. To these studies he added the symphonic influence of Mahler and produced a personal style marked by emotional extremes of tragedy, bizarre wit, humor, and biting sarcasm. Political differences with the Stalinist regime affected his creativity, but in 1953 the appearance of his *10th Symphony* marked the final period of his career and the production of some of his finest works. As one of the 20th Century's great composers, Shostakovich wrote 15 symphonies, 15 quartets, 2 operas, ballets, songs, and film music. These works show mastery of form and technical skill which have overshadowed the piano works in vividness and tension. The piano compositions include 2 concertos, 2 sonatas, numerous préludes in addition to the *24 Préludes and Fugues Op. 87,* 10 *Aphorisms,* and 7 *Dances of the Dolls.*

Spanish School

No mention can be made of Spanish music without reference to the guitar as a musical source. Although musicologists disagree about who "invented" the guitar, it is generally accepted that *Vicente Espinel* in the 16th Century made the guitar a popular instrument with both the upper and lower classes in Spain. It soon became known in Italy and France, and by the end of the 18th Century was fashionable on the European continent and in England.[8]

---

[8] Indicative of the international interest in the guitar, the Italian, Mauro Giuliani (1781-1828), lived in Vienna for 12 years and wrote over 200 guitar pieces, including a concerto published in Vienna by Diabelli. The Italian violin virtuoso, Paganini, wrote quartets for guitar and strings, and his later French contemporary, Berlioz, studied the guitar in his early years.

A few Spanish composers of the 18th Century also wrote for instruments other than the guitar. *Soler* (1729-83), a contemporary of Haydn and Johann Christian Bach, wrote over 70 harpsichord sonatas. His contribution to classical style stood alone for over 100 years.

Meanwhile, *Fernando Sor* (1780-1839), a guitar virtuoso, performed widely and composed for the guitar. He was followed by other Spanish composers, *Tarrega, Rodrigo, Turina, Albeniz,* and *Falla* who reached into the 20th Century to establish the guitar as a serious musical instrument. These composers have found a gifted and enduring interpreter in *Andres Segovia* (1893-   ) who stands out from many excellent colleagues, including his protégé, Julian Bream, as the instrument's greatest contemporary exponent.

At roughly the same time, i.e. the 19th into the 20th Century, Albeniz and Falla, along with their countryman *Granados,* brought Spanish *piano* music into the mainstream. All three endowed their compositions with the flair for rhythmic and melodic idioms and national feeling for folk music now associated with the music of Spain. Their influential teacher and leader was *Felipe Pedrell* (1841-1922) who expounded Spanish musical nationalism in his musicological writings. *Isaac Albeniz* (1860-1909) composed 12 celebrated piano pieces titled *Iberia* (4 volumes) under the influence of the French Romantic writing of Fauré and Dukas. The virtuoso pianist, *Enrique Granados* (1867-1916), wrote poetic piano pieces as well as orchestral suites and operas, the best known of which is *Goyescas,* an opera scored from the piano pieces of the same title. *Manuel de Falla* (1876-1946) was a prize winning pianist and a fluent composer of operas, ballets, chamber music, and orchestral works. His major work for piano solo is *Fantasia Bética* (Andalusia) dedicated to Arthur Rubinstein, but he actually is better known for the flamboyant *Ritual Fire Dance*[9] featured in many of Rubinstein's programs. His most ambitious work for piano and orchestra is *Nights in the Gardens of Spain* which took 7 years to complete.

Joaquin Turina (1882-1949) studied composition in France with d'Indy, but his own composing retained the spirit of Spanish folk music. His works are pleasant if not incisive. Another Spanish composer influenced by French teaching was the Catalan, *Frederico Mompou* (1893-   ), who wrote mainly miniature piano pieces in a "primitive" style without bar lines, key signatures, or cadences. Among them are the *Quatre Melodies* of 1926. *Carlos Surinach* (1915-   ) studied in Spain, Germany, and the U.S. where he became a citizen in 1959. Along with a small number of ballets and orchestral works, he has written a *Concertino* for piano.

With few exceptions, Spanish composers have not contributed major ideas to the musical mainstream as have the French, German, and Italian schools. Rather, in smaller areas, their rhythmic and melodic characteristics and their national flavor have provided attractive ends in themselves. However, this traditional conception of Spanish music may be changing through the efforts of the composer and pianist, *Roberto Gerhard* (1896-1970) who although of Swiss parentage, identified himself with Spanish music, and later became an English citizen. He studied with Granados and Schoenberg

---

[9]   An arrangement by Falla from his ballet *El Amor Brujo.*

but in many of his early compositions used a basic idiom of distinctively Spanish melody and rhythm. After he settled in England in 1940, he at first combined Spanish flavor with tonality, bitonality, and serialism (the opera, *The Duenna*), but from 1952 on his work became completely individualized. In his 3rd symphony, *Collages* (1960), he experimented with electronic tape combined with orchestral sound. He wrote a considerable number of works including 2 operas, ballets *(Don Quixote)*, 4 symphonies and *Concerto for Orchestra*, chamber music with piano, a piano concerto, and a harpsichord concerto. Composers close to the style of Gerhard, including Mompou, are *Joaquin Homs*, also a serialist; *Xavier Monsalvatage* who combines familiar melodies with polyrhythms, as in his piano *Sonatine pour Yvette*; and the *Halffter* brothers, *Ernesto* and *Rodolfo*, who are tonal composers originally taught by Falla but influenced by Schoenberg.

Led by *Luis de Pablo* (1930-   ), important serialists *Blancafort* and *Cristóbal Halffter* (1930-   ), among others, are devoted to freeing Spanish music from folklore and all literary and philosophical ideas. The neo-classicism of Stravinsky and Hindemith has a special appeal to them as a way of achieving this goal.

Japanese School

Modern Japanese musical history began with the Meiji Restoration of 1868. At that time, European music came to Japan through military band performances and Protestant hymn singing. Two decades later, the Tokyo Music School was founded, followed by publication of the first musical journal in 1890. By 1900, the first European opera performance had taken place (a scene from Gounod's *Faust*) and individual piano, violin, and song recitals were popular.

Japan's leading composer of the early 1900's was *Kòsaku Yamada*, a German trained Romanticist. Following the first World War years, European influence switched to Impressionism in the works of *Seifú Yoshida* and *Michio Miyagi*. Miyagi (1894-1956) has been called the father of modern Japanese music. He was successful in creating a European style for traditional Japanese instruments–the *Biwa, Koto, Shakuhachi,* and *Shamisen*.

For many years after the Meiji Restoration, Japanese composers responded to three influences–Japanese traditional music (Buddhist, Shinto, and court[10]); Western traditional music; and international modern trends. The pull of traditional instrumental writing remained strong, but from 1915 to 1930 both Western-style music and contemporary trends were encouraged by visits to Japan from international composers and performers, Prokofiev, Kreisler, Heifetz, Godowsky, and Segovia.

By 1930, Japanese musicians were aware of the European avant garde, and in 1935, 16 composers formed an organization which became the Japanese branch of *I.S.C.M.*[11]

---

[10] This includes the theatrical and courtly genres of *Gagaku* (court), *Noh* (theatre), *Bunraku* (puppet theatre), and *Kabuki* (theatre).

[11] International Society for Contemporary Music.

Since 1945, the trend toward dodecaphony (a variation of the 12 note row) has involved the composers *Kunio Toda, Toru Takemitsu, Yoshio Mamiya,* and *Akira Miyoshi.* In 1953, musique concrète was brought to Japan, and two years later the *NHK Electronic Music* Studio opened in Tokyo.

At present, Japanese composers are often trained in Europe but continue to write for their traditional instruments. Folk songs made into arrangements by professional performers are a popular feature of contemporary music. Even though 20th Century Western music predominates in schools, broadcasts, and commercial enterprises, Japanese composers are preserving the identity of traditional Japanese music through the *Japanese Musicological Society.* The *Society* was formed in 1952 by *Yoshiyuki Kato* and by the mid-1970s listed nearly 1000 members.

The Japanese genius has in turn influenced Western music by its innovations in the field of educational philosophy. In 1933, *Shin'ichi Suzuki* formulated his method of violin teaching which has been applied to other stringed instruments, the flute, and the piano. It has many advocates and is known and used widely in Europe and North America.

Other Schools

Just as the art and architecture of Western Europe vary from country to country, so too the music exhibits qualities peculiar to each nation and area. The main schools have already been discussed; but there are also individual composers who, alone or with a few others, have left a mark on their country's musical progress.

A school of colorful *Czech* composers integrated national feeling into classical structures. Most famous among them were Smetana, Dvorák, Janaćek, and Martinu. *Bedrich Smetana* (1824-1884) was a concert pianist who wrote numerous piano pieces and the masterpiece of folk opera, *The Bartered Bride. Antonin Dvorák* (1841-1904), as Smetana's pupil, inherited Smetana's nationalist drive. He was a prolific and innately lyrical composer of operas, 9 symphonies, concertos, chamber music, songs, and piano pieces including the famous *Humoresque Op. 101 No. 7. Leos Janácek* (1854-1928) in his early career belonged to the world of Smetana and Dvorák but later developed his own extraordinary range of emotion through unusual spacing of chords of the 7th and 9th in numerous operas *(The Makropulos Affair),* orchestra and choral works, songs, and piano pieces. *Bohuslav Martinu* (1890-1959) composed imaginatively but with uneven results. He wrote 5 piano concertos for piano solo and one for 2 pianos.

In Greece, *Nikos Skalkottas* (1904-1949) combined the 12 note system with a feeling for Greek folk music in the *36 Greek Dances* for orchestra of 1933-36. He also wrote 3 piano concertos, the piano *Concertino in C,* and numerous suites, variations, canons, and études for piano. His later compatriot, *Iannis Xenakis* (1922-   ), a Romanian-born Greek now a French citizen, is an architect and mathematician as well as a composer. He has been influenced by the widely divergent styles of Honegger, Milhaud, Messiaen, and Cage. He uses electronics and traditional human forces in a "theory of games,'' somewhat aleatory yet controlled by the composer. He translates computer printouts into scores for conventional instruments or into electronic compositions. He has written for orchestra, ballet, theatre, chorus, tape, and ensemble with piano; also the *Symphonai* for piano and orchestra and the piano solo, *Herma.*

Karol Szymanowski (1882-1937) was the most eminent *Polish* composer after Chopin. While still a young man, he was championed by Arthur Rubinstein and the violinist, Paul Kochansky. His life-long admiration for Chopin showed itself in his nationalism and led, among other works, to his *Mazurek* for piano in 1925, *4 Polish Dances,* and the *Mazurkas* of Opp. *50* and *62.* He was influenced also by Debussy but experimented later with atonality, polytonality, microtones, and elaborate rhythms. In 1933, he toured as piano soloist in his *Symphonie Concertante. Krzysztof Penderecki* (1933-   ) was at one time influenced by Boulez. He continued as an avant garde composer experimenting with freakish sounds such as sawing wood, rustling paper, hissing, screeching, etc. He managed to put these effects to artistic use in his *St. Luke's Passion* of 1966 which was an instant success. He was written opera *(The Devils of Loudun),* orchestral works *(Threnody for the Victims of Hiroshima),* chamber music, and *Psalmus* for tape.

Two *Swiss* composers, born within two years of each other, *Arthur Honegger* (1892-1955) and *Frank Martin* (1890-1974), represent important aspects of the 20th Century. One of Les Six, Honegger demonstrated a many-sided genius–representational, neo-romantic, tonal, and dramatic. In addition to traditional genres, film and radio music, he wrote a concertino for piano and orchestra and chamber music with piano. Martin's works are contrapuntal, delicately colored, and expressive, with free use of the *12 note system* in later years. His works for piano include 2 concertos.

In *Finland, Jean Sibelius* (1865-1957) is considered the national voice of his country. He was influenced by Busoni, Tchaikovsky, and Mahler (Sibelius's style, however, was more concentrated and austere than Mahler's), with a flavor of Palestrina. His mastery of the orchestra shows in his 7 symphonies, but he also excelled in short orchestral forms *(Finlandia),* vocal music, and many piano pieces. Sibelius did not publish a note during the last 26 years of his life.

Liszt and Bartók are the giants of Hungarian music, and their influence is still a living force. Two countrymen, colleagues of Bartók, have provided important, if secondary, material for the mainstream of Hungarian music. *Ernö Dohnányi* (1877-1960) was an internationally known concert pianist. His music has national flavor, although less than that of Bartók or Kodály. He has written operas, 2 symphonies, *Variations on a Nursery Song* for piano and orchestra, chamber music, and piano pieces. *Zoltan Kodály* (1882-1967) became a folk song collector with Bartók, and with him formed an organization for the performance of contemporary music. Less advanced harmonically than Bartók's, Kodály's music won public acceptance through its conviction and melodic drive. His works include *Psalmus Hungaricus for Chorus and Orchestra,* the opera *Hary János, Variations on a Hungarian Folk Song* (the *Peacock*) for orchestra, many singing exercises, and dozens of works for children's voices as well as a method for teaching music.

The most prominent Dutch composer of his generation was *Willem Pijper* (1894-1947). He was a music critic, teacher, and composer of a limited number of works. These include 3 symphonies, 6 *Symphonic Epigrammata,* a piano concerto, 4 piano quartets, and chamber music.

Today the music of *Latin America* commands the serious attention of the musical world. Its flair for color and folk idiom, harnessed to advanced procedures, has attracted the respect of international composers and audiences. *Heitor Villa-Lobos (Brazil, 1887-1959)* was influenced by the Russian nationalists, by Stravinsky, Strauss, Milhaud, and the pianist Arthur Rubinstein who performed his music. He was a Romantic melodist, and his many compositions (9 *Bachianas Brasileiras* for orchestra and different instrumental combinations, *14 Chôros* for orchestra and different instrumental combinations, 17 string quartets, and 12 symphonies) suggest Brazil through their color and rhythm. Villa-Lobos also wrote 5 piano concertos and piano pieces which include *Suite Infantil* and *Prole do Bebê.* For the guitar, he wrote 12 *Études* and 15 *Préludes. Carlos Chavez (Mexico, 1899-1978)* was a composer, conductor, and educator associated with the National Conservatory of Mexico and the Mexican National Institute of Fine Arts. Essentially a Mexican nationalist, he rarely used actual folk material. The *Chilean* composer, *Domingo Santa Cruz* (1899-   ), also an educator, is dean of the Santiago National Conservatory, vice-rector of Chile University, and founder of leading Chilean musical institutions, including the Bach Society and National Symphony concerts. *Alberto Ginastera* (1916-1983) has founded various music schools in *Argentina* including the *Centre for Advanced Music Studies* in Buenos Aires. Until about 1958, he wrote in a national idiom and then adopted serialism and the use of microtones and aleatory rhythm. His operas, particularly *Bomarzo,* have received general recognition. His works for piano include 2 piano concertos, a piano sonata, and a piano quintet with strings.

9 | ENCORE

Those of us who are making and enjoying music today share actively in the last 300 years of musical development. Bringing this development to the threshold of the 21st Century, composers, teachers and virtuosos continue to create a steadily evolving piano repertoire; contemporary ideas are exchanged between individuals and international organizations; the harpsichord, respected forerunner of the piano, comes full circle as an enduring keyboard resource.

Composers, Teachers, Virtuosos: A Brief Encounter

The mutual needs of composer and pianist are obvious: without one, there would be no music; without the other, the music would live only on the printed page. But composing and performing do not remain static. Musical ideas and styles change for the composer, while innovations in structure modify the potential of the instrument. Herein lies the pianist's and the teacher's challenge.

The early harpsichords which supported the intentions of Bach and Handel were followed by the early pianos of Mozart and Muzio Clementi. Adopting the Viennese piano in mid-career, Mozart became the first of the great pianists. Clementi chose the heavier English piano for his specific legato approach. Beethoven also endorsed the English piano and used it widely in his concerts. Composers who were performers as well, flourished in Beethoven's time and took advantage of the mechanical growth of the instrument. These were Carl Czerny, Johann Nepomuk Hummel, Friedrich Kalkbrenner, the Irishman John Field, and the German-Bohemian Ignaz Moscheles. With

Carl Maria von Weber, they helped to form a kind of bridge in performance style from the refinement of the Classical era to the emotional liberation of the Romantic.

Franz Liszt was the epitome of Romanticism, the most extraordinary teacher and virtuoso the piano world has known. His contemporaries, Ferdinand Hiller, Hans von Bülow, and Sigismond Thalberg (Liszt's greatest rival) all lived under the shadow, if not the inspiration, of his pervading genius. A few of his illustrious pupils were the young Carl Tausig (who died at 30), Eugen d'Albert, Moriz Rosenthal, Alexander Siloti, and Sophie Menter. It was not until the appearance of the Polish-born Theodor Leschetitsky that piano instruction found a teacher of Liszt's importance and magnetism.

Born within a few years of Liszt, Felix Mendelssohn, Frédéric Chopin, and Clara Schumann made their individual and controlled styles clear among many Romantic pianists crowding the scene. The latter were frequently regarded as salonists and showmen–Alkan, Henry Litolff, Adolf von Henselt, Henri Herz, Louis Moreau Gottschalk, William Sterndale Bennett, Alexander Dreyschock, Ferdinand Hiller, and Stephen Heller.

Following Liszt, piano teaching went into the hands of Leschetitsky, Antoine Marmontel of the Paris Conservatory, Louis Diémer, Marmontel's successor, and Isidor Philipp. Among them, these men trained generations of pianists: Leschetitsky (Paderewski, Ignaz Friedman, Ossip Gabrilowitsch, Artur Schnabel); Marmontel (Debussy); Diémer (Alfred Cortot, E. Robert Schmitz, Robert Casadesus); Philipp (Guiomar Novaes). Saint-Saëns, an eminent composer, was not a pianist as such but was one of the first to make recordings.

Pianists of the last part of the 19th Century who were heralding the coming changes of the 20th were the stupendous Liszt performer, Ferrucio Busoni, and a group of Russians, Annette Essipoff, Anton Rubinstein, Vladimir de Pachmann, Josef Lhevinne and his fellow student at the Moscow Conservatory Sergey Rachmaninov, and Alexander Siloti. Mauritz Rosenthal who was Polish and his Hungarian teacher Rafael Joseffy were two of the finest pianists of the 19th Century, combining virtuosity with poetry. Josef Hofmann and Harold Bauer, the first Polish-born, the second English-born, settled in America, Hofmann as one of the greatest players of Chopin and Bauer as an interpreter of Beethoven and of French music.

German pianists of the first half of the 20th century had an abundance of varied gifts. Artur Schnabel became famous for his scholarly Beethoven and Schubert interpretations. Paul Wittgenstein lost his right arm in World War I but went on to commission and perform left hand concertos by Ravel, Richard Strauss, Prokofiev, and Benjamin Britten. Wilhelm Backhaus recorded most of the Beethoven Sonatas after his 80th birthday. Walter Gieseking was renowned for his playing of Debussy and Ravel and his ability to control gradations of pianissimo. Edward Steuermann was a specialist in the Viennese atonalists.

Women have graced and stimulated the piano field as performers and teachers since Clara Schumann. She was followed by Sophie Menter, Annette Essipoff, Fannie Bloomfield Zeisler, Teresa Carreño, Ethel Leginska, Elly Ney, Cecile Chaminade, and the Americans Amy Fay and Julie Rivé-King. Clara Haskil and Dame Myra Hess respected the written note without the embellishments frequently added by their colleagues and reinforced their natural warmth with intellectuality. Wanda Landowska was a harpsichordist and pianist whose name became synonymous with the dramatic possibilities of harpsichord performance. Gina Bachauer was a powerful Romantic virtuoso in the style of her teachers, Cortot and Rachmaninov. Marguérite Long (d. 1966), Yvonne Lefébure, and Jeanne-Marie Darré embody the elegance, facility, and proportion of French music. Alicia de Larrocha specializes in Albeniz, Granados, and early Spanish keyboard music. Bela Davidovitch brings to her playing the accurate and brilliant stamp of Russian training.

Many of the younger generation of pianists in America have been trained by foreign-born women teachers with roots in the 19th Century repertoire–Isabella Vengerova, Rosina Lhevinne, and Nadia Reisenberg. Olga Samaroff (née Hickenlooper) was American-born but studied abroad and later taught at the Julliard School in New York. Her pupil Rosalyn Tureck has an inspiring reputation as a teacher and Bach specialist. The list of contemporary American pianists, some of whom have studied with these teachers, is imposing–John Browning, Daniel Barenboim, Van Cliburn, Misha Dichter, Malcolm Frager, Stephen Bishop-Kovacevich, Gary Graffman, Murray Perahia, Lorin Hollander, Andre Watts, Eugene Istomin, Grant Johanneson, Byron Janis, the late Julius Katchen, the late William Kapell, and the late Dinu Lipatti–to name a *few*. From other parts of the world come the additional distinguished pianists Arthur Rubinstein (d. 1982), Claudio Arrau, Rudolf Serkin, Rudolf Firkusny, Jean-Phillippe Collard, Philippe Entremont, Christoph Eschenbach, Vladimir Ashkenazy, Emil Gilels, Sviatoslav Richter, Vladimir Horowitz, the late Clifford Curzon, the late Glenn Gould, and Alfred Brendel.

The interaction of composers, teachers, and virtuosos is the very core of musical life. One cannot function effectively without the other. Some combine these gifts as triple crown winners, like Mozart, Beethoven, Mendelssohn, Chopin, and Liszt. One can only admire the dedicated teachers who tried to guide other 19th Century performers–the spirited salonists, thunderers, and showpersons–in the direction of performance integrity.

Performance integrity is the standard of the present. With the legacy of instrumental music's largest repertoire, and the musicianship of those who brought it about, the pianist of today can revel in the variety and imagination of his spiritual forebears.

Modern International Exchange

Two international organizations dedicated to the performance and dissemination of contemporary music have helped the cross-pollination of 20th Century musical ideas among the major Western European countries and America:

1. *I.S.C.M.* (International Society for Contemporary Music) founded in Salzburg in 1922 is an annual festival held in a different place each year and devoted to the works of contemporary composers of all nationalities. Works to be played are chosen by an international jury.

2. *I.R.C.A.M.* (Institut de recherche et de co-ordination acoustique/musique) is part of the Georges Pompidou Centre in Paris. It was inaugurated in 1977 under the directorship of Boulez and houses laboratories and electronic studios for experiment and research in modern composing techniques.

New concepts and methods spread themselves from one country to another through these organizations, by performances of international artists, and in the inspiration of composers who teach outside their own countries.

The United States has been enriched by the number of contemporary composers who have come to its various universities as guest teachers. This is a variation on the exodus of American composers to France in the 1920s when the renowned Parisian teacher, Nadia Boulanger, taught a succession of American musicians like Copland, Harris, Thomson, Carter, and Piston, to name a few. Celebrated composer-teachers, who have visited or lived in the United States as far back as the 1930s, include Varèse (American citizen, 1926), Boulez (Harvard and N.Y. Philharmonic), Messiaen, Schoenberg (U.C.L.A.), Hindemith (Harvard), Stockhausen, Rieti (American Citizen, 1944) Maderna, Berio (Juilliard), Glazunov, Rachmaninov, Stravinsky, Prokofiev, Elgar, Bliss, Tippett, Britten, Musgrave, Maxwell Davies (studied at Princeton with Sessions, 1962-64), Dvorák, Martinu, Xenakis, Penderecki (Yale), Bartók (Columbia), Dohnányi, Kodály, Villa-Lobos, Chavez, Ginastera, and Milhaud (Mills College).

The strides in communication in the 1980s have opened up an extraordinary potential for artists of the 20th Century. Today they have an unparalleled opportunity to share crucial developments with each other and with the public. Mutual understanding, musically, among peoples of the world may be the most valuable contribution a composer can make.

And the piano. Where is it going? Exact answers are unpredictable because they are determined by unexpected social changes in each generation. Nevertheless, bold past accomplishments suggest that the piano's physical properties, technique, and repertoire will continue to evolve in ways that promise originality and fulfillment.

APPENDICES

Albeniz	*Iberia,* 12 Piano Pieces (1906-09)
Bax	*Moy Mell* for 2 pianos (1908-17)
	The Maiden with the Daffodil (1915)
	Mediterranean for piano (1920)
	Hardanger for 2 pianos (1927)
Berg	*Variations on an Original Theme* (1908)
	Piano Sonata (1907-08)
Berio	*5 Variations* (1952)
	Wasserklavier (1965)
	Erdenklavier (1968)
	Memory for 2 pianos (1970)
Bliss	*Concerto* for 2 pianos (1924)
Boulez	*Piano Sonata No. 2* (1947-48)
	3rd Piano Sonata (1957) (Uses indeterminancy in that the 5 movements can be played in any order except for the 3rd which must come in the middle.)
Britten	*Left Hand Concerto* (1940, rev. 1954)
	Scottish Ballad for 2 pianos (1941)
	Holiday Diary for piano solo (1934)
	Night Piece for piano solo (1963)

Cage	Prepared Piano: *Sonatas and Interludes* (1946-48)
	O'OO" to be performed in any way by anyone (1962)
	Cheap imitation (1969)
	Etude Australis, 32 studies in 4 books (1974-75)
Carter	*Piano Sonata* (1945-46)
	Piano Concerto (1966)
	Night Fantasies (1979-80)
Chavez	*Concerto* for piano
Copland	*The Cat and the Mouse* (1919)
	Piano *Suites* from *Billy the Kid* and *Our Town*
Crawford	9 Piano Preludes (1926)
	American Folk Songs for Children
Crumb	*5 Pieces for piano* (1962)
	Makrokosmos I – 12 pieces for amplified piano (1972)
	Makrokosmos II – 12 pieces for amplified piano (1973)
D'Indy	*Promenades*
	Menuet sur le nom de Haydn
Dohnányi	*4 Klavierstücke*
	4 Rhapsodies
	Variations
	Passacaglia
Dvořák	*Concerto for piano in G minor Op. 33* (1876)
	Dumka Op. 35 (1876)
	Suite in A Op. 98 (1894)
	8 Humoresques Op. 101 (1894)
Falla	*El Amor Brujo* arr. by Falla including *Ritual Fire Dance* and *Dance of Fear*
	Suite from 7 *Spanish Popular Songs* arr. by Falla
	Dance of the Miller's Wife and *Miller's Dance* from the ballet *The Three Cornered Hat*
Ginastera	*Sonata* for piano (1952)
	2 *Concertos* for piano (1961; 1972)
Granados	*12 Spanish Dances*
	6 Pieces on Spanish Popular Songs
	7 valses poeticos
	Goyescas – 2 sets of piano pieces, 7 in all, inspired by a painting of Goya, including *Quejas o la Maja y el ruisenor* (1914)
Griffes	*4 Roman Sketches* (incl. No. 1, *The White Peacock*) (1916)
	Sonata for piano (1918-19)
Hindemith	3 *Sonatas* for piano (No. 1 in A; No. 2 in G; No. 3 in B flat) (1936)
	Sonata for 4 hands (1938)

	Ludus Tonalis (The Play of Notes) made up of a prelude, 12 Fugues with 11 interludes, and postlude (inverted version of prelude). A study in counterpoint and piano playing (1942)
Honegger	*Concertino* for piano and orchestra (1924)
Ives	*3-page Sonata* (1905)
	5 Take-Offs (1906-07)
	Studies for piano (1907-09)
	Protests (Varied Air and Variations) (1916)
Janácek	*National Dances of Moravia for 4 hands,* 3 books (1891, 1893)
	10 short pieces (1901)
	Sonata 1:x:1905 (A street scene: Zulice) (the day a worker was killed by a soldier for demonstrating for a Czech university in Brno)
Koechlin	*Paysages et marines* (c. 1916)
	L'Ansienne maison de campagne (1932-33)
Ligeti	*3 Pieces: Monument; Self-Portrait; Bewegung* (for 2 pianos)
Maderna	*Concerto* for 2 pianos and chamber orchestra (1948)
	Concerto for solo piano (1959)
Malipiero	Piano *Concertos* 1-6 (1934; 1937; 1948; 1950; 1958; 1964)
	Dialogo for 2 pianos (1956)
Maxwell Davies	*5 Pieces* (1956)
	5 Little Pieces (1967)
	Sub tuam protectionem (1970)
	Ut re mi (1971)
Messiaen	*Catalogue d'oiseaux* (a collection of pieces in 7 books based on birdsongs noted or remembered by Messiaen) (1956-58)
Milhaud	5 piano *Concertos*
	Concerto for 2 pianos (1942)
	Saudades do Brazil (1920-21)
	Scaramouche for 2 pianos (1939)
Poulenc	*3 mouvements perpetuels* (1918)
	Concerto for 2 pianos and orchestra (1932)
	12 Improvisations (1932-42)
	Concerto for piano (1949)
	Improvisation in D: Hommage à Edith Piaf (1960)
Prokofiev	*Concerto No. 4* for the left hand *Op. 53* (1931)
	Sarcasms Op. 17 (1912-14)
	Visions fugitives Op. 22 (1915-17)
	2 Sonatines Op. 54 (1931)
	Music for Children Op. 65
Rachmaninov	*5 Morceaux de Fantaisie Op. 3* (No. 2 is the *Prelude* in C sharp minor) (1892)
	Sonata No. 1 in D minor (1907)

	Sonata No. 2 in B flat minor (1913)
	Variations on a Theme of Corelli (1931)
Ravel	*Jeux d'eau* (1901)
	Sonatine (1905)
	Miroirs (1905)
	Gaspard de la Nuit (1908)
Riegger	*4 Tone Pictures* (1932)
	New and Old (1944)
	Concerto for piano and orchestra (1952-53)
Satie	*3 Gymnopédies* (1888)
	21 Sports et divertissements (1914)
	Parade for 4 hands (1917)
	5 Nocturnes (1919)
Schmitt	*10 Feuillets de Voyage for 4 hands Op. 26*
Schoenberg	*6 Little Pieces Op. 19* (1911)
	Suite Op. 25 (1921)
	2 Piano Pieces: Op. 33a (1928); *Op. 33b* (1931)
Sessions	*From my Diary* (1939)
	2nd Sonata (1946)
	Piano Concerto (1956)
Shostakovich	*3 Fantastic Dances Op. 5* (1922)
	Polka (Age of Gold) (1935, arr. for 4 hands 1962)
	Children's Notebook Op. 69 (1944-45)
	24 Preludes and Fugues Op. 87 (1950-51)
	Concertino for 2 pianos Op. 94
Sibelius	*6 Finnish Folksongs* (1903)
	3 Sonatinas Op. 67 (1912)
	6 Batagelles Op. 97 (1920)
	5 Esquisses Op. 114 (1929)
Siegmeister	*Folk-Ways U.S.A.* (3 books)
	Theme and Variations for piano (1932)
	On this Ground (1971)
Skalkattos	*Suite* for 2 pianos (1924)
	15 Little Variations (1927)
	32 Pieces (1940)
Skryabin	*Sonata No. 7 in F sharp (White Mass)* (1911)
	Sonata No. 9 in F (Black Mass) (1913)
	Etudes
	Preludes
	Piano Concerto in F sharp minor (1897-98)
Stockhausen	*Klavierstücke I-XI* (1952-56)
	Pole for 2 pianos (1969-70)
	Mantra (1970) for 2 amplified pianos and electronics. The title

comes from the Indian word for a mystical repetition, or "a sound which makes one see."

Stravinsky	Duets – 3 Easy Pieces (1914-1915) and *5 Easy Pieces* (1916-17)
	Piano Rag-Music (1919)
	Sonata (1924)
	Concerto for 2 solo pianos (1935)
	Tango (1940)
	Sonata for 2 pianos (1943-44)
	The Five Fingers (8 easy melodies on 5 notes)
Surinach	3 *Spanish Songs and Dances* (1953)
Szymanowski	*3 Sonatas Opp. 8, 21, 36* (1905; 1909; 1917)
	Fantasy in F minor Op. 14 (1905)
	3 Masks Op. 34 (1916)
	2 Mazurkas Op. 62 (1934)
Takemitsu	*Asterism* for piano and orchestra (1968)
	Far away; Piano distance; Undisturbed rest; for piano solo
Thomson	*Sonata No. 3 for piano* (1930)
Tippett	*3 Sonatas* (1936-37, rev. 1942 and 1954; 1962; 1972-73)
	Piano Concerto (1953-55)
Vaughan Williams	*Concerto for Piano* (1933)
	Introduction and Fugue for 2 pianos (1946)
Villa-Lobos	*5 piano concertos* (1945-54)
	Rudepoema (1921-26)
	Saudades das Selvas Brasileiras (1927)
Webern	*Stück* (1924)
	Variations for piano solo Op. 27 (1936)
Xenakis	*Herma* (1960-61)

A Partial List of 20th Century Harpsichord Music

With the 20th Century harpsichord, we come face to face again with the instrument which started the piano on its way. After developing the "modern" harpsichord with all its tonal resources and registration changes, current American manufacturers are concentrating on bringing back the qualities of the historical instrument. This is a recent approach since the German concert stage featured modern harpsichords during the 1970's. Contemporary composers are providing a repertoire which incorporates the tonal discoveries of new music realized on traditional as well as modern instruments.

Barati, Geo. (1913-   )
    Harpsichord Quartet (1964)
Berio, Luciano (1925-   )
    Rounds for harpsichord (1965)

Cage, John (1912-   )
   HPSCHD for 7 harpsichord soloists and 51 or or any number of tape machines
   (1967-1969)
Carter, Elliot (1908-   )
   Double Concerto for Harpsichord, Piano and 2 Chamber Orchestras (1961)
Dodgson, Stephen (1924-   )
   Duo Concertante for Guitar and Harpsichord (1968)
Evett, Robert (1922-1975)
   Sonata for Harpsichord
Falla, Manuel de (1876-1946)
   Concerto in D for Harpsichord, Flute, Oboe, Clarinet, Violin, and Cello (1923-26)
Gerhard, Roberto (1896-1970)
   Concerto for Harpsichord (1955-56)
Ghezzo, Dinu (1941-   )
   Kanones for Flute, Cello, and Harpsichord (1972)
Jarrett, Keith (1945-   )
   Fughata for Harpsichord
Lessard, John (1920-   )
   Toccata for Harpsichord
Malcolm, George (1917-   )
   Variations on a Theme of Mozart, for 4 Harpsichords
Martin, Frank (1890-1974)
   Concerto for Harpsichord and Small Orchestra (1951-1952)
Morgan, Robert P. (1934-   )
   Trio for Flute, Cello, and Harpsichord (1974)
Penn, William (1943-   )
   Fantasy for Harpsichord
Phillips, Burrill (1907-   )
   Sonata for Violin and Harpsichord
Porter, Quincy (1897-1966)
   Concerto for Harpsichord and Orchestra (1960)
Poulenc, Francis (1899-1963)
   Concert champetre for Harpsichord (1927-28)
Rieti, Vittorio (1898-   )
   Partita for Harpsichord and Quartet
Rochberg, George (1918-   )
   Nach Bach, for Harpsichord
Rorem, Ned (1923-   )
   Lovers, for Harpsichord, Oboe, Cello, Percussion (1964)
Roussakis, Nicolas (1934-)
   Night Speech; Sonata for Harpsichord
Sauget, Henri (1901-   )
   Suite Royale for Harpsichord solo

Suggested Editions

Where available, the following authoritative editions are recommended:[1]

Bach	Henle; Wiener Urtext; Kalmus
Handel	Henle; Wiener Urtext; Peters
Haydn	Henle; Wiener Urtext; Universal
Mozart	Henle; Wiener Urtext; Dover
Beethoven	Henle; Wiener Urtext; Kalmus; Dover; Schirmer Urtext
Schubert	Henle; Wiener Urtext; Breitkopf; Dover
Mendelssohn	Henle; Wiener Urtext; Dover
Schumann	Henle; Wiener Urtext; Dover; Kalmus; Breitkopf
Chopin	Henle; Wiener Urtext; Paderewski
Liszt	Barenreiter; Editio Musica Budapest
Brahms	Henle; Wiener Urtext; Peters; Dover; International; Schirmer Urtext
Franck	Peters
Tchaikovsky	Kalmus; Peters; Schirmer Urtext
Grieg	Peters
MacDowell	Kalmus
Debussy	Dover; Durand
Bartok	Boosey and Hawkes Original Edition

Bibliography

Abraham, Gerald, ed. *The Music of Tchaikovsky*. New York, W.W. Norton, 1974.

Apel, Willi. *Harvard Dictionary of Music*. 2nd ed., revised and enlarged. Cambridge, Mass., Harvard University Press, 1969.

Brendel, Alfred. *Musical Thoughts and Afterthoughts*. Princeton, N.J., Princeton University Press, 1976.

Concise Oxford Dictionary of Music. 3rd ed. Michael Kennedy, ed., based on the original ed. by Percy Scholes. London and New York, Oxford University Press, 1980.

Davies, Laurence. *Franck*. Master Musicians Series. London, J.M. Dent and Sons, 1973.

Einstein, Alfred. *Mozart: His Character and His Work*. London and New York, Oxford University Press, 1945.

Geiringer, Karl. *Brahms, His Life and Work*. 2nd ed. London, Allen and Unwin, 1948.

Geiringer, Karl. *Johann Sebastian Bach, The Culmination of an Era*. New York, Oxford University Press, 1966.

---

[1] See additional information on editions given at the end of each chapter.

Grove, Sir George. *Dictionary of Music and Musicians.* 5th ed. Eric Blom, ed. New York, St. Martin's Press, 1960.

Hildesheimer, Wolfgang. *Mozart.* New York, Farrar Straus Giroux, 1982.

Horton, John. *Grieg.* Master Musicians Series. London, J.M. Dent and Sons, 1974.

Hughes, Rosemary. *Haydn.* Master Musicians Series. London, J.M. Dent and Sons, 1962.

Landon, H.C. Robbins. *Haydn: Chronicle and Works.* Vol. III. Bloomington, Ind., Indiana University Press, 1978.

Lang, Paul Henry. *George Frideric Handel.* New York, W.W. Norton, 1966.

Lockspeiser, Edward. *Debussy, His Life and Mind.* Vol. I and II. New York, Cambridge University Press, 1979.

New Grove Dictionary of Music and Musicians. Stanley Sadie, ed. 20 vols. London, Macmillan; Washington, D.C., Grove's Dictionaries of Music, Inc., 1980.

Pleasants, Henry. Translated, edited, annotated. *The Musical World of Robert Schumann: A Selection from his own Writing.* New York, St. Martin's Press, 1965.

Radcliffe, Philip. *Schubert Piano Sonatas.* London, B.B.C., 1967.

Rosen, Charles. *The Classical Style: Haydn, Mozart, Beethoven.* New York, Viking Press, 1971.

Schoenberg, Harold C. *The Great Pianists from Mozart to the Present.* New York, Simon and Schuster, 1963.

Solomon, Maynard. *Beethoven.* New York, Schirmer Books, 1977.

Stevens, Halsey. *The Life and Music of Bela Bartok.* Rev. ed. London, Oxford University Press, 1978.

Thayer, Alexander Wheelock. *The Life of Ludwig van Beethoven.* London, Centaur Press, 1960.

Walker, Alan. *Franz Liszt, The Virtuoso Years. 1811-1847.* New York, Alfred A. Knopf, Inc., 1983.

Walker, Alan, ed. *Frederic Chopin: Profiles of the Man and the Musician.* New York, Taplinger. 1967.

Wechsberg, Joseph. *Schubert: His Life, His Work, His Time.* New York, Rizzoli Press, 1977.

Weinstock, Herbert. *Handel.* New York, Alfred A. Knopf, 1946.

Werner, Erich. *Mendelssohn,* London, Collier-Macmillan, 1936.

INDEX